Living and Studying Abroad

LANGUAGES FOR INTERCULTURAL COMMUNICATION AND EDUCATION
Editors: Michael Byram, *University of Durham, UK* and Alison Phipps, *University of Glasgow, UK*

The overall aim of this series is to publish books which will ultimately inform learning and teaching, but whose primary focus is on the analysis of intercultural relationships, whether in textual form or in people's experience. There will also be books which deal directly with pedagogy, with the relationships between language learning and cultural learning, between processes inside the classroom and beyond. They will all have in common a concern with the relationship between language and culture, and the development of intercultural communicative competence.

Other Books in the Series
Developing Intercultural Competence in Practice
    Michael Byram, Adam Nichols and David Stevens (eds)
Intercultural Experience and Education
    Geof Alred, Michael Byram and Mike Fleming (eds)
Critical Citizens for an Intercultural World: Foreign Language Education as Cultural Politics
    Manuela Guilherme
How Different Are We? Spoken Discourse in Intercultural Communication
    Helen Fitzgerald
Audible Difference: ESL and Social Identity in Schools
    Jennifer Miller
Context and Culture in Language Teaching and Learning
    Michael Byram and Peter Grundy (eds)
An Intercultural Approach to English language Teaching
    John Corbett
Critical Pedagogy: Political Approaches to Language and Intercultural Communication
    Alison Phipps and Manuela Guilherme (eds)
Vernacular Palaver: Imaginations of the Local and Non-native Languages in West Africa
    Moradewun Adejunmobi
Foreign Language Teachers and Intercultural Competence: An International Investigation
    Lies Sercu with Ewa Bandura, Paloma Castro, Leah Davcheva, Chryssa Laskaridou, Ulla Lundgren, María del Carmen Méndez García and Phyllis Ryan
Language and Culture: Global Flows and Local Complexity
    Karen Risager
Education for Intercultural Citizenship: Concepts and Comparisons
    Geof Alred, Michael Byram and Mike Fleming (eds)

Other Books of Interest
Age, Accent and Experience in Second Language Acquisition
    Alene Moyer
Language Teachers, Politics and Cultures
    Michael Byram and Karen Risager

For more details of these or any other of our publications, please contact:
Multilingual Matters, Frankfurt Lodge, Clevedon Hall,
Victoria Road, Clevedon, BS21 7HH, England
http://www.multilingual-matters.com

LANGUAGES FOR INTERCULTURAL
COMMUNICATION AND EDUCATION 12
Series Editors: Michael Byram and Alison Phipps

Living and Studying Abroad
Research and Practice

Edited by
Michael Byram and Anwei Feng

MULTILINGUAL MATTERS LTD
Clevedon • Buffalo • Toronto

Library of Congress Cataloging in Publication Data
Living and Studying Abroad: Research and Practice/Edited by Michael Byram and
Anwei Feng.
Languages for Intercultural Communication and Education: 12
Includes bibliographical references and index.
1. Foreign study. 2. Foreign study–Research. 3. Foreign study–Research–Methodology.
I. Byram, Michael. II. Feng, Anwei. III. Series.
LB2375.L58 2006
370.116–dc22   2006010931

British Library Cataloguing in Publication Data
A catalogue entry for this book is available from the British Library.

ISBN 1-85359-911-5 / EAN 978-1-85359-911-8 (hbk)
ISBN 1-85359-910-7 / EAN 978-1-85359-910-1 (pbk)

Multilingual Matters Ltd
UK: Frankfurt Lodge, Clevedon Hall, Victoria Road, Clevedon BS21 7HH.
USA: UTP, 2250 Military Road, Tonawanda, NY 14150, USA.
Canada: UTP, 5201 Dufferin Street, North York, Ontario M3H 5T8, Canada.

Typeset by Techset Ltd.
Printed and bound in Great Britain by MPG Books Ltd.

Contents

Part 3: Short-Term Sojourns

Part 4: Lasting Effects on Sojourners

Part 5: Evaluating the Impact

Foreword

ROBERT CRAWSHAW

The publication of this research anthology on residence abroad coincides with the convergence of a number of historic initiatives in the field of transnational educational mobility. 2005 was the centenary of the foundation of the Language Teaching Assistants programme, the visionary accord of 1905 between Great Britain, France and Prussia. According to the text of the original agreement, the programme's objectives were as much educational as they were political. The initiative was designed as an ambassadorial catalyst, whose elements were intended to offer at least equal benefit to the sojourners as to the pupils whose learning they were destined to support. Its aim was to reach beyond the limitations of wealth and privilege and, for the first time, to place intercultural encounter within an agreed international educational framework. The programme's longevity remains the enduring mark of its efficacy and life-changing properties. Fortuitously, 2006 marks in its turn the 20th anniversary of the European Union's Erasmus project, which has made it possible for a generation of young people, the children of the post-war baby-boom, to experience at first hand, from a specifically educational perspective, the wonder of Europe's cultural diversity. It is also 10 years since the EU's Socrates programme extended the funded support for EU educational cooperation under Comenius to secondary and further education. These structures, together with the pioneering work of The Council of Europe, have enabled mobility within Europe to become a multinational reality, an institutional given which is no longer dependent exclusively on material privilege and bilateral agreements between individual states.

It has taken time for the experience of structured periods of residence abroad in the post-war, post-colonial environment of modern Europe to be properly assessed. Even now, its longer term impact on the wider cultures from which the sojourners emanate can only be guessed at. Records were of course kept by the former Central Bureau for Educational

Visits and Exchanges in London and by equivalent agencies in the different European countries involved in exchange programmes. Reports were
written by schools where the students taught and, to a greater or lesser
extent, universities noted the outcomes of overseas sojourn and fed
them into their final degree assessments. But, for the most part, the
developmental benefits were taken for granted; residence abroad was
not a compulsory component even of modern languages degrees in the
UK, and after the enforced colonial travel imposed by national service
on the majority of young British men during the decade following
the trauma of the second world war, philanthropic education abroad for
the few, like Voluntary Service Overseas (VSO), was seen as an adjunct
to mainstream study, a trapping which would enhance the cultural
outlook of the prospective language teacher, diplomat, international
businessman or civil servant.

I think it is fair to say that, as far as Europe is concerned, serious
attempts to evaluate residence abroad from a theorised, academic, developmental perspective took root partly as a consequence of the need to
account for student mobility in terms of cost-benefit and partly as an
outcome of the wider movement in the 1970s to promote languages
for all to a minimal threshold of communication (*niveau-seuil*), regardless
of ability, within the secondary system. Lines of investigation were
pursued more or less in parallel at two different levels of education.
First, it became clear that survival language tools for children travelling
abroad, mostly for leisure purposes, was deemed not in itself to be a
sufficient educational goal. For deep learning to take place, it was important for the 'lifeworlds' of the learners to change. While they might never
attain native speaker proficiency in the foreign languages to which they
were exposed, they could at least come to appreciate and respect difference and thus use foreign language learning as a means of developing
qualities of tolerance and humanity. However, these abstract, idealistic
aims needed to be translated into practical pedagogical goals. For this
to happen, much closer definition of terms was required, together with
a more acute understanding of how progression towards some new
order of being could realistically be assessed. The Council of Europe,
through the pioneering work of a few committed individuals, was instrumental in enabling these investigations to take place. Through the late
1980s and into the 1990s, a framework for defining cultural awareness
as an educational objective was established. This framework has now
achieved global prominence and, as the papers in the present volume
make clear, has become one of the key benchmarks against which the
attainment of intercultural competence is measured.

At the same time, the successful integration of the residence abroad experience into Higher Education became a growing preoccupation within Europe, not simply from the infrastructural perspective inherent in the European Union's Bologna agreement and the subsequent work of organisations such as the European Universities Association (EUA), but also, complementarily, in terms of its impact on the outlook of young people themselves. Once again, this interest has in part been bound up with financial concerns, especially in the UK. What tangible benefits have accrued from study and work abroad, both to the learners and to the environments within which they have been learning? How has their potential as an economic resource been enhanced as a result of intercultural encounter? Is the period of residence abroad being used to best advantage? How can participants be better prepared for such experiences, so that these benefits can be maximised? It has also been fuelled by the universal upsurge of interest in the social and psychological processes involved in the experience of mobility. Perhaps not surprisingly, this interest in process and developmental outcomes has coincided with the simultaneous enlargement of the European Union, the increased predominance of the English language and the emergence of local, ethnic identities as indices of cultural diversity within nation states. For all these reasons, cultural interaction through mobility has become widely recognised as a materially significant field of research.

The other major development in intercultural research to which this volume bears witness, is the extension of opportunities for study abroad from Europe and North America to the wider world and vice versa. Over the last decade, educationally sponsored mobility has become a global phenomenon, particularly in the UK and Ireland, due to the HE sector's increasing dependence on overseas students as a source of revenue and the attractiveness of English-speaking environments as places of learning. Exchange programmes between European countries and the Americas, China, Japan, India, Malaysia and Africa are now becoming more commonplace. It has become essential to address not just the practical study problems confronted by students engaged in intercontinental educational mobility but the attitudinal changes and pragmatic communication issues which these sojourns entail. Of equal interest is the extent to which these issues continue to underline deep-seated differences in cultural outlook. While the physical opportunities for students to work and study abroad have diversified, the impact of global student mobility on research has been multiple. It has broadened the types of educational intercultural encounter which have been investigated, and, at the same time, brought together different research traditions. The study of intercultural experience within educational contexts has now itself become a trans-national, trans-disciplinary exercise. At the very moment when it might have been thought that intra-European student mobility was running out of steam as a object of research, it has received a new impetus as the scope of the field has expanded.

All of the above points towards the timeliness of the present anthology. As the introduction by Mike Byram and Anwei Feng makes clear, the aim of the editors has been to report on current research from the perspective of recent practitioners. This lends the volume a freshness and directness of tone, even where mobility within Europe is concerned. One of its defining features is that the traditional sequence whereby initial methodological description is followed by analysis and conclusions has been deliberately reversed. In virtually all cases, the papers start with a summary of the findings and then give a close analysis of the methodology followed. Anyone reading the book with limited prior knowledge of the field, will immediately obtain an informative overview of the diverse methodologies currently being applied in educational sojourner research. They will also very quickly identify the major bibliographical reference points.

Of particular interest is the emphasis given to qualititative techniques and 'grounded theory' approaches based on personal narration by sojourners, either recorded in writing in diaries or derived from oral accounts obtained through interview. These techniques are rarely used in isolation, however, but are normally combined with quantitative data from questionnaires or straightforward statistics. In several cases, such data has been analysed electronically using different software packages. The strengths and weaknesses of each are honestly assessed without the sense that the researcher has had to defend at all costs the methodology or the software employed. In addition, the evaluation of mobility to and from certain countries which has hitherto been relatively underresearched is here conducted with unusual candour. The cultural obstacles encountered, for example by Japanese students in Britain or by mainland Chinese in Hong Kong, are extremely explicit. At the same time, the volume includes a clear analysis of the definitions of 'intercultural awareness' currently in use and, in at least one of the papers, the background to grounded theory is fully explained. Finally, the importance of more systematic longitudinal investigation is suggestively indicated as a potential direction for future research. *Living and Studying Abroad* bears valuable testimony to a field in transition. It will give new researchers a strong sense of what is possible and underlines the limitations inherent in certain types of approach. It is a book to be enjoyed and used as a methodological reference by anyone interested in the cultural impacts of study and work abroad.

Lancaster January 2006

About the Authors

Geof Alred is a BPS Chartered Psychologist, counsellor trainer, former student counsellor, and currently counsels in the NHS and in private practice. His research interests include metaphorical understanding and language in therapy, mentoring, and intercultural experience, in particular student residence abroad. He is co-author of *The Mentoring Pocketbook* (1998), and co-editor of *Intercultural Experience and Education* (2003) and *Experiences of Counsellor Training: Challenge, Surprise and Change* (2004).

Mari Ayano is a PhD student in the School of Education, University of Durham, a career counsellor at the Career Centre, Chubu University in Japan and a counsellor in Nagoya area in Japan. For her PhD, she researched intercultural experience and the process of psychological adjustment of Japanese students (University of Durham). She received her MEd in clinical psychology from the Fukuoka University of Education and MA in counselling and guidance from the University of Durham. She has experiences of teaching in clinical psychology, developmental psychology, preschool education and mental health in Japan and the UK. She is a co-author of *Shinrigaku Zusetsu* (Atlas of Psychology) and *Sekushual Saikoloji* (Sexual Psychology), published in Japan. Her main research interests are psychological adjustment process to different environments, especially intercultural adjustment, school adjustment and vocational adjustment of Japanese students and pupils. She is also interested in imagery and metaphor in counselling.

Christine Burnett is a teacher at a large multicultural school in Belfast with responsibility for international students. She has been involved in research into the educational experiences of children from minority ethnic groups in Northern Ireland and of international students at sixth form level. Her PhD thesis focused on the acculturation of Chinese undergraduate students at Queen's University, Belfast and she has presented papers on her work at the conference of the International Communication Association 2003 in San Diego and at the International Conference on Intercultural Research 2004 in Taipei.

Michael Byram is Professor of Education at the University of Durham, England. He first taught French and German at secondary school level and in adult education in an English comprehensive community school. Since being appointed to a post in teacher education at the University of Durham in 1980, he has carried out research into the education of linguistic minorities, foreign language education and student residence abroad, and is now Director of Research Degrees. He has published many books and articles including, most recently, *Teaching and Assessing Intercultural Communicative Competence*; *Language Teachers, Politics and Cultures* (with Karen Risager); *Intercultural Experience and Education* (edited with G. Alred and M. Fleming); and is the editor of the *Routledge Encyclopedia of Language Teaching and Learning*. He is a Programme Adviser to the Council of Europe Language Policy Division, and is currently interested in language education policy and the politics of language teaching.

Darla K. Deardorff received her doctorate in higher education administration and is an international education administrator at Duke University in Durham, North Carolina, United States. She currently holds an elected national office with NAFSA: Association of International Educator, as well as serving as Executive Director of the Association of International Education Administrators. She is an experienced cross-cultural trainer and English-as-a-Second Language instructor/teacher trainer. Her international experience includes working in Germany, Japan and Switzerland. Her research interests include outcomes assessment of internationalization, intercultural competence, and learning styles across cultures.

Susanne Ehrenreich is Lecturer (Wissenschaftliche Assistentin) at the Ludwig-Maximilian-University of Munich, where she teaches Applied Linguistics and ELT Methodology (Englische Fachdidaktik). For her PhD she researched the impact of the year abroad as language assistant on prospective foreign language teachers (*Auslandsaufenthalt und Fremdsprachenlehrerbildung*, Langenscheidt, 2004). Her main research interests include intercultural learning, foreign language teacher education as well as English as a global language. In her current research project she is investigating English as a Lingua Franca (ELF) in international business contexts and the way it impacts on the linguistic and professional identities of ELF users. She holds a BEd (University of Education, Ludwigsburg) and an MA in English and Theology (Tuebingen University). She is a qualified teacher and taught for several years at secondary schools in Heidelberg and Munich, and as *Lektorin für Deutsch* for two years in Ireland at Mary Immaculate College, University of Limerick.

Anwei Feng teaches and supervises Education Doctorate and PhD students in the School of Education at the University of Durham. His research interests include intercultural studies in language education, student mobility, bilingual education, international business communication and TESOL. He has published many book chapters and journal articles in these areas. Currently, he is guest-editing a Special Issue on Chinese bilingual education for the *International Journal of Bilingual Education and Bilingualism* and is leading a research project on synergetic culture focusing on the experiences of students from Confucian heritage cultures studying in the UK.

John Gardner is Professor of Education in the School of Education at Queen's University, Belfast. His main research areas include policy and practice in education, particularly in assessment and information technology in education. Since 1990, he has been principal investigator in over 20 large and small-scale projects involving over £1.6 million including research on, for example, the reliability and validity of the 11-plus tests in Northern Ireland, consumer education needs, Reading Recovery and virtual learning environments. He is currently part of a team conducting an Economic and Social Research Council (ESRC)-funded project on pupils' participation in the assessment of their own learning.

Jane Jackson is Professor in the English Department at the Chinese University of Hong Kong where she teaches undergraduate and postgraduate courses in applied linguistics/intercultural communication and supervises MPhil/PhD research. She serves as coordinator of a study and residence abroad programme for English majors. She received her PhD in applied linguistics/cross-cultural communication from the University of Toronto (Ontario Institute for Studies in Education) and MEd in bilingual (French-English) education from the University of Calgary. She has experience in ESL/EFL, TESOL teacher education, applied linguistics, and intercultural communication in Canada, Egypt, Oman, the US and China (Beijing and Hong Kong). Her main research interests include intercultural and cross-cultural communication, student residence abroad and case-based teaching and learning in diverse settings. She has published many research-based articles, most recently in *The International Journal of Intercultural Relations, Frontiers: The Interdisciplinary Journal of Study Abroad, RELC Journal, System,* and *English for Specific Purposes.* Her book, *Language, Identity, and Study Abroad: Sociocultural Perspectives* (edited by C. Candlin and S. Sarangi) will be published by Equinox.

Carol Lam first started her ESL teaching in the community colleges in Los Angeles, United States. After returning to Hong Kong, she joined the Language Centre of the Hong Kong Baptist University in Hong Kong. Her initial research interests and areas focused more on ESL teaching and second language acquisition. Through her doctorate studies in cultural adjustment and intercultural communication, she has expanded her research areas into identity and intercultural communication, intercultural communicative competence and the promotion of multiculturalism in higher education. With colleagues in other countries, she has carried out a variety of comparative studies including internationalization among primary students from Japan, Hong Kong and Macau, willingness to communicate in English among students from Mainland and Hong Kong, and the change of identity and language choice among the tertiary students in Hong Kong.

Vassiliki Papatsiba is currently a Marie Curie Intra-European Senior Research Fellow at the Department of Educational Studies, University of Oxford. Supported by an individual grant under the 'EU Framework 6, Human Resources and Mobility', her current research focuses on the study of the Bologna Process and the comparative analysis of higher education reforms in several European countries. For her doctorate (Université Paris X, 2001), she investigated the experiences of French Erasmus students and policy on mobility. She has authored a book on Erasmus mobility of students (*Des Etudiants Européens: ERASMUS et l'Aventure de l'Altérité*, Peter Lang, 2003) and has publications on issues such as European identity, intercultural learning, EU policy in higher education, the Europeanisation of higher education and the methodology of textual (discourse) analyses of data. She was a national expert for the French unit of Eurydice at the Ministry of National Education in France and has teaching and research experience at several universities in France.

Aileen Pearson-Evans is a Senior Lecturer in Intercultural Studies in SALIS, DCU. She is Director of the European Intercultural Workplace (EIW) Project, a Leonardo-funded project investigating the impact of cultural diversity in 10 European countries and developing training materials to enhance intercultural communication at work. She trained and worked for many years as a language teacher (French, German, Japanese, EFL) before specialising in Intercultural Studies. She holds a doctorate from Trinity College Dublin, which focused on the cross-cultural adjustment of Irish students in Japan. Her research interests include: cross-cultural adaptation; identities in multilingual and multicultural environments; intercultural dimensions of language teaching; East-West communication; training for managing in intercultural environments; the roles of food and social networks in cross-cultural adjustment.

Gertrud Tarp received her PhD in intercultural learning at the Department of Education and Learning, Aalborg University, Denmark. Currently she teaches English and French at a business school. She has taught English and French at upper-secondary school and university level. In addition she has taught causes and supervised projects on the master's programme, Master of Learning Processes. Her international experience includes teaching at an American high school and being in charge of school internationalisation programmes. She is co-author of a book on linguistics and has written articles on intercultural learning and research methodology. She is interested in exploring agent agendas in educational contexts by means of an ethnographic approach and a grounded theory methodology with an emphasis on student perspectives and student inclusion. Her research interests also include foreign language education and intercultural competence.

Chapter 1
Introduction

Study abroad is a fast-growing phenomenon, urged on by ease of travel, by political changes, by economic need, by cultural interaction. Travel is part of the lives of many young people of university age, and of the majority of those living in developed and wealthy countries; to travel for study is an extension of the travel for pleasure which many have known from an early age. Political changes have made study abroad in many countries easier, not least in the countries of the European Union which actively encourages young people to study in other member states. In some circumstances, political change makes study abroad more difficult, as in the United States after 11th September attacks in New York and Washington. In other circumstances, politicians actively encourage their universities to seek new students from new countries, as in the United Kingdom. There is also an economic rationale for study abroad, particularly where students from Asian and African countries study in Europe and North America. For those students there is the hope of economic benefit in the future, with the status of a qualification from abroad rather than their own country. For the universities receiving them, there is the certainty of economic profit from fees.

Another factor, cultural interaction, is less often considered, but it is implicit that study abroad will lead to increased cultural capital for the individual, improved international relations, and an extra dimension to the educational experience. The tradition of the 19th century 'grand tour' for the children, usually the sons, of the aristocracy is now accessible, it is hoped, to all. Indeed, it can be argued that routine study abroad, rather than the exoticism of the grand tour, is more likely to change people significantly, and give them an educational experience of other countries which will be more intense and enriching.

For study abroad necessitates living abroad, experiencing another way of life, changing one's habits of thought as well as those of eating, drinking and daily life. Or that is at least the expectation. The reality may be different. Foreign students often live in isolation, on the margins of the

1

society in which they reside. This may be their choice, and a resistance to the input of life in 'the West' by those from 'the East'. It may equally be a result of social processes which do not offer an entry even to the most willing student committed to the idea of integration. In many universities, there exist communities within the community, and the ideal of the university as a community of scholars is seldom a reality for those from elsewhere.

The title of our book thus recognises that the reality of study may not involve living abroad in an enriching sense. The living simply serves the purpose of studying, as many of our chapters reveal. This is not desirable but it is often the case, and in order to provide circumstances for studying *and* living abroad we need to understand what is already happening – and to identify the conditions where success in living, as well as studying, is achieved.

This book collects research on different groups and types of students experiencing residence abroad for shorter or longer periods, in countries near and far from their own. Its purpose is to bring the latest high-quality research together and to show what has already been achieved, how it has been achieved, and what might still be done.

It is with the need for more research in mind that we have a dual purpose: to allow researchers to present their findings and to invite them to explain their methods. All our contributors share with the reader the details of their research to a degree which is not often found in research reports. It is thus possible to read 'across' the chapters with a focus on the findings or alternatively with an emphasis on the methods.

The chapters have been placed in five sections to reflect some of the parameters of sojourns: time and space – geographical and cultural distance, length of stay; and the impact of the experience – on the individual personally and professionally, and on the institution to or from which they travel. Other divisions would have been possible, in particular the purpose of the sojourn. People who are language learners, who study languages at university, and then spend a period of residence in a target-language country may see the sojourn as a continuation of their studies, as a natural culmination of their work. For others who seek new study opportunities in other countries, and may not speak the language well, the purpose and the mindset involved bear a different relationship to the sojourn. Such parameters are however only a preliminary differentiation and the significance and the nature of the experience vary despite these, as the following chapters show.

The Results of Research

From the perspective of counselling, Ayano conducted longitudinal studies into psychological states of Japanese students in their year in the United Kingdom. Using different psychological tests and interviews as research tools, Ayano reveals that throughout the whole year the Japanese students suffered psychological distress and their general well-being level remained low. On the basis of these findings, Ayano makes recommendations on how their psychological problems could be better dealt with in the new environment and how the social networks could be improved to ease the anxiety and anguish of the students. These revelations clearly challenge many developmental models of cross-cultural adaptation that suggest an overall stress-adjustment-progress trend.

While the Japanese students in Ayano's case experienced psychological problems in the United Kingdom throughout the year, the Irish students Pearson-Evans studied as a whole apparently experienced increased confidence over time and succeeded in cross-cultural adjustment in their year in Japan. Using diaries as a research instrument, Pearson-Evans analysed three themes that naturally emerged in them, namely social networks, food and language. She reported that, though common stages of cross-cultural adjustment are identifiable, individuals differed greatly in terms of timing and duration of the stages due to numerous contextual factors. These findings, Pearson-Evans argues, are significant as they help us make informed decisions on planning residence abroad, preparing students for the sojourn and providing better support for them during their stay.

With the ever-increasing population of Chinese students studying abroad, the literature on how these students adapt or acculturate into their host cultures is growing in proportion. In reporting findings of an essentially qualitative research study, Burnett and Gardner go beyond description to relate the experience of Chinese students studying in Northern Ireland, to well-established models of intercultural adaptation and acculturation. As a result, a new model has emerged to better reflect the experience of this group of students. This new model, Burnett and Gardner argue, is not meant to replace existing models, but to remind us of the complexity that constitutes each individual's path of acculturation.

In Hong Kong, Lam also studied how a group of students from Mainland China adapted themselves into the local environment. Lam's findings clearly indicate that the adaptation process was, and should be, reciprocal. Great efforts were made by both the sojourners and the local counter-parts. Particularly interesting in Lam's study is the finding that this group of Chinese students, owing to their 'cream of the crop' background as they came from a top university in China, consciously or unconsciously negotiated their unique identities (social, economic and academic) inside and outside their classrooms. These sojourners obviously created intermediate spaces with local counter-parts and tutors. Her findings remind us that it is not only sojourners who constantly adapt to the new culture. The impact of sojourners on local people and thus the local culture should never be overlooked.

In the European context, Papatsiba looks into the experience of French students in the European Union's 'Erasmus' exchange programmes through a qualitative analysis of a large corpus of self-accounts of studying and living in neighbouring European countries, such as the United Kingdom, Austria and Germany. She found in this corpus a continuum of 'subjective positioning' between a 'tourist-guide' type of stereotypical descriptions and 'attitudes of proximity' demonstrating willingness and skills to understand another culture from within. This continuum of subjective positioning not only reveals individual perceptions of otherness and studying abroad but also a model of progression from gaining an encyclopaedic knowledge to conceptual constructing interculturalism and empathy in experiencing a different culture.

While most authors in this volume and the literature on study abroad in general deal with the experience of student 'year abroad' and even longer stays, chapters by Jackson and Tarp focus on short stay sojourners. Jackson's chapter reports findings of her ethnographic study among a group of Hong Kong students who travelled to England and spent five weeks with local families in order to experience their culture and to improve their English. Though short, the experience provides further evidence of gains in terms of cognitive and affective development and intercultural skills, as well as widely-reported symptoms of sojourners in an unfamiliar land at the initial stage. Jackson argues that the gains in short stays could be further enhanced with appropriate pedagogical interventions such as ethnographic training.

Using grounded theory, Tarp conducted research into short-stay programmes in Danish upper-secondary schools. These programmes include common initiatives such as school visits and the European Union's 'Socrates Lingua exchanges' which have a dual purpose of increasing students' intercultural understanding and competence and improving proficiency in a modern foreign language. The findings suggest that institutional perceptions or requirements for the short-stay exchange programmes do not usually correspond with the conceived agenda of the students themselves. This impinges on the educational significance of the programmes. In order for the short stay to be meaning-ful, Tarp argues that it is important to include students in the decision-making process, i.e. to make students' voices heard in exchange curricu-lum design.

In Ehrenreich's chapter, long-term effects of residence abroad on sojourners are explored from the perspective of personal, linguistic, cultural and professional attainment. In this chapter, Ehrenreich reports findings from her research among German foreign language student tea-chers who lived and taught one to eight years ago as teaching assistants in an English-speaking country such as the UK. Data from retrospective interviews highlight the complexity of assessing lasting effects of resi-dence abroad and the necessity to help maximise the potential benefits of the learning opportunities abroad and strengthen positive outcomes for sustainable personal and professional development.

The chapter by Alred and Byram is another longitudinal study which attempts to trace the impact of a long period of residence on people's lives. They used different methods in two studies 10 years apart to talk to a group of university students before and after their sojourn and again 10 years later. They focus here on the second study and on the ways in which the 'year abroad' which is obligatory for language learners in English universities has lasting effects for some and not for others. They show how the experience for some is part of their everyday professional lives, especially if they are teachers. It is not particularly the language learning which was important, even though that might have been the initial purpose, but the intercultural competence they achieved, the sense of an international identity and the importance of passing on their enthusiasm to others. On the other hand, there were those for whom the 'year abroad' had been a difficult experience and one on which they turned a page in order to seek a different kind of life and career. The long-term educational influence of residence abroad is this dif-ficult to guarantee and universities may find it difficult to justify in times of short-term targets but there is no doubt of the meaningfulness of the experience irrespective of whether it can be measured.

The final chapter takes up the question of the institutional perspective. Tertiary institutions in the United States and elsewhere make tremendous efforts to internationalise their curricula and to facilitate the experience of study abroad. Their endeavour is usually based on the belief that students will become more interculturally competent through these educational investments. Recent literature has also shown a keen interest in defining what intercultural competence is and how this competence can be measured. There is, however, hardly any consensus among intercultural studies experts and administrators in universities on these issues. Deardorff in the last chapter reports her innovative study in these two groups through a survey and a Delphi study. She found that despite differences in terms of priorities, agreement exists among top scholars in their conceptions of what constitutes intercultural competence. The identified components are clearly valuable in helping those involved in study abroad programmes to assess effectiveness and to make informed decisions.

It is clear that study abroad will continue to grow, that the financial implications are a major issue, that the policies of institutions will be under scrutiny and that the short and long term effects will be observed and evaluated. There will therefore be a continuing need, too, for research, and in the following section we turn to the methods our contributors used.

The Methods of Research

As editors, we knew that contributors were mainly people who had conducted research for a doctorate, and in so doing had learnt by experience – 'the hard way' – much about choice of methods and applications. They knew that what is discussed in methods textbooks is helpful but needs to be adapted to the vagaries of actual research: drop-out from samples, the change of direction of the researcher's thinking, discovery of new methods half way through, the choices to be made when analysis takes place. Perhaps all this must be learnt 'the hard way' but our experience also tells us that junior researchers can often learn from each other. They do so when they talk to each other in seminars and conferences, but not everyone meets just the right person in a conference, and furthermore our contributors live thousands of miles apart.

For all of these reasons, we decided to have a smaller number of chapters but allow contributors some 10,000 words and encourage them to divide their chapters roughly into two halves, with the first part being an account of their findings and the second being a report of their methods – as they actually happened, not in a sanitised form.

The reader who reads across the second part of each of the 9 chapters will find similarities and differences. All of the chapters are written with the purpose of understanding the experience of residence abroad and its impact on people and institutions, from the perspective of those involved. The research is thus firmly placed within an interpretative paradigm but this is not to be equated with an exclusive use of qualitative data, even though the latter may be predominant.

For example, Ayano in the first chapter uses both questionnaires and interviews, and in the questionnaires she includes sections based on standardised psychological tests. Similarly, her interviews draw upon an established method of eliciting data in a systematic way, 'visual case processing'. She does not rely only on semi-structured interview schedule as many researchers think an interpretative approach must do. As a consequence of this combination of methods, Ayano has a variety of approaches to data analysis, using statistics from SPSS, as well as thematic analysis of her interview transcripts.

Pearson-Evans' study is based on student journals kept doing a long period of residence. These are not structured by the researcher and yet Pearson-Evans describes the significance of the relationship of researcher and participants as being crucial to the success of data collection. Here too there is a long process of data preparation once the data in the form of journals have been collected. She describes this in detail including the problem of anonymising the data which are by their very nature highly personalised. Like a number of other contributors, Pearson-Evans decided on grounded theory for her analysis and explains it considerable detail how she did this.

Burnett and Gardner use interviews which lead to the production and analysis of visual material. Their interviewees are asked to represent their experience in diagrams and colour because they argue that their verbal accounts may be inhibited. The analysis of the data is however, not easy because, unlike the many discussions of how to analyse interview transcripts and the hundreds of books on statistical analysis for social scientists, there is little help on how to analyse visual data. Burnett and Gardner therefore explains in detail how they did this and how they created models of students' adjustment to represent different stages in their experience.

Lam took another approach by engaging in an ethnographic study of a small group of students. She too included methods to elicit quantitative data but admits that this did not succeed on this occasion. Like other contributions, this one describes both successes and failures in fieldwork and data collection, a revelation which is often suppressed in textbooks and research reports. Lam also takes further the discussion of the interview, explaining how some interviews were arranged and recorded – but not all were recorded, as some participants were unwilling – and other interviews were 'friendly conversations' which took place occasionally over a long period of field work.

Papatsiba's data are different again. She discovered what historians would call 'primary sources' in the archived accounts produced by

'Erasmus' students reporting on their residence in a wide range of countries. Data collection was not necessary therefore, but preparation of the data, the creation of a corpus, was an essential part of the process, the equivalent of analysing questionnaires or transcribing interviews for other researchers. Once the corpus and sub-corpora were established, Papatsiba could then carry out analyses from a number of perspectives. She was concerned to 'make the experience intelligible' to others, to understand the experience. She was concerned however also to analyse the discourse of the corpus critically, to reveal underlying concepts and assumptions. She did this by four types of textual analysis: content analysis, lexical analysis – which involves quantification – critical discourse analysis, and conceptual analysis. On the basis of a corpus of primary sources, she thus demonstrates a range of methods and the complex issues they reveal.

Jackson, like Lam, focuses on ethnography. She also places emphasis on the evaluation of the experience of her students, since in this case the residence abroad is of shorter duration and more structured by the teacher than is the case in other studies. Jackson draws attention to the use of narrative analysis and the option of using software in the analysis of data, in the form of the package called NVivo. Researchers working with qualitative data have as many opportunities to use the power of the computer as do those working with quantitative data.

Several contributors refer to grounded theory, but it is Tarp who provides the fullest account because grounded theory became just as important in her work as the data collection and analysis process itself. Readers are given an historical explanation of grounded theory and its purposes, as well as a detailed account of its application to Tarp's data. She too had a variety of data collection methods, including semi-open questionnaires, student diaries and semi-structured interviews. All of these were analysed from a grounded theory perspective, and Tarp provides detailed illustrative extracts from her analysis. She also discusses questions of validity and reliability and the arguments in the textbooks about these and alternative criteria of 'trustworthiness' in qualitative data analysis. She finishes her chapter by reflecting upon the pedagogical dimension of interviewing.

The recurring question of quantitative and qualitative data was central to Ehrenreich's early decisions about her research project. As she points out, there is ample opportunity for quantitative study since hundreds and thousands of students are involved in different schemes for residence abroad in Europe alone, and many thousands of others in the rest of the world.[1] Ultimately however she decided that a study which is interpretative and seeking understanding about the longer term impact of residence on interviewees' professional work had to be focused on qualitative data. She then discusses the questions of quality and of sampling and is as rigorous in her sampling as any quantitative survey. She ensured that her own interviews were systematic, were well validated through triangulation, and were as near the ideal described by the textbooks as possible. She too describes in detail her thematic analysis, and a combination with quantification, but also discusses the importance of the researcher's own reflections and her 'research companion', her diary.

Ehrenreich used narrative incentives in her interviews and Byram and Alred also based some of their research interviews on narrative theory. Their research project was funded by a public body. It is the only longitudinal research which attempts to evaluate the long term effects of residence abroad by carrying out interviews on two occasions, 10 years apart. They explain how the demands of funding meant that there was a common theme but also different emphases over the two periods, which were in fact two projects. In the early interviews they included the use of Repertory Grid techniques and in the later ones they elicited narrative. Their analysis was reported in two forms, for the funding body and in academic publications, and they discuss the differences this creates.

In the final chapter, Deardorff is also concerned to understand her participants' experience, but in this case the participants are those who organise residence abroad rather than the students. Like others, she uses questionnaires, but she also introduces the Delphi technique of eliciting data from informants. Her point is that there is a lack of consensus on how to define the desirable outcomes from residence abroad and other forms of internationalisation of higher education, and without this it is impossible to evaluate the impact. The Delphi technique involved collecting the views of experts and using statistical methods to find the common ground in their discussion of desirable outcomes. This technique could be equally used with students and combined with one or more of the many other methods described by other contributors.

Selecting and combining methods of data collection and analysis to find the best way to address a particular set of research questions requires imagination and is one of the most exciting parts of empirical research. There are no recipes, whatever the textbooks might imply. Research on residence and study abroad is a new field often being investigated by junior researchers. They define their own approaches, they invent their own methods, they borrow and replicate, they learn from each other, and more senior researchers need to do the same. The accounts of doing research in the following chapters will provide inspiration and warnings – about the real difficulties of research as well as the triumph of success.

Note

1. Coleman's work on residence abroad has been largely quantitative and will be part of another book on this topic in this same series. The Interculture Project (www.lancs.ac.uk/users/interculture/) surveyed and interviewed a large number of students studying abroad and provides a databank of materials for potential sojourners and their teachers.

Chapter 2
Japanese Students in Britain

MARI AYANO

Introduction

As a consequence of the increases in the number of international students and because of growing interest in multicultural issues, there has been much discussion of the psychological adjustment and support systems for them from different research perspectives. However, there are few studies that explore what happens in such students' mind during the course of study abroad. I was very conscious of the need to investigate the psychological experiences of international students, because of my personal experiences as an international student. I knew from this that international students experience different kinds of psychological stress during their study abroad and such psychological states influence their performance in host countries. As a counsellor who was trained in a person-centred approach, I thought it crucial to look closely at those students' psychological phenomena in order to support them.

In this chapter, by presenting some of the findings of my research, I will explore the psychological experiences of Japanese international students and discuss the implications for a support system which really meets their needs.

Study Abroad and Japanese People

According to recent statistics, the annual number of Japanese who go to study abroad increased every year during the 1990s (ICS Kokusai Bunka Kyoiku Senta, n.d.). In 2000, it numbered over 190,000 (The Ministry of Justice, Immigration Control Office, 2001). The most common destination is the United States, but the number has been gradually decreasing. Instead, the United Kingdom has become more popular in recent years. In 1990, the number of Japanese who went to the United Kingdom to study was approximately 12,000 (ICS Kokusai Bunka Kyoiku Senta, n.d.), but it climbed to more than 26,000 in 2000 (The Ministry of Justice, Immigration Control Office, 2001) of whom approximately 5300 were students in higher education (The Ministry of Education, 2001). Economic growth after World War II in Japan and the Japanese government's policy in the light of recent worldwide movements towards globalisation has made studying abroad accessible for more young Japanese. It is not only accessible for the elite few but also for anyone who has the desire and the financial support. One option now available for example, is when a Japanese university has a branch in a foreign country or a programme for study abroad as a course requirement (Hayashi, 2000). In the project described here, the majority of my research participants come under this latter group. They belong to a Japanese university and go to England to spend one year as a course requirement right after they enter the university. Most of them do not have any special language or other cultural training before they come to England.

The investigation involved collection of data over a period of two years from a total number of students, including questionnaire and test data, and interviews at three points during their stay.

Findings

What happens in students' minds when they encounter a new environment during the study abroad?

My research was a longitudinal project with a combination of interviews and questionnaires. Both of them cover similar questions and also contain different questions to supplement each other. After two years of data collection, I had obtained a vast amount of data. In this section, I would like to illustrate Japanese international students' psychological experiences during the period of their study abroad in the United Kingdom by selecting some of the most significant findings from both kinds of data.

In my interview research, I especially focused upon imagery and metaphors in students' narratives. Metaphors here are treated differently from in linguistic research where the focus might be on the formulation of metaphor. In counselling, metaphors are treated in a similar way to imagery and it is thought that imagery and metaphors can moderate difficult feelings often caused by talking about psychological issues (Morgan, 1996; Siegelman, 1990). For this reason, many counsellors use imagery and metaphors in their counselling practice and also for their own training. It is, therefore, appropriate to take this approach with metaphor in my research to explore international students' psychological experiences. In the presentation here, I shall link these qualitative data with quantitative data from the questionnaires in order to give as rich a picture as possible.

Adjustment levels over the year

First of all, I will present the results of three psychological tests which I used in my questionnaires. They are Dundee Relocation Inventory (DRI) (Fisher, 1989), Cognitive Failure Questionnaire (CFQ) (Broadbent *et al.*, 1982) and General Well-Being Schedule (GWB) (Fazio, 1977). The first test measures a degree of homesickness, the second test measures a level of psychological fatigue and the third test measures the individual's well-being on the whole.

Figure 2.1 presents the average score of the DRI for the students over the year. The average DRI score of the research participants in the middle of the year was 32.48. Comparing it with the average DRI score (17.5) in Fisher's (1989) study of homesickness in students, this clearly shows that the Japanese students suffered severely from homesickness. The students in Fisher's study entered university in their own country, therefore they only moved from their home town to the town where their university is located. My research participants moved to a different country very far from their home country. It is natural that differences and unfamiliarity experienced by the students in the current study are greater than those in Fisher's study. The result implies that the distance from home and the degree of differences and unfamiliarity in a host town are positively related to the degree of homesickness. It is also apparent that homesickness experienced by my research participants remained at the same level throughout the year, a question I shall return to below.

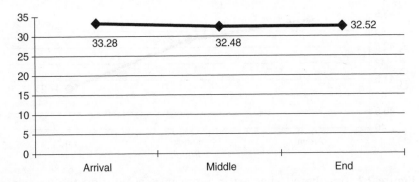

Figure 2.1 DRI score in Japanese international students over the year

Figure 2.2 shows the changes in the CFQ score during the year. The higher the score the stronger the indication that an individual experiences more failures in perception, memory and motor function and is thus psychologically tired (Broadbent *et al.*, 1982). The CFQ score for the middle period was a mean of 42.74. This was higher than the CFQ score in Fisher and Hood's (1987) study, where the score was 39.46 in the sixth week of the autumn term. This suggests that the participants in my research experienced psychological fatigue more severely and for longer.

Figure 2.3 gives the GWB scores for the Japanese students over the year. The higher the score, the stronger the indication of good conditions in psychological well-being.

The GWB score is divided into three levels depending upon the score. The lowest level is from 0 to 55 and it is labelled 'clinically significant distress'. The middle level is from 56 to 70 and it is called 'problem-indicative stress'. The top level is from 71 to 110 and it is named 'positive well-being'. Each level is further divided into three to five sub-levels. Here I have just presented the lower and middle parts of the scale within which the students' score fell. The black line is the average score of the Japanese students. The lower grey horizontal line is the border between severe and moderate in 'problem-indicative stress' level and the upper pale horizontal line shows the border with mild problem-indicative stress level. Comparing the Japanese students' scores to the standardised score of the GWB, we can see that the scores in all of the three periods reached problem-indicative stress level. The scores at the arrival and in the middle period indicate severe problem-indicative stress level.

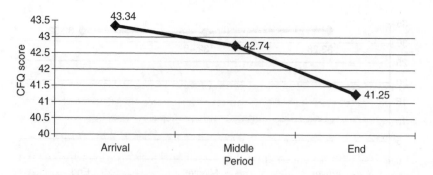

Figure 2.2 Time-based changes in score on CFQ during the studying abroad in Japanese students

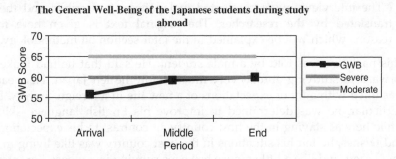

Figure 2.3 GWB scores over time

According to the above indications, the scores of the Japanese students over the year fall into the middle level, 'problem-indicative stress'. In fact, scores at the arrival point and in the middle of the year are both in the severe level. At the end of the period, scores slightly went up, but not high enough to reach the moderate level.

All three psychological tests imply that the Japanese international students in the United Kingdom suffered homesickness and psychological fatigue and their general well-being level remained very low over the year.

Through examining the results of these tests, it is possible to grasp the students' psychological conditions in general. Now, I would like to investigate what actually happened in their minds when they felt so tired, lonely and unhappy. To do so, I would like to examine students' narratives and the metaphors in the following subsections.

Narratives and metaphors of adjustment
Arrival and the following weeks: Trapped, restrained
Kago-ni haitta nezumi (a mouse in a cage)*

Kago-ni haitta nezumi-mitaina-mono. Jiyu-ni mie-te jiyu-ja-nai-yo-ne.... Koko-ni kite-ne, 1-shuukantte sugoku hayai-tte omotta-kedo, kekkyoku onajikoto-no kurikaeshi-dakara-sa, kooyatte nezumi-ga gara-gara hashitteru-janai, anna kanji-dayo. (Ted 1: 286–287, 304)

I am like a mouse in a cage. We seem to have more freedom but we don't. Since I came here, I felt a week has gone so quickly. But I just repeat the same things over and over. I feel like running in a wheel like a mouse in a cage.

(*The interviews were conducted in Japanese, transcribed and then translated by the researcher. The original text is given here for reasons which will be explained in the later section on methodology.)

This narrative was told by a male student. He said that he had looked forward to studying abroad very much before he left Japan. His heart was filled with a lot of expectations of a new life in a foreign country. In particular, he was determined to improve his English language skills while he was staying in the host country. In contrast to his expectations and wishes, he felt his situations in the host country was like living in a small cage, and like a little mouse he keeps running in a wheel. For international students, the first few weeks after arrival are hectic. They have to sort out a lot of things, e.g. moving into accommodation, registering for the academic course, learning about basic rules for living, settling down into a new environment. Furthermore, they had to use English to do all these things. During these busy weeks, the students feel that they have to 'run in a wheel' all the time. The metaphor of a cage seems to represent the idea that international students have only a limited amount of information about experiences in the host environment and therefore, feel trapped in a small cage.

Tasuketee! (help!)

So-desu-ne. Yappari Nihon-to-wa chiga-tte, jibun-no sukinakoto-ga dekinaitte- yu-no-ga.... Iya nanka taihentte-yu-ka, jyujitu-kan-wa nai-desu-ne. Aa, doronuma-ni hamatta-kibun. Aa, tanbo-no naka-de ashi-ga . . . nagagutsu-haite nagagutsu-ga nukenai-mitai-na hagayui-kanji desu-ne. Chotto iyada-na-tte- yu-teido-de. Jiyu-ga kikanaitte yuuno-wa arimasu-yo-ne. "Tasuketee!" desu-ka-ne. (Tom 1: 47–48, 52–53, 97–99)

Well, here, I cannot do what I want unlike myself in Japan. I don't feel I am fulfilled. Well, I feel like being trapped in mud. In a muddy rice field, I cannot pull out my feet... wearing a long boot... I cannot pull out my feet in a long boot and I feel impatient with it. I feel uncomfortable quite a bit. I cannot move freely. "Help!" That is my feeling.

In his narrative, Tom complained about a situation in which he cannot do what he wants and expressed his impatient feelings with the word 'Tasuketee!', 'Help' in Japanese. His non-verbal expressions also indicated how hard his struggles were and his imagery of being held down by a muddy rice field was his way of expressing the sense of despair. People cry out 'tasuketee' or 'help' when they have almost given up trying to help themselves after much effort. There were many other students who described their situations and feelings using metaphors whose theme was similar to the stories above, i.e. trapped and restrained.

The next narrative does not express difficulties and struggles directly. However, it implies subtle psychological strains in every day life in a host environment. Andrew complained about food, the bath and shower in his college and described his feelings as follows:

Kokoro-no yori-dokoro (spiritual anchorage)

Ma hyomen-teki-ni-wa sonna-ni ki-ni-shite-nain-desu-kedo, jissai, tabun, seishin-teki-ni-wa tashoo eikyo- suru-tokoro-wa aru-to-omoi-masu-ne. Uun, nanika...soko-made ima-wa ishiki-shite-nai-desu-kedo, tabun, nagai- aida- toka iru-to, ato-ato arun-ja-nai-kana-tte. Ma, itte-mire-ba kokoro-no yori-dokoro-tte-yuu bamen-demo tsuka-ware-te-ta–tokoro-nande, o-furo-toka shokuji-tte-no-wa. Sore-ga nakunaru-tte-koto-wa dan-dan sutoresu-toka tamatte-kita-toki-ni, hassan-suru-basho-ga nai-tte-yu-ka. (Andrew 1: 153–155)

Well, consciously, I do not mind it, but I think probably I am mentally affected by this. I am o.k. now but I will feel it stressful after a long time. Bath and meals are often considered to be kokoro no yoridokoro (spiritual anchorage) do not have them enough, you would not have anything to control stress.

According to Andrew, there is something which people usually use or do to comfort or unwind themselves. For him, this was food and a bath. By moving to a host country, international students lose such things. The effect seems subtle and many of them may not notice it. However, as Andrew said it can cause severe problems in a certain period of time.

In the middle of the year: Fatigue

Five to six months after the students' arrival, I conducted the second round of data collection, at the beginning of the second term after the holidays.

Tsukareta (I am tired)

[...] Yappari sugoi tukaretan-desu-yo. Mo, sutoresu-mo tamatte-kite, un, tanoshii-kedo yappari nihonjin-tomo iru-koto-mo ooi-desu-kedo, eigo shabera-nakucha-naranai-koto-mo ookute...Sutoresu-toka, shiranai-hito-to ikki-ni ippai attarishitan-de, moo...Hito-to sonna-ni zutto issho-ni irutte-koto-ga, nihon-de-wa nakatta-kara. Jikka-dattan-de. Ima-wa, nanika asa-kara ban-made, dareka-ni awana-kucha ikenai-kara, sooyuu-no-de, sugoi sutoresu-ga tamattet-te. Moo, kekkoo, sakunen kaeru-chokuzen-gurai-wa, kekkoo, bakuhatsu-shiso-na-hodo-ni tsukarete-te, de, nihon kaetta-kara, nihon-wa iina-to omotte. Zutto, kaette-kuru-no sugoi iyadattan-desu-kedo. (Nancy 2: 9)

I felt so tired. The stress was cumulating and . . . it's fun, of course, I spent a lot of time with Japanese friends, but I had to speak in English a lot. . .that was stressful and I've had met a lot of strangers at once and . . .
I haven't previously spent so much time with someone without my family because I was living with my parents back in Japan. Now, I have to meet people from morning to night. That is stressful, too. Then, I was so exhausted that I was almost bursting with my emotion, before I went back home to Japan during the holidays. I felt so relaxed in Japan that I really didn't want to come back here.

This interview took place six months after Nancy's arrival in England and she had just gone home to Japan during the Christmas holidays. Nancy talked about how stressful her daily life had been during the first term. As she said, to meet people of other cultures for the first time and speak in English with them were exciting experiences for most of the Japanese international students since they said these were the top two purposes for study abroad. Even so, keeping speaking in a foreign language and meeting strange people can make international students very tired. That is to say, the difference between the old environment and the new was so overwhelmingly large for her that she was unable to handle it efficiently and needed to go back to the old for a while. This therefore is one explanation of the tiredness indicated in the CFQ test described above. Nonetheless Nancy did make local friends despite the stress.

Issen-o hikare-teru (draw the line)

Honto-wa moo, doppuri tsukatte, koo, kaeroo-to omottetanda-kedo, nanka. . .
Nante-yuundaroo. Aisoreeto-sareterutte-yuu-ka. . .
(Igirisu-jin-no-guruupu-ni hairo-to doryoku-shita-no?)
Un, shita shita. Shita-kedo yappa-nanka, soremadette yuuka . . . Issen-o hikarerutte-yu-ka . . .
[. . .] Igirisujin-no naka-de-no tukiai-kata-o, watashi-ni taishite, onaji-yoo-ni shitekure-nai. [. . .] Tatoeba kurabu-toka-ni itte-mo, hanashi-kaketari shite-kureru-kedo, minna, yappa, jibun-no motto kyoomi-no-aru hitotachi-to, atsumattecchau-kara, jibun-wa, don-don, don-don, oite-ikarechau. Karera- wa sooyuu-fuu-ni, ishiki-teki-ni yatterun-ja-nai-to omounda-kedo. Nanka, jibun-teki-ni-wa imaichi sono-naka-ni haitte-ike-naiutte-yuu . . . . (Sandy 2: 5–7)

Honestly, I wanted to be immersed into British students' groups. But, the reality is . . . I feel isolated.
(Did you try to join a British students' group?)
Oh, yes, yes, I did. But, I felt they draw the line between them and me. For example, if I went to a club meeting, they came to talk to me kindly but they soon left me and went to someone else with whom they can talk about something more interesting. So, I felt left behind by them. They may have not noticed but I felt I couldn't join them.

Unlike Nancy, Sandy had difficulty making friends with host students. International students like Sandy often realise that there is a line between host students and themselves. Similar phenomena are also reported in studies of friendship patterns between international students and host students (Bochner *et al.*, 1985; Yokota, 1991) and this is considered stressful for international students. This example also brings out another important point, for when we look at the first sentence in the quotation, 'I wanted to be immersed into British students' group', it is clear that this was her expectation, but the reality was that she 'felt isolated'. There is thus another factor which makes Sandy's case different from Nancy's case, the gap between expectations and reality.

Fuan-desu-ne, tsune-ni (I feel anxious all the time)

Un, hiru-ma-wa issho-kenmei nanika-o yattete, sore-dokoro-ja-nai-kedo, yoru-ni-naru-to nani-mo suru-koto-ga naku-naru-kara, hen-na-koto, kangae-chaunda-to omoun-desu-kedo.
[. . .] Eigo-wa jotatsu-suru-noka-tka, fuan-kan desu-ne. Tsune-ni.
[. . .]Iya . . . Nihon-ni iru-toki-mo atta-to-omoun-desu-kedo. Demo, sore-wa, Nihon-dewa kontororu-dekiteta-mono-ga . . . nandaka, mo, wake-ga wakara-naku, sugoi ochikon-dari-shiterun-desu-ne. (Martha 2: 100–101, 168)

Well, I am too busy to think about anything during the day, but I start thinking about a lot of things at night because I don't have anything to do. For example, I am wondering whether my English can be improved or not . . . I have anxious feelings all the time.
I think I also had such feelings when I was in Japan, but I could control my feelings at that time. But I cannot manage it. I don't know why but now I feel so depressed.

This is another example of psychological distress experienced by the students in this period. Martha was a hard worker and joined a few clubs and circles including two orchestras and a swimming club besides classes in university. She seemed on the surface to be enjoying her life in the host country. However, inside her, it was not so easy. She was afraid of having free time because she started thinking of something not constructive and getting depressed and so she tried to make her schedule very busy. She also said that she felt anxious continuously and was suffering from depression. She was anxious about all sorts of things but first of all, it was about her English proficiency. By this time, they had already spent more than half of their study abroad period and some of them were worried about the achievement of the targets they had set for themselves before their sojourn.

At the end of the sojourn: Going home and cultural learning
   In the third and final interviews at the end of the year, it was time for the students to think about and to prepare for going back to Japan, and to plan a new life in Japan.

> Mo hayaku kaeritai. Hayaku kaette, hayaku moto-no seikatsu-ni mod-oshite, subete-o moto-ni ... risettotte-wake-demo-nai-kedo. Suggoi iyana-no-ga, yappari kocchi-no-go-hantte futorimasu-yo-ne. Suggoi, sore-ga, suggoi iya-de, yappari, Nihon-ni kaettara, are-yatte, kore-yatte, sore-de, ko-yatte yaserutte-yu-no-ga, yappari mokuhyoo-dakara. Dakara, hayaku kaette, hayaku moto-ni modoshi-taitte-yuuka. (Julie 2: 3–62–63)

> Oh, I want to go home soon. Then, I want to return my life style to a former one and return things as they were before I came here ... something like reset things. What I hate most here is that food is very high in calorie and I have gained a lot of weight. I really hate it. So, first of all, I do everything to lose my weight when I go back to Japan. That is my goal. So, I want to go back to Japan soon to make things normal.

Julie talked about what she was planning after she went back to Japan in the final interview. She was so bubbly and kept talking what she planned to do to lose weight, e.g. going for swimming lesson, eating Japanese food and so on, and also to rejoin a social group of Japanese in her generation in Japan, for example buying a mobile phone, going to a hair dresser and buying new fashionable clothes. At the end of the study abroad period, students' longing to go home seemed to become much stronger than before. The feelings were not vague and subtle anymore but clearer.
   Another significant theme in this period is cultural learning and cul-tural awareness. Although it was still at a shallow level, we can see some of the evidence for it in Sarah's story.

> Nanka, maikai au-tabi-ni, koe-o-kakete-kurerutte, soo-yuu-notte anmari Nihon-ja anmari nai-yoo-na-koto.... Soo-yuu, goku-

shitashii-hito-ja-nai-to hanasa-nainda-kedo, kocchi-wa, zettai, zen-zen hanashita-koto-nai-yoo-na-hito-demo, me-ga au-to, nanka, haro-tokatte ittari, so-yu-koto-toka, sesshi-kata-mitaina-no-ga wakatte-kita. (Sarah 3: 23)

It is rare in Japan that people say hello or something whenever they meet. In Japan we do such a thing only between people in close relationships. But here, even strangers greet each other when their eyes meet. I became used to it and got to understand how to do it.

Having seen Japanese students' narratives, and what they were feeling and thinking during their study abroad, it became clear that their psychological conditions were not so positive. Examining the findings from the quantitative research and the qualitative research, I found that the influential culture shock theories (e.g. Lysgaard, 1955; Oberg, 1960) do not seem to explain the findings of my study. Oberg (1960) argues that when individuals encounter a different culture, their reactions in the initial period are optimistic and he named this the honeymoon period. Then, such positive reactions gradually turned into negative ones. After a while, as people become adjusted to the new environment, their negative reactions towards the environment turn into more positive ones again. Lysgaard (1955) and his colleagues described individuals' adjustment levels towards unfamiliar environments using a u-shaped line. Thus, the adjustment levels at the beginning and the end of the sojourn period are higher than that in the middle.

The Japanese students in my study suffered from psychological strain almost throughout the year. There was no optimistic honeymoon period or significant adjustment period. The experience was difficult for much of the time although there were high and low moments reported in the interviews. The quantitative results showed a general tendency to experience difficulty. The question thus arises what help they could find and would turn to, and what further help they needed.

Seeking Help

To obtain data on this issue from the questionnaires, I asked students to pick the first five people whom they considered important for them in their host environment. This shows that establishing and maintaining relationships with others, Japanese or non-Japanese, are large concerns for many students. I asked the students to select five individuals who they thought were close to them. Figure 2.4 shows the results concerning the first three choices.

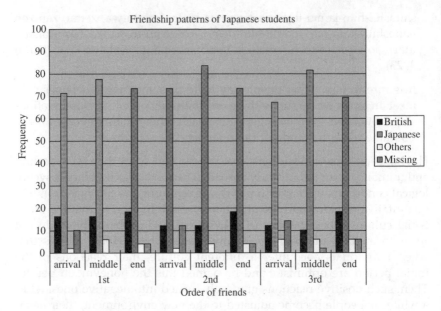

Figure 2.4 Friendship patterns of Japanese students

It is quite obvious that most of the students selected other Japanese people (about 70.0% on average) as their first three closest persons over the year and only a few selected British people (less than 20.0%). The result is very similar to the research by Bochner *et al.* (1985) with international students in England in 1985. The difficulty of establishing friendships between international students and host students in Japan is also reported by Yokota (1991).

Despite the fact that the students experienced psychological distresses and difficulties in establishing friendships with host students, most of the students did not find currently available support systems helpful and struggled to cope with the situations by themselves.

Figure 2.5 shows how many students visited current available supportive professionals. Only 20.0% or under students sought the professionals. So they had to find other ways to solve their problems and Figure 2.6 shows their strategies to cope with difficulties. The most common strategy is to listen to music in their own room. The second most common strategy is to talk to Japanese friends in England and the third is to phone someone in Japan. So here again it is evident that students tended very much to rely on people of their own nationality, around them or at a distance.

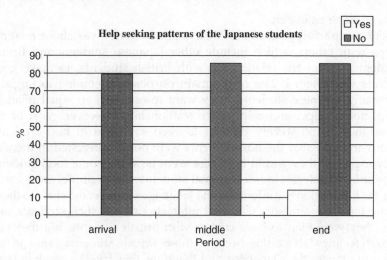

Figure 2.5 Help-seeking patterns of the Japanese students

What are the implications of this for offering more systematic support? I argue that there are three which could be discussed here:

- host students as friends;
- Japanese network;
- listener.

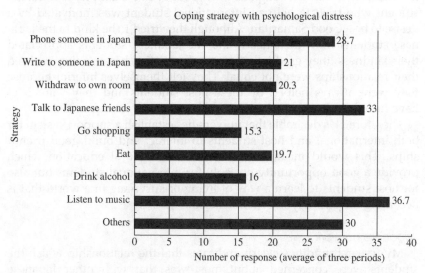

Figure 2.6 Coping strategy with psychological stress

Host students as friends

For my participants, one of their main concerns was about relationships with others, which include other Japanese students and British students. As for the relationship with British students, to make good friends with them is one of the main purposes of coming to England for many Japanese students. They want to establish an equal relationship, not a helper-and-help-seeker relationship. However, most of the time, they found it very difficult to even say hello to host students, and many said that the host students were not as interested in them as they expected they would be. There were however some local students who showed interest in international students. For example, those learning the international students' home language would come close to them. Some Japanese students who had interactions with such students said that they were glad to have contact with British students, but they had mixed feelings about this because those British students came to see them to practise their Japanese, and therefore, they tried to speak in Japanese and they felt this was not good for them because they could not practice their English. Some other Japanese students said that they were not very happy to be with these local students who are learning Japanese because they came to them with their own purpose, not for to befriend them.

Another group of people who tend to be kind to the Japanese students are those who have a religious background. For example, a Christian student who tried to help an international student was motivated by a desire to be a Good Samaritan. Although they tried to be kind to the Japanese students from their heart, and the Japanese students appreciated their kindness, they gradually became dissatisfied because they realised their relationships were not equal. They felt themselves inferior because they were always helped by these host students and they wanted to have host friends on equal terms.

Therefore, it is desirable that universities establish a support system for both international and host students to interact and build good friendships. This would mean some kind of intercultural education which provide a good opportunity not only for international students but also for host students to learn a way of living or surviving in a world that is becoming increasingly internationalised.

Japanese network

My research findings clearly indicates that the relationship which the students were concerned about most was that with other Japanese students within their own group. For international students who have difficulty in building a good close relationship with the host students, it is crucial to have a supportive relationship within their own national group, and it is even more important for their survival in daily life in an unfamiliar environment. The participants were very much concerned about how other Japanese students think of them and seemed afraid of being isolated from them. Since the community of the Japanese students was very small and limited, they became very close friends in a relatively short time. However, this relationship cannot be taken for granted. The dynamics among the members sometimes could become very tense. Jack's story tells vividly about such tensions within the Japanese group:

> Dakara, nanka...anmari gohatto-desu-toka-yu-kanji-no (laugh).**
> Nihongo-gakka-de manan-deru hito-to tomodachi-ni naru-to, nihonjin-ga 3,4-nin atsumaru-kara, butsukaru-wake-desu-ne. ...Tomodachi-tokat-te 2-tai-1-ja-naku-te, 1-tai-1-janai-desu-ka, akiraka-ni...ano...hanasu-toki. Demo, aru-teido-no nihonjin- dooshi-no kiyaku...kiyaku-kankei-ppoku, futari-de hitori-no tokoro-ni ikut-te yuuno-wa, akiraka-ni, ano, sore-wa kizuke-nai-desu-ne, tomodati-kankei. ...toriai-toka.... "nani hanasi-ten-da-yoo aitsu"...toka, nari-kane-nai-desu-ne. (Jack 3: 123–128)

> ...So, it's something like a taboo... to make a friend with a (British) student in the Japanese language course.
> Because... because if you make a friend with a (British) student in the Japanese language course, 3 or 4 Japanese students interact with one (British student). It is obvious that a conversation goes better if you are a pair (with a British student), not two (Japanese) to one (British). It's not good to come between other people's one-to-one relationships by tacit agreement within the Japanese students' group. It disturbs other's friendship.
> [...] Scrambling for a British friend [...] or searching how others are doing... something like, "Hey! What are they talking about together?"
> ** Words in parentheses were added by the researcher.

The use of the word 'taboo' is the indication here of the tension they were experiencing. As some students said, it is crucial, but very difficult for them to establish a close relationship with British students on the one hand, while maintaining a friendship with other Japanese students on the other hand. These two kinds of relationships are often incompatible with each other. This is because to have a British friend often causes other Japanese students to be jealous, which often leads to exclusion from the Japanese network.

I think that there are two main factors in this problematic situation. The first one is a lack of opportunity to establish close relationships with host students, discussed in the previous subsection. The second one is too much density of relationships among co-nationals. To over-come this kind of problem, it would be necessary to loosen the tight cohesion of the Japanese group. Before the students came to England, most of them had been educated in Japan in the Japanese culture in which harmony within a group is important and to be different or to do something different from others is regarded as bad because it destroys this harmony. Yet in this new situation they naturally are anxious to make friends with host students leaving their co-national friends behind. To handle the problems this creates, they need systema-tic training to learn to be independent and to accept being different from others. This could be done for example in language or cultural learning classes, where activities and assignments which the students have to accomplish individually, e.g. to interview a host student in college and report it in the classroom, can be introduced with help and advice from teachers.

Listener

Some interview participants said that the researcher played an import-ant role as a listener from outside their group to ease such tension within the Japanese group and release their psychological stress in daily life. For ethical reasons, I asked my interview participants after each session, if they felt uncomfortable in talking about their experiences and feelings to me, and if they had any comments on my research. All of the intervie-wees said that they felt good after each session or at least they did not have any difficulties to explore their problems and feelings with me.

One female student said that she talked a lot and felt so good every time because she could talk about what she never felt secure to talk about to her friends, and longed to see me the following time. She saw me as a visiting listener who came round regularly. To clarify what is meant by 'a listener', the following points need to be considered:

- I am a Japanese and I can talk to them in their own language (insider).
- I am an outsider to their group and I am not influenced by their group dynamics.

- I am not a counsellor for them at the time of the interviews, but nonetheless a trained counsellor. They feel secure about exposing their emotional problems to me without recognising that they have a psychological problem and they are being helped by a counsellor.
- They volunteered to participate in my research, at my request, and contributed to it. Therefore our relationship was on equal terms with each other or they were even in a higher position as people to whom I was in debt.

In order to fulfil this listener role in general, I suggest that universities and other educational institutions which invite international students or send their students to different countries should consider training some staff to be listeners, e.g. a counsellor or a lay person if she has a basic training to be a good listener, who is from the students' home country or who speaks the students' first language well. If the students are at a level in the host language where they can express their thoughts and feelings, a counsellor who is an expert in intercultural counselling or a trained lay person in the host country can take the role of listener.

In short, it is important for support to be successful that people work together from different directions, including host students who support international students to perform effectively during their study abroad. This process of working together is not only important for the international students but also for host students and staff who interact with them in terms of development of intercultural perspectives.

Research Design and Methods

Research participants and data collection

I collected data from Japanese international students in higher education in England from spring in 1999 to early spring in 2001. I collected data from two cohorts of these one-year sojourners and had data from three different groups in all: (1) students at a branch of a Japanese university in 1999; (2) students at a British university in 1999 and (3) students at a branch of a Japanese university in 2000.

I collected data three times from each group of students. The first data collection was done one to two months after their arrival. The second data collection was immediately after the first holidays, which was from five to six months after their arrival. The final data collection was less than one month prior to their departure for Japan and about 10 months after their arrival.

Choice of instruments

In this study, I used both questionnaires and interview methods as research instruments. In the following pages, firstly, I will explain why I chose those instruments, comparing the characteristics of quantitative and qualitative methods. Then I will move to describe the structure of the questionnaire and the content of the interview.

A review of the literature showed that it is commonly accepted that data collected by a qualitative method are more subjective but contain richer information than those by a quantitative method (Coolican, 1990). On the contrary, quantitative data are more objective in the sense that they can be generalisable, but they can also be superficial. The research setting when qualitative data are collected, is realistic and naturalistic contrasting with artificiality in the other (Coolican, 1990). Like many other education researchers, therefore, I decided to collect both types of data. The demographic information, psychological adjustment level and past experience of going abroad are examples of the quantitative data. Since I was interested in metaphor and imagery, I also needed students' stories about their experiences of studying abroad which would contain expressions using imagery and metaphors. These are necessarily more naturalistic and subjective and I chose a qualitative method – an in-depth and semi-structured interview – for collecting the data of this kind.

My main research questions are as follows:

(1) What psychological process is experienced by Japanese international students, as described in terms of imagery and metaphor, when those students encounter new environments and during the period of their studying and living abroad?
(2) What factors, e.g. past experience of going abroad, a student's personality, proficiency in a host language, and stressful life events, influence international students' psychological experiences in the process of adjustment to a host country?
(3) What are the advantages and disadvantages of studying abroad for these students?
(4) How can we help international students who experience psychological difficulty to go through their period of study?

Data collection

In order to collect data which might answer these research questions, I produced a questionnaire, considering formulations of questions, the number, length and order of questions, and a format which would be convenient for both the students to fill in and the researcher to operate the data analysis. The questions in the questionnaire cover the following issues:

- students' personal demographical information and other information about their background;
- students' feelings about their experiences;
- students' experiences in the host country;
- students' self evaluation of adjustment to the host country;
- students' self evaluation of their host language proficiency;
- students' involvement with the host environment.

I adapted three standardised or widely used psychological tests by other researchers to handle these questions because when I looked for a standardised psychological test for measuring the level of culture shock or intercultural adjustment, I found nothing after searching through all the available catalogues of psychological tests on the internet and the university library and asking for an advice from specialists in psychology and counselling. Through the literature review on culture shock (e.g. Church, 1982; Furnham & Bochner, 1986; Oberg, 1960), my MA study and my personal experiences, I considered that three kinds of psychological reactions, i.e. homesickness, absent-mindedness and self perception of well-being of self, are important indicators psychological difficulties following a geographic movement, and therefore, can be used as an indicator of psychological adjustment level. For homesickness, I chose Dundee Relocation Inventory (DRI) by Fisher (1989) because it has been validated by herself and her colleagues (e.g. Fisher and Hood, 1987) and also most of the statements in the original were applicable to the situation of my research participants. For absent mindedness, I used the Cognitive Failures Questionnaire (CFQ) by Broadbent *et al.* (1982). Although there was no significant evidence that stressful experiences cause any change in the CFQ score, there were some studies in which the test was used and show correlations between the CFQ score and life stress following a geographical movement (e.g. Fisher and Hood, 1987). Each statement in the questionnaire was suitable to the current study as well.

For psychological well-being, I chose a standardised test which is made up of the sub-questions of the General Well-Being Schedule (GWB) developed by Fazio (1977). The aim of this measurement is to assess self-representations of subjective well-being, which met my research purposes, and the validity and reliability of the test are established (Robinson *et al.*, 1991). Each statement in the instrument was also examined and was found appropriate to my research. All the three psychological measurements were published in English and therefore I translated them into Japanese for the use in the current research in order to collect accurate data from the Japanese students. I maintained the main meaning of each question as much as possible in order not to decrease the value of the tests. The translation was checked by a Japanese who was a bilingual in Japanese and English.

Help-seeking strategies and problem-solving strategies were also asked about every data collection. The questions about help-seeking strategies were adapted from another set of sub-question of the GWB and those about problem-solving were based on a pilot study with other Japanese students. Interactions with the host environment, in terms of socialisation and friendship, were also asked commonly in all of the three questionnaires. With respect to socialisation, the statements in the question were based on the pilot research and my MA research. As for friendship, I adapted material from a series of study of the friendship patterns of international students by Bochner and his colleagues (Bochner *et al.*, 1977, 1985). The self-evaluation of host language proficiency was assessed in each period of data collection in terms of reading, listening, speaking and writing. I also asked students to describe freely, in open questions, their experiences in daily life and studying abroad and their self-image.

Before conducting the main research, all the three questionnaires were piloted by a group of Japanese international students and their spouses who discussed if there were any grammatical errors or difficulties in completing the questionnaires.

The main part of the questionnaire consists of four sections. The first section is to collect the demographic information about a participant. The second section contains three psychological tests, i.e. DRI, CFQ and GWB to measure the adjustment level to the host country. The third section consists of questions about students' experiences of study abroad at a given point in time. The fourth section investigates self evaluations of their study abroad. The questionnaire was administered three times to the same students, with the main part of the questionnaires identical for all of the questionnaires. I also added some questions appropriate to the time of the data collection: questions about past experiences of going or living abroad in the first questionnaire; and I asked participants to comment on my research in the third questionnaire. All of the questionnaires requested participants' names in order to match individual data from three points of data collection.

Turning now to the interviews, I adapted Visual Case Processing (VCP) by Ishiyama (1988). The technique was developed to facilitate the elicitation of the imagery and metaphors of counsellor trainees in a supervision session in order to focus on their psychological experiences in counselling sessions and analyse them. The technique involves four activities: (1) initial non-visual case description; (2) visual case description; (3) case drawing and (4) case presentation and description. Each step contains several clear instructions and it seemed suitable to my research. I modified the original instructions and questions for my aim and translated them into Japanese, but the original meanings of the method were not changed. I prepared different sizes (A3 and A4) of paper and different colours of pens, felt tips, pencils and crayons to try which method works best. I again asked some Japanese students to help me to test the instrument. When I asked them to draw something on a sheet of paper in Step (3), almost all of the students reacted in the same way. They politely hesitated and refused to draw anything, saying, 'E-wa chotto jishin-ga nai-na' (I am not confident with my drawings) or 'E-wa heta-dakara' (I am not good at drawing at all). I told them that it did not matter but they were never satisfied. Then, I showed them an example in the article by Ishiyama, which was not very good in artistic terms but well drawn in psychological terms. Some laughed at it and some others smiled, but all of them looked relieved and started drawing their visual images in the mind. The technique worked very well and the students talked about their psychological experiences much more easily than before after a practice using the modified VCP (MVCP). I decided to use this method in my main interview research. For the preparation for the main interview, I made four cards on which instructions were written for each of the four steps. This is because many students asked me the instructions repeatedly and or to show my note of them. I also prepared plenty of A3 and A4 paper, pens, pencils, felt tips, crayons as well as a pair of scissors and glue for students who wanted to do a handicraft.

The interviews were semi-structured and the main questions were common for all three groups. The language used in the interviews was Japanese which is the first language for both the interviewees and the interviewer. I asked the students freely about their experiences, their feelings and emotions, problems, friendships and anything they want to say about their daily life and themselves. The length of each interview was 45 to 90 minutes. The first meeting began with introducing myself and having a short conversation about trifling matters in order to thaw the students' hesitation and my nervousness as a researcher. Then, I briefly described the purpose and the procedure of the interview. I also explained to the students that they had the freedom to drop out of the research anytime, that what they told me in the interviews was only to be used for the purpose of my study and that their confidentiality was guaranteed.

I asked them to sign the consent form when they agreed. This was followed with a warm-up using MVCP and after the MVCP practice, I started asking about their daily experience and how they felt about it. For some students who chose one of their daily experiences for the MVCP practice, the step four in the MVCP moved onto the main interview without any break.

I began the main interview with a question about their daily life, e.g. 'Saikin wa doo desu ka'. (How are you doing these days?) or 'Are kara doo shite mashita ka'. (How have you been doing since you came to Britain?) I usually encouraged students to talk freely about their experiences, thoughts and feelings related to those experiences. I asked some questions in my list only when I needed, trying not to interrupt the thread of the students' stories. I sometimes asked the students how they felt or what kind of image they had about their experiences, the people and environments appearing in their stories, using MVCP when it was appropriate.

For the second and the third interviews, I did not take time for MVCP particularly because I wanted to use more time for listening to the students' stories. However, I used the practice in MVCP when I considered it appropriate. For example, when a student talked about one incident, I asked them to have a visual image in their mind and to talk about it. I sometimes asked her to draw some pictures of their images. I also asked her to express what she experienced using another word, i.e. metaphors and talked about them, asking further questions.

In the last interview, I asked the students about their view of their whole experience during their study abroad. Adding to that, I asked them to give some comments on my research and on their experiences of participating in the research. All of the interviews were recorded with audiotape with the permission of the students. I made some notes during and after the other interviews as well.

Data analysis

I used computer software SPSS to analyse the data from the questionnaires. In order to run this programme, I entered the data into SPSS using a Data Editor in this software. I used only descriptive statistics so far and have not used all the possibilities of looking for causal relationships between factors, for example, previous experience and adjustment. Like many researchers I found I have more data than I need for the immediate purposes of the research, in this case the PhD thesis. So I chose the most relevant and left the remaining data for future study.

I applied the methods of thematic analysis and grounded theory analysis for analysing the interview data. In the initial plan of my research, I proposed to conduct a grounded theory approach to analyse my qualitative data. Strauss and Corbin (1990: 23) define grounded theory as follows:

A grounded theory is one that is inductively derived from the study of the phenomenon it represents. That is, it is discovered, developed, and provisionally verified through systematic data collection and analysis of data pertaining to that phenomenon. Therefore, data collection, analysis, and theory stand in reciprocal relationship with each other. One does not begin with a theory, then prove it. Rather, one begins with an area of study and what is relevant to that area is allowed to emerge.

Thus, I read through the interview transcripts making notes and memos in the margin or in a notebook. Considering the aims of my research, i.e. to examine psychological experiences of Japanese international students and to attempt to generate a theory from the collected data, the grounded theory seemed appropriate to my study. However, the amount of the data which I obtained after two years of the data collection was overwhelming for me to analyse with this method from the beginning to the end in the limited time for the PhD study, and I decided to apply the thematic analysis method, to reduce the amount of data to manageable size.

Thematic analysis is a widely known qualitative analysis methods which was introduced by Boyatzis who argues:

... thematic analysis, is a process that many have used in the past without articulating the specific techniques. It is a process used as part of many qualitative methods. In this sense, it is not a separate method, such as grounded theory or ethnography, but something to be used to assist the researcher in the search for insight. (Boyatzis, 1998: vi)

Those two approaches have similarities to and differences from each other. A main difference between them is that, on one hand, in the thematic analysis, researchers firstly decide themes to look at and then select data which are relevant to each theme before analysis; this enables them to focus on what they are looking for. The weakness of this method is that it was originally invented to transfer qualitative data into quantitative data and therefore, there is no further technique to analyse the qualitative data in depth. On the other hand, in grounded theory, researchers do not have any assumptions or predictions to examine prior to analysis, but a systematic analysis method leads them to discover the theory (Strauss & Corbin, 1990). Thus, this method leads researchers to 'break through assumptions and to create new order out of the old' (Strauss & Corbin, 1990: 27). It includes a higher level of analysis than the thematic analysis and therefore, I consider that it is suitable to analyse my data in depth. The disadvantage of this method is, as I mentioned above, that it demands a lot of time and patience.

As for the similarities, both of the methods are for analysing qualitative data and involve coding, categorising and linking data by comparisons in basic procedure. Considering those points, I decided to adopt two analysis methods for analysing the qualitative data.

Before I actually started analysing data, I made some preparations for handling my data safely. I copied each interview tape to another tape to prevent the original from being damaged through the transcribing process. Each master and copied tape was labelled with the informant's code name and the date of the interview. The original tapes were stored in a secure place in my room at home which no one else was able to access without my permission. I tried to start transcribing interview tapes as much as possible as soon as I finish each interview. However, it was often very difficult to find time for me to do so while I had to prepare for other interviews and questionnaires besides my daily routines as a mother. I really wished I had 48 hours per a day or I could work without sleep or rest. I often felt it was overwhelming and realised that if I did not take enough rest, I could not concentrate on listening to the students' story very well, and deal with a lot of different kinds of data carefully. To minimise the disadvantages of not transcribing the interview tapes immediately after each interview session within a limited time and energy, instead of transcribing the interview tapes, I always sat and recalled what happened in an interview session for a while in my car or alone in the room which I used for the interviews and jotted down in my research journal whatever came up my mind right after each interview. I also showed the original text as well for the same leason.

Therefore, it was when I had almost finished all of my data collection that I actually started transcribing the tapes. I typed the transcripts using a computer listening to tapes using a transcriber with which I could play, stop, rewind, forward and replay a tape relatively easily with a pedal switch. Although the transcriber enabled me to shorten time to transcribe the tapes, it still took several months for me to finish more than 500 hours of interview tapes. I printed the transcripts and made a few copies of each transcript for analysis. I kept two sets of original copies of the transcripts as well as two sets of copies of floppy discs in different places ensuring that no one could access them without my permission.

One more thing which I would like to discuss here is an issue of language. I conducted all of my research in Japanese since it is the first language for both my research participants and myself and then, in order to meet the regulation for the thesis submission in my university, which states that a thesis should be written in English, I had to translate my data when I need to cite them in my thesis. As Spradley (1979) suggested, it is very important for qualitative researchers not to impose their own meanings on their participants' stories, but to make an attempt to find specific meanings which were personally intended by each individual. I was concerned that translation from Japanese to English might change the original meaning of the data and that I might impose my meanings on the participants' statements especially when they contain metaphors and imagery as is often the case in my research. Therefore, I decided to wait to translate all of my data until I started writing my thesis. This enabled me to keep the original meaning by ana-lysing the data in my participants' words unless I needed, for instance, to discuss it with my supervisors or other PhD students in seminars or con-ferences. After that process, I finally started analysis of the interviews. I also showed the original text as well for the same reason.

I actually started analysing data after I finished transcribing a few of the interview tapes referring to the methodological textbook (Strauss & Corbin, 1990) and others' work. I read through the transcripts taking notes in the margin and underlining words, phrases and sentences which I thought interesting, fascinating, meaningful, or remarkable in some way. It was an exciting experience because I found so many interest-ing words and sentences in the interviews and when I looked simul-taneously at the interviews with different students, I noticed that there were some similarities, which I could look at more carefully later.

After the initial reading, I compared my notes, underlined words, phrases, sentences and paragraphs, tried to group the similar phenomena and put a possible label on each group. In this process, I actually cut lines and paragraphs of each interview out and glued them on a sheet of paper titled with a possible label. It was not so simple to find an appropriate name for grouped occurrences. Strauss and Corbin (1990) emphasise the importance of conceptualising, saying that it is crucial for further analysis, i.e. categorising, linking and discovering a theory behind the data. Therefore, the names of each category should preferably be abstract rather than descriptive. The names I gave to each category were often descriptive at the beginning, but gradually became more conceptual. I changed names whenever I found better ones, as Strauss and Corbin suggest. Strauss and Corbin (1990: 198) also emphasised the importance of memoing and diagramming as follows: 'Memoing and diagramming are important elements of analysis and should *never* be omitted, regardless of how pressed the analyst might be for time'.

Open coding is the first step of analysis process and it involves. It is regarded as the process of breaking down of data. That is to say, I read through the data analysing line by line, putting a conceptual label on whatever I found fascinating. There were more than ten pages of a list of the conceptual labels. I compare each of them and categorised depending upon their similarity and put more abstract categorical labels on them as Strauss and Corbin (1990) suggested. Then, the categorised data were developed by identifying their properties and dimensional locations. It was when I was doing open coding following grounded theory method that I decided to adopt the thematic analysis method for the reasons which I described above. In order to increase the reliability of the selection of relevant stories, I decided to adopt the criteria of a thematic code. Boyatzis (1998: 31) lists five elements of a good thematic code as follows:

(1)   a label (i.e. a name);
(2)   a definition of what the theme concerns (i.e. the characteristic or issue constituting the theme);
(3)   a description of how to know when the theme occurs (i.e. indicators on how to 'flag' the theme);
(4)   a description of any qualifications or exclusions to the identification of the theme;
(5)   examples, both positive and negative, to eliminate possible confusion when looking for the theme.

The following step is axial coding which refers to putting those categorised data together in different ways by 'making connections between a category and its sub-categories' (Boyatzis, 1998: 97). In my case, I compared each category to find similarities and connections. Then I worked out a large chart of those categories and links. It looked like a complicated family tree. Through this process, the categories developed further by specifying the conditions in which a phenomenon occurred. The conditions consist of three elements, i.e. the context in which a phenomenon takes place, the strategies by which the phenomenon is dealt with, and the consequences of the strategies. Those elements are regarded as subcategories of the phenomenon. Although a potential structure of the theoretical formulation becomes more apparent, it is still premature and has to wait for the final process.

Selective coding is the final process of the grounded theory. In this final process, the data which have been identified in the open coding and categorised in the axial coding are put together to find 'a grounded theory' (Strauss & Corbin, 1990: 116). This process requires more detailed work of the researcher. I tried to rearrange and reconnect all the categories I made in the axial coding process. The process was like completing a jigsaw puzzle, for which there is no model and you never know what it will be like when it is complete. Sometimes, I felt so excited because all pieces seemed to fit in and soon I was disappointed because I found the last piece did not fit in. Then, I started it again from the beginning. I repeated this going back to the former coding processes, i.e. axial coding and open coding, from time to time or even to the original data. It was when I found satisfactory answers to my research question that I decided to stop the selective coding. I had to meet the time limit for the doctoral study.

Reflections

Through the present study, I obtained a great amount of data which were also very rich. The results from the questionnaires showed me a map or an outline of the inner world of Japanese international students. Then students' narratives invited me into the world which was filled with each individual's unique experiences of studying abroad. It was a really exciting journey.

The research I conducted, which is longitudinal with a combination of qualitative and quantitative research, was a time and energy consuming method. However, through this study, I have learnt not only a practical method of doing research but also a way of being a researcher in contact with other individuals, which you cannot learn from a textbook.

Chapter 3

Recording the Journey: Diaries of Irish Students in Japan

AILEEN PEARSON-EVANS

Introduction

This chapter examines the dynamics of individuals' cross-cultural adjustment and learning during residence abroad, which emerged from case studies of six Irish university students living and working in Japan for a year. Methodologically, qualitative data were provided by personal diaries written by the students while in Japan, and analysed using a grounded theory (Glaser & Strauss, 1967) approach. Findings highlight the significance of three themes affecting and mirroring the students' adjustment process – social networks, food and language – and reveal, in each, a dynamic tension between home culture, host culture and other foreigners while living abroad. The research underlines the individual and complex nature of the adjustment process. Examining existing theories in the light of new findings, it raises questions as to what exactly constitutes adequate adjustment/learning during residence abroad and (if we can define it) how can it be facilitated and assessed. It is also in part a meta-case study of the diary methodology used in the process of conducting the research.

Setting the Scene

The impetus for this study had its roots in both my personal and professional background. Living in Japan (1985–1987, 1992–1995) and subsequently teaching Japanese in Ireland (1989–1992) made me acutely aware of the challenges of dealing with ways of seeing the world that are very different from one's own, and of the potential for learning through the experience of residence abroad. The International Marketing and Japanese four-year degree programme at Dublin City University

(DCU) required all students to spend their third year in Japan, to develop their cross-cultural communicative competence. However, very little was concretely known about the process or extent of their learning while abroad: they were largely left to their own devices, the only university assessment being of their linguistic ability in their final year. Visiting the students each year in Japan, and organising pre-departure and post-return workshops, I realised individuals had very different learning experiences. Some experienced major adjustment problems and home-sickness; others sailed through the year, seeing it as one long party, vir-tually untouched by cross-cultural interaction; some others adjusted well and gained in cross-cultural competence. Some returned home with increased ethnocentric attitudes, their prejudices and stereotypes confirmed by personal experience; others developed new perspectives, and stressed unexpected learning and skills developed abroad. Emphasis-ing only academic learning during that year, I felt we were ignoring issues of possibly greater educational value, which seemed to be of primary importance to the students concerned. It was obvious that residence abroad was an undervalued and under-explored potential source of student development and of research-based insight, and I began doctoral research in this area.

Research questions and design

My aim was to discover more about the learning/adjustment process of students during residence abroad, with a view to informing educational practice, contributing to research in the field, and maximising the devel-opment of intercultural sensitivity among students. My research ques-tions were:

- What processes and patterns are evident in each individual stu-dent's adjustment?
- What do students learn while in Japan; what factors facilitate or inhibit such learning?
- What challenges are encountered while living in Japan and what coping strategies are developed?
- Are there significant changes in attitudes, behaviours and perspec-tives on their host culture, themselves and their home culture?
- Can we establish from the research what factors encourage or block the development of greater self-awareness and intercultural sensitivity?

Such questions have attracted the interest of researchers in disciplines as varied as anthropology, sociology, psychology, language education and resulted in a vast range of theories and models conceptualising cross-cultural adjustment. The process has been variously construed as: a linear development through set stages from 'culture-shock' to recovery (Adler, 1987; Lysgaard, 1955; Oberg, 1960; Yoshikawa, 1987), a process of culture learning (Furnham & Bochner, 1994), a developmental journey in self-awareness (Bennett, 1986), a homeostasis mechanism, as individuals strive to reduce inner tension resulting from interaction with the foreign environment (Gudykunst & Hammer, 1987; Torbiorn, 1982). Other research has focused on identifying predictors of stress and coping strategies (Bochner, 1982; Searle & Ward, 1990; Babiker *et al.*, 1980), and the effect of individuals' attitudes, expectations, perceptions and values on the adjustment process (Klineberg & Hull, 1979; Burgoon, 1995). In addition, integrative models developed by Kim (1988) and Anderson (1994) offer multidimensional frameworks attempting to synthesise existing approaches, to achieve a more comprehensive and accurate explanation of the cross-cultural adjustment process.

Given the potential relevance of all the above to investigating the research questions I wished to address, I decided to adopt a qualitative case-study design, which would not restrict analysis to any one perspective, and which would facilitate further exploration. I was also interested in seeing how the integrative models would apply to real life cases. Church's (1982) emphasis on the paucity of qualitative longitudinal studies, new theory and new methodological design in cross-cultural adjustment research, was the basis of my choice of diaries as a research instrument, and the grounded theory analytic approach.

Participants' details

Diaries from six Irish students, written while living in Japan (1994/1995 and 1995/1996) provide the data for this study. Having completed two years of Japanese language and culture study at DCU, this academic year in Japan was a compulsory part of their four-year degree pro-gramme. In Japan, they spent the first three months studying Japanese language and culture at a Japanese university, followed by six months working in a Japanese company. While at university, five students lived with Japanese host families and one in a student dormitory; during their company placement two students lived in company dormitories, one in an apartment complex for foreigners, and three in company apartments. Four students were female, two male. Their ages ranged from 19 to 24. Two students were of mixed nationality: Irish/American and Irish/Japanese. All had travelled abroad on holiday, although only one had previously visited Japan. Their Japanese language ability ranged from elementary, intermediate to advanced. To preserve their anonymity, all personal and place names were changed in the data.

Findings

The diaries were analysed first horizontally, to identify common themes, and then vertically, to examine in depth individual adjustment patterns. Relating the six analytic adjustment stories to literature in the field, I extracted key elements to generate a grounded theory, which explained the nature and process of cross-cultural adjustment according to the data in this study. Given the limitations of this chapter, I can only briefly outline some of the key findings, which are however available to the interested reader elsewhere (Pearson-Evans, 1998, 1999, 2000, 2001).

Three common themes: Social networks, food, language

Across all six diaries three themes emerged as significant in both reflecting and affecting the students' cross-cultural adjustment process: social networks, food and language. Interestingly, they correspond to three basic concerns common to students going to study abroad: Will I be able to make friends? Will I be able to eat the foreign food? Will I understand and be able to communicate in the foreign language? Cross-cultural researchers have identified and examined the important roles played by social networks (Bochner, 1982) and language (Kim, 1988) in both determining and reflecting adjustment. The diaries were able to provide insights in both areas and highlight exactly how they interacted with other variables in the real lives of individuals. Food, although the subject of much anthropological research (Douglas, 1966; Levi-Strauss, 1968) has not previously been studied in relation to cross-cultural adjustment, and for that reason I will focus on it here. The diaries showed food to be, like language, a symbolic code, which students used, consciously and unconsciously, to express their changing identities and allegiances during the year. Running through each of the themes was a dynamic tension between home culture, host culture and other foreign cultures while living abroad, as the students strove to maintain a balance between the familiar and the strange, security and adventure in their host country. Adjustment was reflected in changing memberships of and attraction to different cultures at different times throughout the year: whether they sought Irish, *Gaijin* (foreigner) or Japanese friends, wanted Irish, Western or Japanese food, or communicated in Irish,

English or Japanese language, indicated their current attitude and level of adjustment to their host culture.

Social networks

Social networks are considered to play a major role in determining how a person interprets and responds to their environment, and are particularly relevant in the cross-cultural context (Kim, 1988). Students abroad are especially vulnerable and reliant on support from social networks: not only coping with the temporary loss of their familiar home network, they must simultaneously balance the conflicting pressures to maintain contact with home and create new networks in their host country. Bochner *et al.* (1986) identified three types of networks developed by international students in their host culture: monocultural (home culture/ethnic), bicultural (host culture) and multicultural (other foreigners). The Irish students' diaries revealed how a fourth monocultural network, consisting of friends and family at home, also played a significant role in adjustment abroad. Figure 3.1 illustrates the connections between the four networks:

Movement from left to right across the networks represents a movement away from similarity and safety of one's home culture toward increasing degrees of difference and potential threat (to one's identity, way of thinking, etc.) represented by foreign/host cultures. Cross-cultural adjustment lessened the students' reliance on home and increased the number and closeness of host culture ties (Kim, 1988), with resultant loosening and questioning of relationships with home. The network of *gaijin* (foreigners) in Japan, a first encounter with difference, could be a stepping stone to the host culture, or block further adjustment by becoming an end

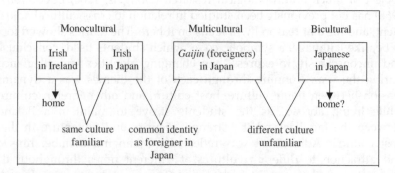

Figure 3.1 Four social networks of Irish students in Japan

in itself. Sharing the common experience of being foreigners in Japan, the *gaijin* network represented an extended ethnic network abroad. Earlier studies have found that ethnic network support facilitates adjustment in the early stages, but hinders it later on (Anderson, 1994; Kim, 1988); and that international students tend to emotionally depend on and mix mainly with ethnic/foreign friends abroad, developing few, and mainly utilitarian, host culture contacts (Klineberg & Hull, 1979). The Irish students' diaries indicated a more nuanced reality. They showed how all four social networks were valued by the students, providing both psychological support and cultural information for different students at different times depending on their level of cross-cultural adjustment; all could potentially encourage or impede adjustment, depending on the context.

The Irish students drew on their ethnic network, at home and in Japan, for emotional support, advice and practical help, as well as a temporary escape from dealing with host culture difficulties. Letters and phone-calls from people in Ireland were crucial to their sense of stability in the early days, but could intensify rather than alleviate homesickness:

Well its 5.20 pm and I just got off the phone to Mom. Okay I finally admit it, I'm well and truly homesick. I would do anything to be sitting in my house in Ireland eating Sunday roast and instead I'm on my way into the house to try and hold a conversation with strangers. I miss everyone so much, if they were here I'd have the best time ever 'cause its not Japan that I don't like. (Lucy, 1.10.95)

Lucy's experience echoes Simmel's (1950) defining paradox of 'the stranger', physically distant from people one is emotionally close to, and emotionally distant from those in one's physical proximity. Emotional involvement with home regularly intruded on the Irish students' experience abroad. Bad news from Ireland undermined the value of being in Japan: 6000 miles distance imparted a sense of uselessness to help those at home. Strong attachments to home lessened motivation to develop host culture relationships, often due to fear of resultant adjustment difficulties on return: two students, emotionally dependent on boyfriends in Ireland, developed no close Japanese friends. Willingness to accept change in oneself and one's relationship with home is essential for adjustment to a foreign culture (Anderson, 1994; Kim, 1988). As students adjusted, contact with home was less frequent and less satisfying, underlining how little people in Ireland understood or cared about life in Japan; Japan and Ireland had switched places in the students' emotional world and they became increasingly apprehensive about difficulties readjusting to 'home'.

The network of Irish friends who shared the Japan experience provided solidarity and support: exploring the new culture together turned a potentially threatening experience into an adventure; when homesick it helped to know others felt the same. When overwhelmed by difference, they could recreate a familiar social life within a more exotic setting, and had no need to deal with the real Japan. The danger inherent in this group was that its reinforcement of Irish values and pressure to spend time together discouraged adjustment to Japan. The Irish 'in-group' encouraged superior and negative attitudes towards their host 'out-group' (Barth, 1994) rather than empathy. Lucy became depressed about the amount of time they all spent 'bitching about Japan': useful for releasing stress, it ultimately reduced motivation to adjust. Mixing with Japanese often incurred negative comments from classmates about disloyalty and guilt feelings, strong 'in-group' boundaries placing restrictions on 'out-group' interactions (Barth, 1994). And for some students, relationship problems and competition within the Irish group compounded their difficulties in Japan. Friendships did not always provide the support expected: all were dealing with the cross-cultural experience in different ways and reactions were unpredictable even to themselves. The uncontrollable 'rollercoaster of emotions' many experienced abroad, resulted in relationships often becoming quite superficial:

> I think that now I understand a bit more why people don't talk to each other as much over here about things that matter; I think that when you feel great and when you're enjoying yourself, it's harder to listen to other people's problems because it's very easy for them to drag you down here. I know it sounds cruel and heartless, but if you listen too hard or get involved too much, it will eventually pull you under. (Naomi, 27.3.96)

The *gaijin* (foreigner) network, as a type of extended ethnic network, provided emotional support and information on Japan, but also blocked further adjustment if it became an end in itself, replacing the motivation to meet Japanese. *Gaijin* literally means 'outside person': exclusion from the Japanese 'in-group' contrasted with automatic inclusion in this foreigner 'out-group', or in Bridget's words 'The *Gaijin* Club'. Three students found this an exciting new network of international friends: highly visible among Japanese, *gaijin* always greeted each other, and making friends was easy, with English as the international language and assumed similar values (Barth, 1969). Some students felt happy and totally adjusted to their host culture, although mixing exclusively within the *gaijin* world of international foreigners in Japan. For students whose priority was finding Japanese friends, *gaijin* were a stumbling block: Naomi complained her university only offered '*gaijin* and stress'; Liam claimed *gaijin* were his main source of problems in Japan; Aidan tried to avoid *gaijin*, frustrated by their culturally insensitive behaviour and appalled that Japanese considered him to be one. But, later in the year, encountering major cross-cultural problems with Japanese colleagues, Aidan wished for *gaijin* friends who could empathise with his point of view, supporting Bochner's (1982) findings that a balance between ethnic and host culture networks is most beneficial to adjustment. In collectivist (Hofstede, 1994) Japan, individuals are defined in terms of group memberships: the *gaijin* community is a foreigner's designated group, whether one ascribes oneself to it or not, and it is unwise to reject its support.

Relationships with *Japanese* were crucial to the students' adjustment, as through them they developed a deeper understanding of Japanese language/culture and increased motivation to integrate into the host culture. These were more difficult to establish and more demanding, and not all students had the motivation to seek them out. It was only once a certain level of general adjustment to the language/culture had been achieved, that students actively sought to develop closer contacts with Japanese, beyond the utilitarian nature of initial contacts (Tanaka *et al.*, 1997). The development of host culture relationships was strongly influenced by the host environment's 'interaction potential' and 'conformity pressure' (Kim, 1988): the receptivity of Japanese to newly arrived foreigners with low language skills facilitated adjustment, whereas later continuing strong pressure to conform to the *gaijin* stereotype or to Japanese rules negatively affected adjustment. Four of the Irish students made close host culture friends: Liam's closest relationships were with his host family and Japanese girlfriend; Aidan had exclusively Japanese friends and a Japanese boyfriend; Naomi and Lucy moved through the *gaijin* circle to developing close Japanese friends by the end of the year. These relationships involved a much deeper emotional involvement than the purely utilitarian level found in earlier studies of international students (Klineberg & Hull, 1979). Liam's and Aidan's Japanese relationships provided crucial emotional support and a positive contact with their host culture when experiencing cross-cultural difficulties; through Naomi's friendships with Japanese colleagues and relations she finally felt part of Japanese culture. For these students, host culture friends were at times more important than ethnic friends. Findings support Klineberg's (1982) *Modified Culture Contact Hypothesis*, that for cross-cultural relationships to be successful they should ideally be of equal status, involve superordinate goals, satisfy the needs of individuals and be free from discrimination and condescension. The Irish students consistently sought such features in relationships and only friendships satisfying these criteria developed beyond initial superficial contacts. In contrast, they developed increasingly negative attitudes towards Japanese when contacts were superficial, feeling used as 'token *gaijin*' or 'free English practice'. Many contacts provided by the university fit this latter type, underlining the need for careful rethinking of how such contacts are organised.

Food

Food, described as 'the symbolic medium par excellence' (Morse, 1994), has been widely studied as a cultural artefact by sociologists and anthropologists to uncover underlying cultural values and beliefs (Douglas, 1966; Levi-Strauss, 1968). The theoretically 'omnivorous' nature of human beings suggests our food choices and practices are culturally conditioned (Fischler, 1988); food has been shown to be of central importance in creating and maintaining social relations, both within and between cultures, and food preferences to be intimately connected with individual, group and national identity (Bourdieu, 1986; Fischler, 1988). Food is therefore a salient area of study in the cross-cultural adjustment process, where social relations and identities are brought into question by exposure to different customs and values.

For the Irish students in Japan, becoming familiar with new tastes and textures, learning to eat things they would normally not consider as food, and mastering a new mode of eating with chopsticks, all required considerable adjustment. Since eating is a basic necessity for survival, it was part of the host culture that the students could not avoid interacting with on a daily basis. The diaries showed that depending on their tastes and stage of adjustment, food could be a source of constant pressure, a trial, a challenge or an adventure.

Food as membership of culture

Bourdieu's (1986) findings that food choices reflect an individual's attempt to control their environment were supported by the students' to-and-fro dynamic between Irish/Western and Japanese food, alternating between times-in and times-out of their host culture. *Irish food* had a special value for them: not only was it expensive and often impossible to find in Japan, but it had power to evoke memories and the feeling of 'home' (Grossman, 1996). Although chocolate was their major 'comfort food', anything Irish became irresistible abroad, as Naomi comments about Tayto crisps:

> I never used to touch them last year, but when I got them last night, you'd think they were the best thing since sliced pan! (Naomi, 29.3.96)

The students agreed that *Western food* in Japan was bland, but it still represented the taste of 'home', so they chose Western restaurants to celebrate special occasions like birthdays and Christmas. Fast-food chains like MacDonalds and MrDonuts, with their familiar tastes and atmosphere, provided a refuge from Japanese culture especially in the early days.

> MacDonalds never tasted so good, I've never eaten there as much as since I've been in Japan. Some days the thought of more rice and *miso* is just too much! (Roisin, 5.11.94)

MacDonalds was a regular venue where the female students met to 'chat' about Japan, where they felt comfortable and could talk openly and frankly. Likewise, Irish pubs and foreigners' bars were places to relax on home territory – there the students understood the rules of behaviour better than the Japanese, foreigners were in the majority and the main language of communication was English. As the year progressed, Western food and Irish bars became a means of sharing their home culture with Japanese friends and an indication of closer cross-cultural relationships.

Similarly, eating *Japanese food* as an important way of taking part in Japanese culture (Douglas, 1966; Fischler, 1988). Symbolic of their hosts' invitation to be part of Japanese society and the students' willingness to participate in their host culture, it mirrored participation and adjustment in other areas of Japanese life. Since refusal to eat Japanese food felt like rejection of Japanese culture, they made valiant efforts to eat what they were given, even when seemingly inedible from an Irish viewpoint:

> I arrived home to be offered some sweets. *'Oishii, oishii'* Honest? I couldn't refuse outright so I ate one – YUCK! That scummy, rubbery tasteless rice-cake gunk in the middle, with that revolting sweet bean-paste on top . . . But I lied happily and said yes, it was delicious. And promptly drank a big cup of tea to get rid of the taste. (Roisin, 27.11.94)

Babiker *et al.*'s (1980) *Culture Distance Hypothesis* suggests the extreme differences between Japanese and Irish food should exacerbate adjustment problems for Irish students in Japan. The diaries revealed however that alimentary difference sometimes facilitated adjustment: eating exotic Japanese food was part of the novelty of exploring Japan and it could ease communication in their host families, compensating for weak language skills. For Lucy, sharing Japanese food was central to feeling part of her host family, so their attempts to accommodate her difficulties with chopsticks and Japanese food by serving Western food caused great distress:

> Naomi (Host family sister) made me a piece of fish and everyone else got this amazing fish rice and soup mixed up with chopsticks and I got a knife and fork. I'm so pissed off. She wouldn't even give me rice. Why is she singling me out. Dad came home and gave me a cake, but I wasn't in the mood to talk to him so I said I had to study. Jesus I can't believe how upset I am. Hopefully I can sleep this off. I can't stop crying oh please let this week be good, I don't think I'll make it through the year. I'm so lonely. (1.10.95)

Lucy's interpretation that receiving different food symbolised exclusion from the family unit, underlines the central importance of food in creating and maintaining social relations (Fischler, 1988).

Food as mirror of cross-cultural adjustment: Changing tastes mirroring adjustment

The students' cross-cultural adjustment showed parallel changes in their alimentary tastes, and they suddenly found themselves liking Japanese foods they had initially found off-putting. In November, Roisin reacted negatively to raw fish in a *sushi* bar: 'I looked at all these slimy bits going around on the conveyor belt and felt ill' (4.11.94). Yet by December she was commenting on how delicious *sushi* was (4.12), and her first real feeling of being 'at home' in Japan was when wandering round a Japanese shrine eating *yakisoba* like all the other Japanese tourists (2.1.95). Closer identification with their host society saw them consciously choosing Japanese over Western food, sometimes in contrast to their Japanese friends: 'It was a bit strange, I was the one eating rice and fish with chopsticks, while Seda-*san* had her curried rice, salad, knife and fork' (Roisin, 30.1.95).

Bourdieu's (1986) assertion that food preferences are often a conscious expression of changing identity is supported in the diaries. It is most clearly expressed by Lucy, for whom eating Japanese food was somehow a way of 'being Japanese' (Fischler, 1988): cooking Japanese food for her family in Ireland at Christmas helped counteract feelings of reverse culture-shock, recreating an atmosphere of 'home': 'All the cousins arrived, we had *ramen* for starters, it reminded me of home, we served all the Japanese snacks it was a laugh, we served *sake* and loads of other grub . . . ' (27.12.95).

Since food and food rituals embody a culture's values (Douglas, 1966; Levi-Strauss, 1968), the students' reactions often indicated to what extent they understood and appreciated Japanese core values. While their tastes adapted over time, problems related to cultural value differences persisted, and difficulties they had with other aspects of Japanese culture reappeared at mealtimes too. They complained of the lack of individual choice in their collectivist (Hofstede, 1994) host culture, and of conformity pressure to adhere to the strict role definitions of what *gaijin* or females could or could not eat. As with social networks, findings support Kim's (1988) and Anderson's (1994) emphasis on the influence of the host culture environment's 'conformity pressure' and 'receptivity' on adjustment. Japanese culture exerts strong conformity pressure on both Japanese and foreigners to adhere to strict codes of behaviour and strong in-group/out-group boundaries make integration difficult for a foreigner. As 'adapted *gaijin*' students often encountered difficulties around food and food practices with Japanese hosts, due to no longer fitting the expected stereotype. This resulted in the paradox that the more they cross-culturally adjusted to Japan, the more they tended to feel excluded from Japanese society (Gudykunst, 1983). These findings refine understanding of Babiker *et al.*'s (1980) *Culture Distance Hypothesis*, suggesting that although surface differences in variables such as food may predict cross-cultural problems, of far more relevance are the differences in underlying core values of cultures, which may then find their expression through these variables.

Language

Given the centrality of language to human communication activities, host language proficiency is assumed to be one of the most important determinants of successful culture learning. It has therefore been included in almost all studies of cross-cultural adjustment (Kim, 1988). Bourdieu (1991) considers linguistic proficiency as 'cultural capital', and host language competence has been found to provide access to status and power for foreigners (Kim, 1988). Since interpersonal communication does not happen in a social vacuum, research on concerns of 'face' (Goffman, 1967; Siegal, 1996) and social identity (Turner, 1987) provide further insights into an individual's communication patterns in a cross-cultural context. Research into linguistic relativity suggests a complex relationship between language, perception, thought and culture (Whorf, 1998): learning a foreign language has been equated with potentially opening up a new world view or developing a second or even multicultural personality. Kim (1988) defines language as encompassing three levels: words, paralinguistic features, underlying communication rules. Pearson-Evans (2000, 2001) has combined Agar's (1994) term *languaculture* with the culture iceberg metaphor, to explore challenges posed to one's identity on all three levels of the '*languaculture* iceberg'.

The learning of language and culture is recognised as a complex process, which happens both consciously and unconsciously, is affected by the social context of the learner, and affects various levels of the learners' identity. The Irish students' diaries provide rich data illustrating all of the above issues. Three languages – Irish, English and Japanese – appear in the diaries, reflecting their sense of inclusion/exclusion, attachment to/rejection of home culture, Western culture or host culture throughout the year. Like food, language is shown to be a highly symbolic medium, intimately connected with maintaining and developing relationships within their social networks in Japan.

The diaries support findings of studies on language use in bilingual and multilingual societies, in that the Irish students saw their choice of language code in Japan as an 'act of identity' (Le Page & Tabouret-Keller, 1985) and power (Bourdieu, 1991). Although English was their native language and none spoke Irish fluently, they used *Irish* to accentuate their Irish identity. After an evening in the Irish Pub with Irish friends, Naomi said she had to leave early as: 'being the salarywoman that I am, I had to head home to *me leaba*' (29.3.96). Her use of Irish and the pronoun 'me', common in inner city Dublin speech patterns, reflects a conscious attempt to create a 'stylised persona' (Rampton, 1991) with a stage-Irish expression, not reflective of her normal speech. For Bridget and Lucy, speaking Irish strengthened group solidarity when intimidated by incomprehensible Japanese all around them. On the plane to Japan, Lucy wrote: 'it's crazy, we're surrounded by Japs so we keep speaking in Irish, we're having a great laugh' (19.9.05), and a few days after arrival Bridget stated: I've spoken more Irish in the last few days than I have in the past year at home' (23.9.95). Speaking Irish, like switching l/r as a parody of Japanese speakers' English, replaced feelings of inadequacy with superiority, of exclusion with inclusion. By reinforcing 'in-group' loyalties, this behaviour encouraged negative attitudes towards their host culture and was counterproductive to adjustment. As an 'in-group' code, students used Irish to create privacy and power: Lucy told an Irish friend she was working as a *muinteoir* (teacher) (12.4.95), not wanting Japanese colleagues to understand; Aidan used a newspaper article about Ireland to get his own back on Japanese students, who insisted on emphasising how difficult the Japanese language was for foreigners:

> I showed it to nearly everybody in the dorm I was so proud. I got some of them to read *Uimher a hAon* which none of them could make head nor

tail of. I was able to use the *'Airurando go wa muzukashi, ne'* lines. Revenge is so sweet! (1.11.94)

English, the normal language of communication among foreigners in Japan, expressed the students' *gaijin* identity in their host culture. Speaking English among themselves or with other foreigners was relaxing, and a welcome opportunity to 'be themselves' again: even students with high host language skills expressed frustration at being unable to present an adequate 'face' (Siegal, 1996) in Japanese. But mixing within an English-speaking ethnic network could have negative effects on adjustment, as suggested by Giles and Smith's (1979) *Speech Accommodation Theory*: not only was such communication less demanding and often more satisfying than host language interactions, but it reinforced ethnic language and thought patterns, and their underlying cultural values. While students were happy to speak English with *gaijin*, they were reluctant to do so with Japanese, and suspected the motivation of any Japanese person who initiated conversation in English.

> I was standing on the platform waiting to get the train home when I saw this down and out heading straight toward me. I just thought to myself 'no God! Please not today!' God was not listening. I wonder sometimes if I have a sign on my back that says 'Practise your English on me!' I tried to be as polite as I could but when my train came I pushed my way into the crush as deep as I could to escape. (Aidan, 17.4.96)

Even students with low language skills expected to speak Japanese with host culture members and interpreted unwillingness on the part of their hosts to do so as a way of excluding them from Japanese culture. Being intuitively aware of the power associated with host language competence and the question of who decides what language is spoken in an interaction (Bourdieu, 1991; Kim, 1988), they reacted with resentment and sarcasm on such occasions. They felt most comfortable when they sensed equality in their relationships with Japanese: linguistically this was expressed by conversing in a mixture of Japanese/English (*eigoni-hongo*) or by mutual help with each others' language difficulties. This arrangement meant both parties learnt something from the interaction and was a perfect solution for those with limited host language skills.

At the start of their year, all students were highly motivated to become fluent in *Japanese*, seeing it as the primary aim of their year abroad. Their interest was in developing pragmatic communicative competence in real situations with host culture members, rather than success in university exams. Opportunities to speak Japanese increased motivation, helping them feel part of Japanese culture; conversely, rejection of their host culture was reflected in refusal to speak the host language. The diaries showed the students grappling with the process of coming to terms with a radically different 'languaculture' (Agar, 1994). It was a 'two steps forward, one step back' process, full of excitement and challenges but also fraught with uncertainties. Progress was highly dependent on context and the state of their relations with host culture members: Liam managed to have complicated discussions with his host family on a wide range of topics, but at work, feeling like 'an unwanted child' (11.2.96) and 'the bottom of all agendas' (2.2.95), he could barely compose a correct sentence in Japanese. As in their normal lives at home, students were concerned with constructing a positive 'face' (Goffman, 1967) in their host culture: success was often hampered by limited language skills, inadequate understanding of pragmatics, or reluctance to embrace a 'face' appropriate to the host culture but conflicting with their own culture's values (Siegal, 1996).

While high language skills are generally thought to facilitate adjustment (Kim, 1988), the diaries showed that language proficiency alone did not determine the readiness with which students embraced their host culture during the year. Low language skills could be compensated for by non-verbal behaviour and the indulgent attitude of Japanese hosts; only when seeking a deeper level of communication with host culture members did they become a barrier. High language skills provided potential for deeper communication with host culture members, but did not automatically facilitate adjustment. Proficiency in Japanese brought the students into an ambiguous realm where neither host nor guest was clear what extent of fluency had been attained – the host culture's attitude oscillated between treating them as *gaijin* unable to speak Japanese, and expecting native-like proficiency, interpreting mistakes in register as deliberate insults. Neither attitude encouraged cross-cultural adjustment. Such experiences may explain recent findings of decreased sojourner satisfaction among more proficient speakers of Japanese within the international student body in Japan (Tanaka *et al.*, 1997). Deeper involvement with their host culture inevitably entailed dealing with the different 'cultural logic' informing Japanese values and behaviour. The ensuing 'clash of consciousness' (Clarke, 1976) has been recognised as the most challenging level in cross-cultural encounters (Condon, 1974). Frustration at this level produced negative attitudes to the host culture and undermined progress on a purely linguistic level. While all students encountered this level at some stage, higher language skills brought it on sooner and involved higher expectations of being able to deal with it.

Key elements in the adjustment process

This section addresses briefly some of the key findings relating to the cross-cultural adjustment process elucidated by both horizontal and vertical analysis of the Irish students' diaries.

Relating the students' stories to existing literature, it was clear that no one theory of adjustment fits all cases. All existing theories found resonance in the students' diaries, and shed light on elements of individuals' experiences, but none could adequately explain all aspects of an individual's adjustment process. The integrative models (Anderson, 1994; Kim, 1988), which synthesise existing approaches, were supported by these findings. However, their multi-dimensional frameworks, though valuable in graphically combining all elements of the adjustment process, do not explain how different variables interact or why they modify each other in different ways in individual cases. The diaries provided such detail, proving to be an effective method of extending our understanding of the dynamics of the complex web of variables involved in cross-cultural adjustment.

The diaries show cross-cultural adjustment to be a process of growing familiarity and deepening involvement between the individual student and his/her host culture. In this dynamic process of interaction, no two individuals' characteristics and no two host culture contexts are exactly the same, with the result that adjustment processes and outcomes are highly individual and subjective. Leaving Japan, all students are satisfied with having achieved a certain level of adjustment and host communication competence, enabling them to participate in host culture activities with host culture members. Yet, since not all aim at the same depth of involvement, they are satisfied with very different adjustment levels at the end of their year. Adjustment is subjective: it means different things to different individuals, and even to the same individual what is valid at one stage is unsatisfying later on. For example, Lucy feels 'totally adjusted' after one week in Japan, but weak language skills enabling only superficial communication soon produce dissatisfaction; mixing exclusively with _gaijin_ she feels comfortable and 'adjusted' again by Christmas, but in January greater host language skills and confidence encourage her to seek deeper involvement with Japanese people. Naomi, likewise, feels 'really adjusted' mixing with her Irish network by March, but outgrowing its support, soon sees it as restricting her development of deeper contact with her host culture. In both cases the individuals seek the level of adjustment, which corresponds to their needs and abilities at the time. These findings question the validity of research that measures adjustment levels according to single variables such as one's 'satisfaction' and 'comfort' in the host culture, or at isolated points during a sojourn, suggesting instead the desirability of investigating how individual patterns develop over time.

Although it is possible to identify some common stages in the students' adjustment patterns, suggesting support for conceptualising adjustment in terms of a Stage model (Oberg, 1960), there is so much variation in individuals' experience of, and the timing and duration of, these stages, that it seems more useful to investigate the causes of such variation in individual patterns than merely describing the stages themselves (Church, 1982). The students' diaries show a common cycle of 5 stages: (1) *A pre-departure/transition stage*, characterised by mixed feelings of apprehension/excitement about what lies ahead, and nostalgia for/fear of losing what is left behind; the balance between the unfamiliarity of the culture one is about to enter, the perceived challenge, and attachment to the culture one is leaving determines which feelings predominate at this stage. (2) *An initial arrival stage*, which can be a honeymoon (Oberg, 1960), a nightmare, an interesting or mixed experience depending on the individual context. (3) *A settling-in stage*, characterised by acute observation of everything in the host culture, comparing everything with home and with one's expectations of how it should be. (4) *A 'roller-coaster' settled stage*, where life has settled into a pattern in the host culture, one has achieved a certain degree of familiarity and competence, but everything is still subject to ups-and-downs and 'adjusting never ends' (Naomi). (5) *A pre-departure/transition stage*: before leaving Japan there is another phase similar to (1), except this time home and host culture have switched places in the individual's emotional world.

This cycle reoccurs every time the students face major cultural changes: entering their host culture, exchanging university life for a company placement, moving to live and work in a new city, facing the prospect of returning home at Christmas or at the end of the year. The U-curve (Lysgaard, 1955) was not upheld by the diaries: all students exhibited different adjustment patterns, none of which resembled a U-curve; Lucy's diary showed four adjustment cycles, in two of which a U-curve was evident, but the high-low-high patterns represent different levels of adjustment. Only Lucy experienced Oberg's (1960) honeymoon phase; for others the initial experience was more muted, suffused by homesickness, or in Naomi's case so extremely stressful she described it as a 'nightmare'.

As Anderson (1994) emphasises, adjustment implies learning and change, and affects all levels of an individual's identity (Kim, 1988). For the Irish students it involved the experience of marginality, which was perceived as positive or negative depending on the individual. The students' stories suggest the importance of being informed about and prepared for this potentially disorientating experience in advance of residence abroad. The Irish students' diaries showed that adjustment resulted in different outcomes for different individuals, but all experienced increased self-confidence and self-reliance having succeeded in meeting the challenges posed by the host environment.

Methodology

For this study I collected qualitative data from students' personal diaries, written while living/studying abroad, and analysed them using a grounded theory (Glaser & Strauss, 1967) approach. The decision to undertake qualitative research was based primarily on the exploratory nature of my research questions. My interest did not focus on testing hypotheses or measuring the students' experience using generalisable statistics, but on finding out more about the nature and process of their cross-cultural adjustment while abroad, with a view to informing educational practice. Although quantitative research still predominates in the fields of education and cross-cultural communication, it has been criticised for the fact that its results, while of theoretical interest, are often difficult to apply to real life situations. This is largely due to the practice of 'context stripping' (Shimahara, 1988) or analysis of isolated variables removed from context. Qualitative research, in contrast, is directly concerned with 'experience as it is 'lived' or 'felt' or 'undergone' (Sherman & Webb, 1988) and emphasises studying events in their natural settings, from the perspective of those being studied. Aiming to collect naturalistic 'slice of life' (Wolf & Tymitz, 1997: 77) data, it favours non-interventionist methods of inquiry, to minimise the influence of the method and researcher on the phenomenon under investigation. Its concern is to produce a holistic account of reality: rather than seeking to measure experience quantitatively and to identify causal relationships, it aims to discover, describe and interpret the meanings of the symbolic patterns of interaction and relationships between events and people. Reviewers of cross-cultural adjustment literature (Church, 1982) have recommended that quantitative studies be informed by more qualitative research, in the form of intensive case-studies of longitudinal design, in order to better understand the dynamics of individual's cross-cultural adjustment processes. The students' diaries in this study represent a response to this call.

Diaries as a research instrument

As a research tool, diaries belong to the anthropological research tradition (Long, 1980), and are a method of naturalistic inquiry (Lincoln & Guba, 1985) which has its origins in ethnography. In such research, diaries constitute data, corresponding to ethnographic field notes, and are used as an alternative to self-reporting and questionnaires. The quality of introspection/retrospection in diary writing is of particular value, for they can reveal 'facets of experience which are normally hidden or largely inaccessible to an external observer' (Bailey & Ochsner, 1983: 190). Diaries therefore seemed to be a valuable way of 'getting inside the lives' (Campbell, 1988) of the students, and seeing their experiences from their perspective.

The value of diaries as research instruments has long been recognised in the field of foreign/second language education (Bailey & Ochsner, 1983), where they have been used to elucidate the learning process and the factors influencing it, both for researchers/teachers and learners themselves (Schumann & Schumann, 1977). As a stimulus to encourage reflection and learning from experience, 'learner diaries' are regularly employed to help engage students' interest and increase their sense of involvement in their own learning process, thereby increasing their intrinsic motivation and autonomy (Parkinson & Howell-Richardson, 1990). Today's broader perspective on language teaching/learning, which includes the dimension of 'culture learning' (Furnham & Bochner, 1994) has naturally led to the transference of the diary methodology to the study of the process of learning/adjusting to a new culture, and the variables influencing it. Since Klineberg's (1981) conceptualisation of the cross-cultural adjustment process as a *mini-life-history*, the autobiographical/biographical approach to investigating this area has been gaining in popularity. Diaries are now regularly integrated into residence abroad programmes, both as ethnographic research tools and as a way of encouraging students to reflect and learn more from their experiences (Interculture Project, 1997–2000; Whalley, 1997).

Unstructured diaries

According to the purpose of diary writing, diaries may be structured in various formats, and students may be asked to respond to specific questions at regular intervals. For this study the diaries were optional and not part of the students' academic programme. I invited the students to take part in a research project that would entail keeping regular diaries about their cross-cultural experiences while in Japan, in whatever form they wished. The purpose behind not specifying a particular structure, content or length was to minimise my influence on the students' thinking. Prescribing certain topics or forms would focus their attention on issues I deemed important, and could have resulted in overlooking other topics of relevance, which were not so obvious and hitherto unexplored. Rather than providing them with a set of questions to address, my idea was to be exploratory and see what would emerge in their writing. Given the inevitability of my influence in the analysis and interpretation phase (Hall, 1982) I wanted to collect raw data that would be as natural and reflective of the students' experience as possible.

Problems with data collection

Collecting diary data was no simple task however. Despite enthusiastic agreement to participate in the research project by all students in the 1994/1995 (12 students) and 1995/1996 (nine students) cohorts going to Japan, between the two classes I collected six fairly complete diaries at the end of two years. This was due to a number of factors.

Both I and the students underestimated the time and effort required to keep regular diaries, especially with the excitement and challenges of learning to live in a foreign culture, which often left little available free time to record and reflect on their experiences. Another factor was that the level of contact I had with the students was not close or regular enough to inspire the kind of trust and commitment necessary for this type of data collection.

In retrospect, the difficulties I experienced in collecting this type of diary data point to a few key elements that would facilitate the process. Bailey (1981) emphasises the importance of developing a close personal working relationship between the researcher and the participants when undertaking a diary study. My experience underlines this. But a relationship of trust requires time and close contact, and cannot be developed in a few short weeks. Living in the same country and city, having frequent and regular contact, as well as providing more regular feedback on the diaries, are essential aids to developing such a relationship. From a total of 21 students, I was extremely fortunate to collect six diaries, three of which were over 200 pages each. Clear specific instructions on what to write, a shorter time-frame, and providing diary notebooks might have produced a greater number of diaries. However, this more structured approach would undoubtedly have resulted in quite different data from the rich and varied unstructured diaries in this study.

Nature of diary data: Rich and varied unstructured data

The freedom ensuing from the unstructured nature of the diaries led to a great variety in style and content. Students differed in the frequency and length of what they wrote, some producing pages daily and others a few lines a few days per week. Individual personalities were clearly visible in the writing styles: Lucy's stream of consciousness and lack of punctuation mirrored her emotional openness and unreflective attitude towards her experiences; Naomi's serious self searching was reflected in writing her diary on computer, allowing her to edit and return to entries, adding comments later which reinterpret earlier events from her present perspective. Writing style and content often reflected the adjustment process: for Liam, who usually wrote brief entries, a difficult period in Japan resulted in longer, more personal accounts, the diary providing a channel for him to air frustrations and, in a way, substituting for the lack of friends in his immediate environment. A variety of languages appeared in the diaries – mostly written in English, they included Irish and Japanese words and original Japanese-English expressions, this *macaronic* format mirroring the students' communication style with each other in Japan.

Common to all diaries was the candour and personal nature of the students' writing. I was surprised by how openly and revealingly they wrote about both pleasant and unpleasant aspects of their experience, and the personal nature of the content. There are several possible explanations. One may have been the agreement that they could edit the diaries prior to submission and that all names would be changed to preserve anonymity. Only two students chose to edit their diaries however, by blocking out certain sections with white paper before submitting for photocopying. Another factor may have been the personal relationship they had with me the researcher – they were writing to someone they knew and trusted, whom they knew cared about their experiences. As time went by however they seemed to forget about a reader altogether, the diary seemed to assume an identity of its own, becoming a confidante to whom they could talk when in trouble and lonely, and in whom they could confide their fears, frustrations and worries.

In subsequent discussion, all mentioned how glad they were to have kept a record of their experiences during that year in Japan. The balance between the research agenda and the educational value raises some interesting questions for me. My research benefited greatly from the rich data they provided. I was however more focused on data collection for research purposes than on the educational potential of diary writing, and I feel the students could have derived more structured learning from the experience had I adopted a different approach. Incorporating diary writing in an academic programme, using the diaries both during and after residence abroad for cross-cultural discussions, as suggested by Whalley (1997), would be an ideal way of ensuring that students benefited from their reflection on such an exercise. In this way, both the participants and the researcher could benefit more equally from the research.

Preparation of data for presentation and analysis

It took approximately six months to transform the original diaries into an appropriate form for presentation and analysis. This process involved a continual tension between wishing to preserve naturalistic data and protect the students' anonymity.

Five of the diaries were hand-written, so the first step was to type all photocopied originals. In the interests of anonymity, I employed a typist who was unfamiliar with the students and Japan. Maintaining the naturalistic quality of the data was simpler in English than in Japanese, which is written in a combination of three alphabets: *hiragana* and *katakana*, both syllabic alphabets, and *kanji*, Chinese characters. Since there are nearly 2000 *kanji* in general usage, students learn to write in the syllabic alphabets, gradually adding in appropriate Chinese characters as they progress. All three alphabets appeared in the diaries, as did Japanese words written in the roman alphabet (*romaji*), and original 'Japlish' words created by the students, for example, combining Japanese nouns and English verb endings. I thought it important to record when a student chose to write in Japanese, which alphabet they used, and whether or not they made mistakes, as all three factors might offer information about their current adjustment stage and process. Computer software was available for typing in Japanese, but it did not extend to recording students' mistakes, for example, when a *kanji* character had too few/many strokes, or looked different from the correct version. So, I typed them in correct Japanese, indicating the original mistake with a footnote. Mistakes in *romaji* versions of Japanese words were reproduced in the text, with both correct and incorrect versions listed in a glossary of Japanese terms. To make the diaries accessible to non-readers of Japanese, I translated into English all Japanese words and phrases that appeared, resulting in a Glossary of 371 items. For words written in Japanese script, I added footnotes indicating the romanised version and translation.

Ensuring the students' anonymity was a complex and time-consuming process. I had agreed to change all names of people and places before presenting the diaries as data, but this proved to be a far more extensive undertaking than I had imagined. In total it required 513 name changes: 237 Western/Irish personal names, 187 Japanese personal names, 19 Irish place names, 41 Japanese place names, 22 company names and 12 university names. Once all changes were completed, I sent each student a copy of the final version of his/her diary. This was to see if they had any problems with the changes made, to allow them a final chance to edit material, to consult them regarding issues I was unclear about and to incorporate their suggestions.

Data analysis: A grounded theory approach

To analyse the data I chose the grounded theory method, developed in the 1960s by sociologists Glaser and Strauss (1967). Not only did it represent a qualitative, inductive approach consistent with my aim of minimising the imposition of an outside structure/interpretation on the data, but it also offered a set of systematic procedures for the analysis of data and building of theory. While collecting and preparing the diaries for analysis, I was constantly thinking about my research questions, and I kept a journal detailing my reactions to and ideas arising from the material. I started thinking about recurrent themes, different students' experiences of similar episodes, and types of learning. My core interest was in investigating the nature and process of their adjustment/learning in Japan, and in the examination of other issues in terms of how they might relate to such adjustment/learning. But since I was still exploring the nature of such adjustment/learning, examining other issues was also a way of clarifying what exactly adjustment/learning meant. So, from the outset, I was simultaneously involved in the process of open, axial and selective coding.

Once the diaries were ready for presentation, I immersed myself in the analysis process. On initial reading, I labelled everything that seemed interesting or potentially relevant. Reviewing these labels I identified 15 different themes across the diaries. These were obvious and mainly descriptive categories: comparing experiences at university, in the host family, in the Japanese company; the role of language; identity changes; contact with home; attitudes to Japan, etc. This represented a preliminary open coding of the data.

Since the volume of the data was so large, including three diaries of over 200 pages each, I needed to somehow reduce it into manageable chunks for analysis. Through further readings, I sorted the data into diary 'maps', using computer tables. I did this diary by diary, simultaneously keeping memos recording comparisons/contrasts with other diaries, ideas, questions and hypotheses for further reflection. Each table contained six columns: date; category; sub-category; a quotation, information or comment; plus two blank columns where I noted connections to other data, and inserted further comments by hand. When I was not sure how to code the information, I left the name of the category blank, until I could see how it might fit into the larger picture. At this stage I included everything, even weather and illness, etc., as I did not know what would ultimately be most useful in revealing the students' cross-cultural adaptation process. Having the data in table form, I could sort and compile information according to different categories, change the names of categories, or assign the same information to different categories. Blank columns enabled me to regroup the data under new headings, as more relevant themes emerged through analysis. Reading and rereading the diary maps, I compared experiences and events across all six diaries, as well as within each individual's story. I used colour coding to highlight students' positive or negative attitudes to their host culture, noting when changes occurred and asking questions and checking hypotheses about possible causes. I drew many sketchy diagrams and graphs, attempting to depict individual adjustment patterns over time, and how different variables interacted in the process. To obtain a clearer picture of patterns within individual diaries, I produced wall-charts showing how different themes interacted on a daily or weekly basis.

Guba (1978) advises one should only consider a limited number of categories in any naturalistic investigation. I had identified and examined numerous categories in the diaries, but gradually three emerged as most dense and promising in relation to the core category of adjustment/learning: social networks, food and language. Initially the significance of all three categories was suggested by one student's (Lucy's) diary: personal relationships were of paramount importance to her, she was fascinated by Japanese food, and her enthusiasm for the Japanese language was reflected in writing regularly in Japanese. In addition, her diary showed clearly marked stages of adjustment, which connected with all three categories. I decided to investigate the importance of these categories for the other students. The amount of name changes necessary from the original diaries had already suggested the importance of relationships for all students while abroad, so I began axial coding, identifying the properties and dimensions of the category 'relationships': what relationships existed, the closeness and frequency of contact, their function for the student, and how they affected adjustment. Three sub-categories were evident: relationships with Japanese people (Host culture), with other foreigners, and with Irish people at home and in Japan (Home culture). It became clear that although students differed in the extent to which they developed or relied on these relationships, there was a definite parallel between the balance of these three sub-categories and the individual's adjustment/learning. The dynamic within the category of relationships was mirrored in food and language: the tension between home, foreign (Western) and host culture suggested a tension between degrees of seeking comfort in the familiar, known world of home/Western and exploring the challenging, unfamiliar world of the host culture. I began to examine how, when and why individuals differed in the degree to which they sought difference or familiarity, adventure or security, the excitement of exploring the new or comfort of reliance on the known. A dynamic to-and-fro between these poles seemed to underlie the cross-cultural adjustment process.

After examining the students' adjustment in terms of these three themes across all six diaries, I felt it was appropriate to trace each individual's story of adjustment, weaving in these themes and other factors relevant to the individual case. Through this process of horizontal and vertical analysis of the data, the major categories were related to the core category of adjustment/learning, which was then highlighted in the analytic stories of the six individual students. From these stories it was possible to identify six principles common to the cross-cultural adjustment of individuals.

The final step in building grounded theory is relating existing literature to one's findings. As Hutchinson explains:

> Grounded theorists generate a theory based on behaviour patterns observed in the field and then turn to the literature to find support for the emergent theory. Literature that illuminates or extends the proposed theory is interwoven with the empirical data. Through its correspondence with 'the real world', literature establishes a vital connection between theory and reality. (Hutchinson, 1988: 137)

A thorough literature review of cross-cultural adjustment research in different disciplines showed that the grounded theory proposed was supported by the literature and in turn extended understanding of existing theories by highlighting new dimensions and relationships in the process.

Conclusion/Reflections

Although separated for the purposes of this chapter, the findings and methodology are intimately connected, the diary methodology being a key factor in determining the findings. Unstructured diaries provided intimate personal accounts of the students' lives, where adjustment stages and issues were revealed unconsciously in recording daily events and concerns. Qualitative analysis of this naturalistic data was able to highlight connections between variables, showing how they interacted in individual stories to produce very different adjustment processes and outcomes. Such an analysis shed light on both the relevance and limit-ations of existing theories in explaining the cross-cultural adjustment process.

This study showed diaries as a research instrument to be a potentially rich source of data, but also a difficult and unpredictable method of data collection. The time, energy and commitment required to write a diary throughout the year indicate that students must have high motivation and regular support in this process. Making diaries a compulsory and possibly graded component of residence abroad, or providing a simpler more structured format, could increase the number collected, although these conditions would ultimately change the nature of the information received and may not result in as fertile a data base. For the type of diaries in this study, a close personal trust relationship between the students and researcher proved to be crucial, as did regular contact and encouragement.

Reflecting on how the research process affected me as researcher, my strongest sense is of having developed a deep insiders' understanding of the complexities involved in individuals' cross-cultural adjustment stories. The grounded theory approach kept me constantly very close to the data, with the result that I felt I was almost living the students' experiences with them. In hindsight, I realise the huge commitment on the part of the students writing the diaries and feel privileged to have been given such a rich volume of data. In future, I would think twice before asking students to keep such diaries, and would more likely favour a structured approach, whereby the educational value for the students would be paramount.

Chapter 4

The One Less Travelled By . . .: The Experience of Chinese Students in a UK University

CHRISTINE BURNETT and JOHN GARDNER

> *A young female student recently arrived from China commented on the confusion of encountering the smiling faces of strangers as she walked along the street. 'At first I think "are you rude or are you mad?" because in China if you don't know that person they will not say hello. Now I know they are just friendly.'*

Such perplexing encounters confront many young people as they join the growing numbers of international students in Britain today. These individuals face not only the demanding transition from school to higher education common to all students, but the stress of adapting to a new country, culture and often language. The numbers of those across the British higher education sector who find themselves in this position every year is increasing rapidly. In 1991, there were approximately 92,000 international students in Britain and this had risen to over 276,000 in 2002 (HESA, 2004). Queen's University, Belfast (the focus for this study) has almost 23,000 full-time and part-time students and in the past the number of students from outside Britain and Ireland has been low compared to many other UK universities. Recently, however, the number of international students has increased markedly with the Higher Education Statistics Agency (HESA) reporting that these students comprised 10.3% of the total student population at Queen's in 2002/2003 only slightly lower than the UK average of 12.7% (HESA, 2004). Among a number of developments designed to increase participation by overseas students, Queen's University entered into a collaborative arrangement with Shenzhen University in southern China in 1999. The link has resulted in an annual intake of undergraduate students with the number of students rising to become the largest national group of overseas students studying at the university (at the time of writing comprising approximately 200 students); and to be by far the largest group from a single university. It is these students who were the primary focus of this research and in this chapter we report how their experiences have been analysed using the theoretical models of acculturation that are currently available.

Acculturation has been defined by Berry (1990) as the changes that an individual experiences when in first-hand contact with another culture. The term is most often used in connection with individuals who make a geographical transition across cultures such as sojourners, immigrants and refugees. Sojourners, according to Furnham (1988), are those individuals who voluntarily spend a medium length of time (six months to five years) in a new and unfamiliar environment with the intention of returning at some point to their home culture. International students fit this definition and form an important group within the category of sojourners. Arising from their location within a university, they tend to be easily accessed by researchers and a significant amount of research has therefore been devoted to their experiences of acculturation (e.g. Barker *et al.*, 1991; Furnham and Bochner, 1982; Klineberg & Hull, 1979; Zheng & Berry, 1991). Much of this research has focused on international students in North America, and, in spite of valuable contributions by researchers such as Murphy-Lejeune (2002), there is comparatively little research within the UK context.

Dion and Dion (1996), in their study of Chinese students in Canada, point out that sojourning students must often adapt, not only to the usual demands of student life, but to a culture with different, if not opposing, values and customs to their home culture. The transition to a new culture is generally accompanied by what Oberg (1960) described as 'culture shock', arising from a loss of the familiar cues and patterns of social interaction. Culture shock often results in feelings of anxiety, helplessness, loneliness, frustration and hostility to the host country. For some, it only takes a short period of time to overcome the psychological distress while for others, it may be longer lasting and debilitating (Chen & Starosta, 1998). The pattern of the stress may differ according to the type of students and the context in which they find themselves. For example, a long-term study by Zheng and Berry (1991), focusing on Chinese students going to study in Canada, found that acculturative stress increases from its original level prior to their departure from home and reaches a peak three to four months after arrival, declining slowly thereafter to the baseline. However, research by Ward *et al.* (1998) into the adaptation of Japanese students in New Zealand found that they experienced the peak in their difficulties on arrival; and that these decreased with time.

For most sojourners, then, culture shock may simply be a stage in their gradual adjustment to cultural difference in the new environment. A number of researchers, including Yoshikawa (1988), Berry (1980, 1990) and Bennett (1993), have attempted to theorise the whole process of intercultural adaptation (including any 'culture shock' stage) through experiential models and it is against these models that we have explored the experiences of the students at Queen's. The models are outlined briefly below and in more detail later in the chapter.

Yoshikawa (1988) drew from his own experience of intercultural adaptation in moving from Japan to the United States. From this experience, he developed a model based on the analogy of a journey, in which the sojourner encounters 'anomalies disturbing enough to shake their existing, customary perceptual foundations' (Yoshikawa, 1988: 146). In this process the individual develops an increasing level of cultural awareness and their self-awareness also grows. In Berry's view (1980, 1990), however, there are two key issues that the sojourner must confront. The first relates to the degree to which they maintain their own cultural distinctiveness and the second is the extent to which they form relations with the host society. The response to these issues of cultural identity determines the four possible outcomes of acculturation, which he terms Assimilation, Integration, Separation and Marginalisation. Bennett's (1993) model of acculturation is, like Yoshikawa's, a developmental one. A central aspect is the need for the sojourner to acquire intercultural sensitivity, and so to move from an ethnocentric to an ethnorelative orientation. The model focuses on the sojourner's 'subjective *experience* of cultural difference', not just their objective behaviour (Bennett, 1993: 22, with original emphasis).

These models are widely acknowledged as influential in the field of intercultural communication research, focusing as they do on the experiences of the sojourner and their relationship with the host culture. In considering the design of our research, the developmental nature of the models pointed to the need to survey the students on more than one occasion, in this case over a period of one year. Choosing Chinese students enabled us to exploit the fact that that the difficulties experienced by sojourners are to some extent a function of the degree of cultural difference between their own culture and the host society (Furnham & Bochner, 1982). According to Chen and Chung (1993), maximum distance exists between Western and Eastern cultures, thereby increasing the acculturative stress on the students and making Chinese students an interesting and fruitful group to study. We therefore, set out to examine how Chinese students negotiate their way through the process of intercultural adaptation in Queen's. In this chapter, we will show that these models were not entirely satisfactory when confronted with our data and that consequently we felt it necessary to develop our own modification of the models.

At the outset of our study we elected to focus on the experiences of the first-year undergraduate students arriving from Shenzhen University, and on a small group of postgraduate students. The immediate benefit for our research design in choosing the students from Shenzhen was that it ensured a reasonable degree of cultural similarity and reduced the number of variables involved in, say, working with a group of students drawn from various universities in China or elsewhere in Asia.

Exploring the Models

Two main methods were used to investigate the students' experience of moving to the UK. The first involved interviews with 40 undergraduate students in the weeks following their arrival and then a year later. The second method was a spontaneous drawing session with each of four students who had been living in the UK for at least two years. The data arising from the interviews were used to critique the existing models of acculturation and the visual method allowed a more in-depth evaluation of these models and the creation of a new model which better fitted the students' experiences. Further details of these methods may be found below.

Berry's model of acculturation

Berry's model of acculturation (1990: 245) focuses on two key questions to which the sojourner must respond:

- Is it considered to be of value to maintain cultural identity and characteristics?
- Is it considered to be of value to maintain relations with larger society?

These questions highlight the dilemma for the sojourner on entry to the host culture. It is the way in which the individual responds that determines, according to Berry, the mode of acculturation they adopt. This is shown in Table 4.1. The dilemma posed by Berry's two questions was implicit in over half of the interview discussions with the undergraduate students and it was clear that they considered maintaining their cultural identity *and* relating to the larger society as valuable. This demonstrated

Table 4.1 Berry's model of acculturation

		Is it considered to be of value to maintain cultural identity and characteristics?	
		Yes	*No*
Is it considered to be of value to maintain relations with larger society?	Yes	Integration	Assimilation
	No	Separation	Marginalisation

Source: Berry (1990: 245)

itself at many levels, from attitudes towards food to decisions about who they wished to relate to as friends.

Berry would term this mode of acculturation 'Integration' and much has been written about the benefits of this approach. However, such an appraisal is open to the charge of being somewhat superficial, arguably failing to appreciate the complexities involved. Several criticisms of the model may be made.

First, the model appears to imply that the sojourner makes a conscious choice in relation to both questions. In fact the choice of not maintaining their own cultural identity did not seem to have been considered by the students and in our view they would probably have been shocked to think that this was an option. The notion of being able to set aside one's cultural identity is one that many people, especially those from collectivistic cultures, would find difficult to embrace. Leung (1996: 254) contends that Chinese individuals believe that the group rather than the individual is the basic unit of society and consequently that 'social relationships and roles constitute the core of the self in the Chinese culture'. Markus and Kitayama (1991: 246) support this view and suggest that in collectivist cultures the emphasis is on the self in connection to others where '...one is conscious of where one belongs with respect to others and ... [is] continually adjusting and accommodating to others'. If these contentions are accurate, for such people, self-identity and collective identity are very closely linked, and this may create problems for this model.

Second, the sojourner may consider that maintaining relations with the host culture is valuable but may not actively pursue it. In the early interviews, relating to the host culture was seen as important in an idealistic sense but was not the priority at that stage of the students' sojourn. For example, a student stated: 'I wish I can live with local students but maybe I need some Chinese; maybe next year.'

By laying greater stress on maintaining their cultural identity than on relating to the larger society, the students were fitting into Berry's category of 'Separation' though this was largely viewed as a temporary strategy rather than a long term goal. By the time of the later interviews, the behaviour of the students reflected more the 'Integration' mode. This highlights the view that the model does not make sufficient distinction between intentions and behaviour and that acculturation strategies may differ at different stages of a sojourn and be more dynamic than the model might suggest.

A third issue relates to the way the model might give the impression that choices regarding acculturation are entirely in the hands of the sojourner, and that the impact of the host culture's attitude to the sojourner is largely ignored. Berry (1990: 244) does, however, acknowledge that 'in some societies, the dominant group virtually dictates the ways in which the non-dominant groups may act'. Consequently, the sojourner may not have the free choices that Berry's model would suggest but there is no development of the model to reflect this. While sojourners may wish to relate to the larger society, factors such as a perceived lack of openness and unfriendliness could make this goal difficult to realise.

A fourth and related problem is that sojourners may choose different modes of acculturation in different aspects of their lives. In the case of most of the students, the basic approach was one of integration by which they tried to relate to the host culture while maintaining their cultural identity. This was largely successful in the social aspect of their lives but within the academic setting, things were very different. To use Berry's language, the dominant group, in this case represented by the university, dictated the way they should act. If the students wished to be successful academically, they had no choice but to conform to the Western educational approach and in that sense turn away from their own cultural values. This Berry terms *assimilation* and illustrates that in different areas of life different modes of acculturation may be appropriate.

The final concern with Berry's model is that it adopts a dichotomous approach to each question, which is clearly an oversimplification. Sojourners may differ in the degree to which they emphasise the two issues at the centre of Berry's questions and the acculturative outcome will consequently be affected. While the students who were interviewed may have considered that maintaining their cultural identity and relating to the host culture were both of value, their relationships within their own cultural group were of greater importance, particularly at the start of their sojourn. A range of options rather than a stark YES or NO response to the Berry model questions would better reflect the actual situation that sojourners face within a host culture.

Setting aside the concerns explored above, Berry's (1990) model proves useful, in a number of important ways, in exploring the experience of the students' acculturation. For example, the issues he raises are resonant of the very practical demands the sojourner must face when adjusting to a new environment. The model recognises that sojourners may adopt different strategies for adapting to the host culture and that these may result in different acculturative outcomes. It also recognises that the construction of a personal identity, within the conflicting claims of the home culture and the host culture, is central to acculturation. However, it is probably fair to say at this stage that we found Berry's model less adequate than the others in explaining the process our students experienced.

Bennett's model of acculturation

Bennett's (1993) model is one of the two developmental models on which we have focused, identifying as it does, the need of the sojourner to develop intercultural sensitivity and in so doing move from a ethnocentric outlook to an ethnorelative one. He charts the movement of the stranger through six stages: Denial, Defence, Minimisation, Acceptance, Adaptation and Integration. The model proposes a personal growth process that focuses on how cultural difference is experienced. It therefore centres on the sojourner's perceptions of, and response to, the cultural differences they encounter. The model assumes that 'intercultural sensitivity is not natural' (Bennett, 1993: 21) and that individuals who have little contact with other cultures will have an ethnocentric outlook. The Chinese students had come from a largely mono-cultural society, part of a vast country, with no experience of travel abroad. It would not be unreasonable, therefore, to expect that they would exhibit ethnocentric attitudes. This was indeed borne out in the early interviews where the lack of cultural awareness implicit in ethnocentrism resulted in confusion and lack of comprehension of the host culture. Each of Bennett's six stages is considered briefly below.

Denial

Bennett categorises the first stage of ethnocentrism as Denial (of difference) where an individual denies the existence of cultural difference. This perspective, he argues, has broad categories for cultural difference and these lead to stereotypes, though these are generally benign. While the students did not deny cultural difference in the new culture they had difficulty in categorising the differences they encountered. Their pre-departure training had given them a general idea of what to expect but this was insufficient to allow them to make sense of the host culture when they were actually experiencing it. Nevertheless, Denial did not appear to be an appropriate categorisation of the Chinese students' attitude to sojourning as they were overwhelmingly aware of the difference between their own and the host culture. It seemed rather that coming in contact with a different culture forced them to become aware of their own cultural perspectives.

Defence

The next stage of Bennett's model is termed Defence; viewed as a reaction to the perceived threat of cultural difference 'to one's sense of reality and thus to one's identity' (Bennett, 1993: 34). This can result in the denigration of the host culture or to a sense of superiority. Moving into an alien culture was a major challenge to the students' cultural assumptions, particularly as they came from a society where conformity to the given way is highly valued. As Brislin (2000) notes, people who come into contact with other cultures will inevitably experience challenges to their ethnocentric feelings.

The students were therefore forced to ask the question, 'Is our way the only way to do this?' In the early interviews, many expressed views which contained the implicit assumption that the Chinese way was best. As one of the students commented: 'We should keep our own culture and study their [the other culture's] good things.'

At times they presented generalised opinions such as 'all the local students are unfriendly' and 'the lecturers are unhelpful'. Whether these can be taken as evidence of the superiority and denigration behaviours that typify Defence is debateable. Much of their early attitudes were simply evidence of the problems of applying a worldview developed in one culture to another culture, though this clearly raises some identity issues as Bennett would claim. The second interviews revealed that during the intervening year the students had gained an appreciation of the host culture that enabled them to interpret the behaviour of others more accurately.

Minimisation

The next stage in the model is Minimisation, when cultural difference is acknowledged but trivialised. In other words: 'human similarity seems more profound than cultural difference' (Bennett, 1993: 41). Bennett observes that Minimisation is often typical of the dominant group in a society and that those in subordinate groups tend to pass quickly through this stage. Such was the situation for the Chinese students, although Bennett would argue that individuals need to go through the stage of Minimisation before they can develop an ethnorelative outlook. An apparent example of this was that in the initial interviews the students stated that they had nothing in common with the local students and so had little to talk about with them. In the later interviews, though, when we asked a group of male Chinese students what they talked about to the local students they replied: 'The same things we talk about to each other – girls, movies and clothes.' Their experiences had shown them that, in contrast to their first impressions, they had a lot in common with the local students. However, we could argue that this realisation was an appreciation of commonalities in the face of cultural difference rather than Bennett's concept of the Minimisation of difference.

Acceptance

The next stage, Acceptance, represents a major shift from an ethno-centric position, where cultural difference is perceived as threatening, to an ethnorelative outlook, where difference is recognised, accepted and even enjoyed. Bennett (1993: 48) observes that 'while superficial differ-ences in verbal and non-verbal behaviour may have been recognised in earlier stages, here the recognition and acceptance are at the deeper level of cultural relativity'. There was little evidence of this deeper under-standing during the initial interviews of the Chinese students where cul-tural difference was perceived as perplexing. However, a year later the students were much more able to interpret the behaviour of host culture members within the host culture context, rather than from a purely Chinese perspective. There were a number of instances, which they recounted, that bore evidence of this ethnorelative outlook. One example of this was in relation to their lecturers, who they initially felt lacked interest in their academic progress because of their habit of giving source material to the students and expecting them to undertake independent study. Later, they understood that the lecturers were encouraging the students to develop the ability to think independently and to formulate their own opinions; skills that are intrinsic to the Western approach to education.

Adaptation

Adaptation is seen as the stage following Acceptance in the acquisition of intercultural sensitivity. Here intercultural communication skills develop so that the sojourner can communicate effectively within another culture. Central to this is empathy which Bennett conceives of as the 'attempt to understand by imagining or comprehending the other's *perspective*' (Bennett, 1993: 53, with original emphasis). One striking example was found in a student's response to the complaints of her Chinese friends that the local students were not interested in them. Her comments on the lack of effort to engage on the part of the Chinese students revealed her understanding of the perspective of the local students: 'Sometimes I would consider it narrow minded because they [Chinese students] can't find something interesting to share with people. They always just quiet standing there doing their own things.'

Bennett contends that a further aspect of Adaptation is pluralism where the individual has internalised a second cultural frame of reference and so has more than one worldview.

Integration

The final ethnorelative stage in Bennett's model is Integration in which the individual is no longer affiliated to their primary cultural group but develops an ethnorelative identity that exists on the margins of two or more cultures. However, this implicit individualistic perspective limits the model's explanatory power for those who come from collectivistic cultures as in our case with students from China. The model has value in that it stresses the importance of the construction of personal identity in the face of cultural difference, an issue which was clearly important to the interviewees, and its developmental approach is clearly an appropriate one for acculturation. In our study it was clear from the student interviews that change and personal growth are central to this experience.

Bennett's view of the movement along a continuum from an ethnocentric to ethnorelative outlook was a useful perspective on the development of intercultural sensitivity which is central to acculturation. However, his proposed stages, particularly the ethnocentric, did not entirely fit with the experiences of the students that were interviewed. It also has the danger of being judgemental in its view of those whom it assesses to be ethnocentric, labelling them as being 'in denial' or 'in defence', and it may lead to misinterpretations of the naïve ethnocentrism of the sojourner who has had little prior intercultural experience. While the model may be appropriate for members of a host culture coming into limited contact with those from other cultures, in which circumstances they have the option of denying their presence, being defensive, etc., it appears less useful in describing the experience of those entering a new culture. There is also, we believe, an implicit individualistic perspective in the model that limits its applicability in the context of those from more collectivist cultures. This, in combination with its linear approach, led us to conclude that it could not accurately reflect our students' experiences.

Yoshikawa's model of acculturation

Yoshikawa also proposes a developmental model, this time of five stages of acculturation; a model that takes account of 'the conscious as well as the unconscious changes in the individual' (Yoshikawa, 1988: 140). His model draws on earlier work by Adler (1975) and identifies the stages as: Contact, Disintegration, Reintegration, Autonomy and Double-swing. As with Bennett, we outline Yoshikawa's stages briefly below.

Contact

In the first stage, Contact, the individual enters a new culture but fails to recognise the new realities as they view the host culture from the perspective of their own worldview. The differences they encounter are generally experienced as exciting and this is often known as the 'honeymoon' period, although for some individuals the differences may be perceived as threatening. This resonated with the findings from our initial interviews with the students, most of whom (approximately three-quarters) described the new culture as interesting and exciting; as one commented, 'When I come here my expectations and my mood is very high.' A small number (less than a quarter), however, found the early days in the new culture difficult and reported feeling homesick from the start of their sojourn.

Disintegration

Yoshikawa (1988: 142) describes the Disintegration stage as occurring when the sojourner is overwhelmed by the cultural differences between the first and second culture and their divergent worldviews. The sense of bewilderment and conflict characterising this stage is often known as culture shock. In the interviews later in their first semester, many of the students (over one-third) appeared perplexed by various aspects of the new culture and expressed much less positive perspectives of the host culture than in the earlier interviews. A few were so overwhelmed by their experiences that they became visibly distressed during the interview.

Reintegration

The Reintegration stage focuses on the sojourner's attempts to adjust to the new environment. Yoshikawa argues that cultural similarities and differences 'are rejected through stereotyping, generalization and judgmental attitudes' (Yoshikawa, 1988: 142). Some individuals experience an identity crisis as they are 'caught in two cultures and in search of a sense of belongingness' and this may lead to a return to the disintegration stage. The comments of the students reflected the difficulty in dealing with cultural difference and there was evidence of negative judgements of, for example, the local students and the academic staff.

Autonomy

In the Autonomy stage the sojourner's outlook becomes more flexible, enabling them to accept and appreciate cultural differences. The individual 'gains the ability to experience new situations in a new way' (Yoshikawa, 1988: 142) and becomes increasingly autonomous in outlook. The students displayed some of the features of this stage in the second interviews. They had largely come to terms with cultural difference and were able to appreciate the perspectives of the local students and others within the host culture. There were features of the new culture, such as the way strangers would smile at them in the streets, which they were able to appreciate and enjoy rather than feel threatened. Yoshikawa suggests that some individuals at this stage begin to create a new cultural identity for themselves; an identity that he calls 'the third culture'. While it was difficult to find explicit evidence for this in the interviews, it was apparent that the cultural outlook of some of the students had changed from a primarily Chinese collectivist approach to one that embraced a more individualist way of dealing with life. One student, for example, described how he felt less obliged here to be involved in the difficulties of others than he would have in China. 'Now I say it's your problem not my problem', a not necessarily good outcome from the stage of Autonomy!

Double-swing

In the last stage, which Yoshikawa termed Double-swing, the sojourner is fully able to enjoy and be enriched by the cultural similarities and differences they encounter; the Double-swing being established when 'one is independent, yet simultaneously interdependent' (Yoshikawa, 1988: 142). As with the final stage of Bennett's model, there was little evidence for this stage in the undergraduate student data but the process of Double-swing was more apparent for the group of longer-term sojourners who took part in the visual imagery. We will return to this later.

The Yoshikawa model related well to the perspectives of our students and proved to be more closely related to their experiences of entering a new culture than the Bennett model. The impact of coming into contact with an alien culture is well described by the model, including the influence of such a move on the personal identity of the sojourner. We feel, however, that the model would benefit from further development of the Reintegration and Autonomy stages in terms of how the cultural perspective of the sojourner shifts to account for the host culture outlook.

The models described above helped inform both aspects of our research with the Chinese students. First, in the interviews, our awareness of the models allowed us to take notice of any comments made by the students which appeared to support them or otherwise. However, we recognised the danger of unwarranted reading of such endorsements into the students' experience and therefore applied caution. In the spontaneous drawing sessions – to be discussed later – a similar approach was taken, although in this case the initiative regarding interpretation was given to the student reducing considerably the danger of imposing the researcher's perspective onto the work.

The Methods

The methods we used to investigate the students' experiences were essentially qualitative in nature and involved interviews with 40 undergraduate students as the main data collection tool.[1] We chose an interview rather than questionnaire approach for the usual reasons. Our primary aim was to try to understand the process from the perspective of the student, rather than in some objective sense, through encouraging the students to talk of their experiences of moving to a new culture. The interview schedules were designed to encourage the students to talk of these experiences and in particular to discover any factors which facilitated or hindered their adaptation. Issues, such as their aspirations, relationships with Chinese and local students and their progress in their studies, were addressed. The initial interview schedule was adapted for use in the final interviews though largely the same topics were addressed in both.

Interviews are well suited to enabling researchers to gain access to the 'meaning-endowing capacities [of the interviewee] and produce rich, deep data' (Brewer, 2000: 66) but we were aware that significant problems could be encountered in using the interview in a cross-cultural setting, the most obvious of which relate to language. Clearly any level of language difficulty has the potential to create problems, both for the interviewee in understanding the questions and for the interviewer in understanding the responses. Another difficulty is that Chinese young people, having been taught to have great respect for both parents and educators (Lee, 1996), are often reluctant to express anything that may reflect negatively on an authority figure or institution. A third issue is that a Western researcher may miss important information due to a lack of awareness of non-verbal cues, so vital to the Chinese 'high-context' approach to communication. Brislin (1986: 163) also points to the danger of the 'courtesy bias' which he suggests occurs 'when respondents try to discover what the questioner wants, and then direct their answers accordingly'. In order to address these issues we chose to use an innovative approach involving a spontaneous drawing session with four individual students in order to gain insights into their perspectives on acculturation.

In justification of our choice to use visual methods, we drew on the work of a number of researchers including Kellogg; Leonard and Davey; Rudenberg, Jansen and Fridjhon; Dalley; and Kübler-Ross. Visually-based data have been used for a number of decades by researchers such as Kellogg (1970), who used children's drawings as a useful way of gaining insight into their perspectives on their everyday lives. According to Leonard and Davey (2001), drawings provide a valuable alternative means of illustrating inner feelings and thoughts before verbal fluency and other forms of expression have been acquired. Children's art has also been used as a therapeutic device for accessing the inner thoughts and feelings of children who have been subjected to an emotionally traumatic experience. Such an approach is seen in research by Rudenberg *et al.* (2001) in which drawings are used to understand the psychological effects of stress among children living in societies characterised by civil unrest. This psychological approach to drawings is based on the premise that people may unconsciously reveal information about their inner world, which would not be possible through direct communication.

Art therapy is based on a similar premise, using art activity as a non-verbal medium 'through which a person can achieve both conscious and unconscious expression' (Dalley, 1984: xii). This largely Jungian approach sees the images and symbols in drawings as a way in which the unconscious may reveal itself (Furth, 1988) and spontaneous drawings are therefore viewed as a powerful analytical tool. According to Kübler-Ross (1988: x), an added advantage of this is that most people enjoy drawing simply because 'it taps into the universal need to express oneself'. We were content, then, that spontaneous drawing sessions would allow some degree of exploration of the students' experiences of acculturation.

There exists little guidance for researchers on the interpretation of such data. Those who use similar methods to research the experience of young children, such as Rudenberg *et al.* (2001), often devise their own framework for interpretation and apply this to the work of each child. We felt, however, that imposing our own interpretation on the drawings would be dangerous, not least because of the cultural divide between subject and researcher. One example may serve to illustrate this danger. One of the subjects used the colour red to depict the harmony she achieved after a significant period of time in the new culture and commented 'red means happiness in Chinese'. Another subject used the same red colour to draw a jagged line on her drawing to which she attached the label 'anxiety'. When asked why she used this colour, she replied that she had used red in the Western not the Chinese way. Our approach, therefore, was to probe for the authors' meaning throughout.

Images of Acculturation

We now turn to the images of acculturation produced by the four longer-term students (all of whom had been at Queen's for at least two years) in the spontaneous drawing sessions. We will first discuss these in the light of the theoretical models and then suggest our own modification which we believe better describes the experience of the Chinese students with whom we worked.

The spontaneous drawing approach required the students to visualise and sketch representations of their experiences over the course of their studies, thereby seeking to avoid some of the potential limitations of the interview method and its reliance on language skills. All four participants were female students; three were postgraduate (one doctoral, two masters students) and one was an undergraduate nearing the end of her final year. Each student was given paper and coloured pens and asked to draw, in whatever way they wished, something that depicted their experiences, both positive and negative, of moving to a new culture. All were told that they could explain their drawing after its completion and the confidential nature of their comments was stressed. The subsequent conversations were recorded on tape and the drawings scanned. The procedure was carried out with the students individually and each session took approximately one hour.

In this section we set out a brief description of the images produced by the students and the discussions that took place. The four students are referred to as students A, B, C and D and excerpts from their verbatim comments, as with those above, are presented as illustrations where appropriate, without corrections of grammar and syntax.

Student A

Student A was 22 years of age, had been studying at the university for almost three years and was approaching the end of her undergraduate

Figure 4.1 Student A: 'Experiences of moving to a new culture'

course. The image she produced (Figure 4.1) depicted her experience of living in a new culture as a series of sections moving from left to right across the page. There was a dynamic quality to the drawing with an emphasis on change, movement and journey.

A major theme was the dissonance between her expectations of moving to a new culture and the reality of her experiences. This was a particular issue in the early days of her sojourn. 'When I first arrive here I think there must be lots of positive things that I will be experiencing.' She pointed to the three wavy red lines and a single black line, which she had drawn on the left side of the page. 'Of course I didn't expect it to be so good so there must be something not very good so I've drawn this black line. Also this up and down.'

Overall, she had expected that her experiences would have ups and downs, mostly positive with some negative, but in some sense predictable. This region of the drawing has a very regular emphatic pattern.

In the next section the regular pattern disappears. 'In the period after I arrive I find that life really is a mess.' This part of the drawing is random, with little pattern, and appears much less definite. She explained that things had not been at all as she had expected, a 'mess' rather than something more comprehensible. This stage of the drawing portrays the chaos that she felt might have overwhelmed her. 'But I didn't lose hope.' Then things began to change: 'I began to act more active than before. I'm getting more involved, being more in control. That's the arrows.'

This next section is bolder, dominated by arrows emerging from the 'mess'. She felt that if she acted positively towards others she should get a positive response, but sometimes the response had been less positive than she would have expected. She represents this by shapes with a black border, 'not solid, not very negative but under my expectations'. Overall though, she felt that she had a greater sense of control over her own life. She illustrates this by red ovals reflecting harmonious outcomes, observing that red is the most positive colour in Chinese culture. These are interspersed with triangles depicting the strange or unexpected experiences that still cause her surprise in the new culture.

The final section on the right hand side of the drawing reflects her life in more recent months. 'I have probably sorted out something. That is why these waves are in order, but not like the waves [at the beginning]. That was my expectation but this is reality.'

She pointed out that the waves have a certain random character but are more settled and harmonious than before. The area to the very right depicts her expectations for the future. 'I hope everything is harmonic – all red and active.'

Student B

Student B was 28 years of age and was over half-way through studying for a PhD. At the beginning of the session she told me that her husband had joined her in Britain some months earlier and that she was expecting their first child.

Student B drew a picture of a large garden with a number of people in it (Figure 4 2). She explained that the drawing was of a public park close to the university where she liked to go to relax. She spoke of the people in the picture: 'I think their life is very easy and comfortable, relaxed. I think it is an aspect of the local life here. I think it's very perfect in my mind to live in such way.' The picture, she stated, was not just a physical place but an image that had been coming into her mind a lot recently during her pregnancy. 'I just try to relax myself and enjoy. So I find this life is perfect, easy life.'

When asked about how difficult she found the experience of moving into a new culture she replied, 'Coming here has been very positive.'

Figure 4.2 Student B: 'Experiences of moving to a new culture'

Although her primary motivation for coming to Britain was for academic and professional reasons, she recognised a wider value in her sojourn: 'It's good for my experience, for my personal growing, to widen my knowledge and experience.'

She felt that the major challenge in the first months after she had come to Britain was the language. However, sharing a flat with two Chinese students who had been in Britain for some time had helped her to understand the local culture. She relished all her encounters with new people and in new situations and felt that the insights she had gained allowed her to interact with the culture in a way that had been impossible at the start of her sojourn.

At the moment I can understand some of the culture here even though it's very limited. So sometime I can explain it in my own way even though I'm Chinese but I try and learn here's culture. At the moment I think I can enter the culture here and the situation here in a way I could not before.

Overall she felt that she had adjusted well to her life in the UK. 'I have become more confident to adapt to living here.' She was looking forward to resuming her PhD studies after her baby was born. 'I will finish it. It's my dream; it's why I've come here.'

Student C

Student C was 25 years of age and was approaching the end of her studies as a masters student. Her drawing was very simple; an undulating black line rather like the line of a graph (Figure 4.3). She was given the opportunity to embellish further the drawing but declined to do so. 'This graph is just a simple line but represents my mood changing in [coming to] Belfast. When I come here my expectations and my mood is very high.' In spite of her high expectations, she felt very homesick during this early stage. 'I miss my friends and my parents' home and my pet dog... his name means "happiness". My mood is going down... but it's gradual because I make some new friends here and I gradually get used to the culture here.' At this point there is a significant gulf between her positive expectations and the reality of her experience. She had expected that making new friends and starting to interact with the new culture would make things easier. '... but I still don't feel as good as I expected before I come. So it's gradual change, we come to the lowest point.'

After successfully completing her masters modules things start to improve. 'After I finish it, I become happier so my mood is going up again.' A summer spent at the university struggling with her dissertation resulted in a second low point, though she pointed out that it was not as deep as the first. However, as she coped with these challenges she regained a sense of being in control. 'I feel so much after I've experienced different challenges and difficulties here I think my moods are quite positive and routine here. I think I'm already in a stable situation.' This is depicted by the line in the drawing going up and down. But eventually the line becomes quite even. Overall her experience was a positive one, a 'wonderful chance to experience different culture and different food or different way of study'. She felt she had changed as a person since

Figure 4.3 Student C: 'Experiences of moving to a new culture'

coming to the new culture. 'I think I am more confident. Here people treat me like an adult. That is not the Chinese way ... there I still feel like a child. Here I learn to be an independent person ... that feel good.'

Although her early high expectations had not been realised she seemed content to leave the ups and downs behind and enjoy the sense of equilibrium she had achieved in her life.

Student D

Student D was 25 years of age who, like Student C, was a masters student nearing the end of her studies. Her drawing consisted of a series of peaks and troughs in three colours, which she had divided into two parts representing the first half and the second half of the course (Figure 4.4). One word, 'anxiety', was written on the page at the beginning of the lines. 'The first half of the year is just like a mess because I have to adapt to everything. The red pen just like the anxiety of how I feel because I have to adapt to the new situation.'

Her drawing shows, in addition to the red line, a green line, which she explained represents her studies, and a blue line, which depicts her life. For the first half of the year, all three lines show dramatic peaks and troughs with the red line of anxiety predominating during the early months after arrival. 'That's all a mess in the first half of year but I try to organise my life and study here.' She felt that the very different teaching philosophy in Britain compared to China was a major challenge. 'The teachers here just introduce this person's idea about this, that person's idea about this, but they never give us the right answer, you know. What I mean the right answer in China.' This absence of the concept of the 'right answer' was a particular problem when she was writing essays where she was expected to give her own point of view.

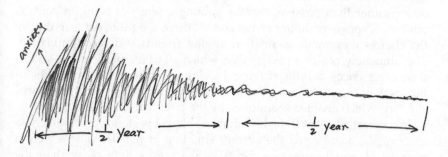

Figure 4.4 Student D: 'Experiences of moving to a new culture'

Even more daunting was being asked to express such personal opinions in class. 'The teachers always ask you "what's your idea about this?" When I first confronted this question I was astonished because this is a quite different way.' In China, she explained, the teacher would ask what the text was about but would never ask for a personal opinion of the text. 'So I was quite astonished. "What's my idea?" I don't have any idea. I just understand what the material say. So that's quite strange for me.'

However, she felt that this interactive approach to learning was overall a very positive experience, which she was keen to bring back to China. The researcher asked if she felt she had changed since coming to the UK. 'I think I've changed just a little bit. I've got more active and more confident than before.' She summarised her current situation by pointing to the right side of her drawing where the red line disappears and the green and blue lines are gently oscillating. 'The anxiety has gone. The study is still there and the life.'

Common Themes in the Drawings

A number of themes are common to the three drawings of Students A, C and D, the most obvious of which is their chronological aspect. All three students chose to represent their sojourning experience as a linear sequence with the positive and negative elements expressed by undulating lines. All three drawings progress from left to right across the page with drawings C and D resembling time-lines.

Another common theme is the dissonance between the students' high expectations at the start of their sojourn and the realities of adjusting to a new culture. A major aspect of these early months was coming to terms with this realisation, and of finding ways to cope. Students A and D spoke about 'acting more active' by which they seemed to mean being active rather than passive, thereby gaining a sense of being in control. Student C spoke in similar terms and all three sought to achieve this by the choices they made in relation to jobs, friends and accommodation. The ultimately positive perspective, which all of the participants had of their experiences, is quite striking. Having coped with the early difficulties, each of the students appeared to have achieved a sense of emotional stability, which enabled them to enjoy the latter part of their sojourn.

In contrast, Student B chose to draw an almost pastoral scene, which, as she explained, reflected the current situation of her life. There were a number of possible reasons for this. She was a little older than the others and married, with her husband accompanying her on her sojourn.

An indication of her greater maturity was that she was the only one to refer to herself as a woman rather than a girl. She was expecting her first baby, an event that she was clearly anticipating with excitement. As a PhD student she was self-motivated and her English was probably the most proficient of the four students. She did not seem to have had the same sense of unrealised expectations early in her sojourn and appeared to have achieved a significant understanding of the local culture. There were, however, many commonalities between her experience and those of the other three students. For example, in common with the other three, she had struggled with the language at the start of her stay and had also sought to interact positively with the local culture.

Modelling the Students' Experiences

The images produced by Students A, C and D stressed the dynamic nature of adapting to a new culture. In each case the process changed with time, reflecting the changes within the individual and their relationship with the new culture. For this reason the models that focused on the developmental, personal growth aspects of acculturation, those of Bennett and Yoshikawa, seemed to have most potential. Indeed, one of the students observed specifically that moving to a new culture had been '...good for my experience [and] for my personal growth'. However, as we argued earlier, neither model worked fully with the experiences as detailed to us in the series of interviews with the undergraduate students, and the inadequacies led us to modify the models in the light of our data, and most notably the data from the spontaneous drawing sessions with the four students.[2] In this last section of the chapter, we propose a refined model that more accurately reflects the experience of our students. As with the two earlier developmental models, our model is also characterised by stages in the process of acculturation, five in all: Encounter, Disorientation, Reaction, Independence and Internalisation.

Stage 1: Encounter

All four of the students in our study highlighted the impact of entering a new culture that had so many new situations to understand and to which they had to respond. All had high expectations of their sojourn and were highly motivated to adapt successfully to the new culture. Their Encounter with the differences therefore generated a positive response to the new environment for the first few weeks. When sojourners enter a new culture they immediately face cultural differences, often to a degree never before experienced. For many, like our students, the

Encounter may be experienced as exciting, particularly since sojourners, being by definition voluntary migrants, tend to be highly motivated to enter a new culture. However, for those with limited experience of cultural differences, the Encounter will tend to be interpreted solely through their own cultural perspective and may therefore be unhappy, confused and even, in the worst cases, frightening.

The Encounter stage is therefore close to Yoshikawa's first stage of Contact and fits with Oberg's (1960) notion of a 'honeymoon period'. We feel, however, that the term Encounter better describes the notion of meeting or confronting the new experiences than the suggested passivity of mere Contact.

Stage 2: Disorientation

Without previous experience of cultural differences, sojourners who are highly motivated may react to their Encounter with the new environment with excitement while those who retreat into an own-culture perspective may become unsure and confused, and perhaps homesick. However, our results suggest that even those who are initially excited will, at some relatively early point in time after arrival, begin to recognise the possibly vast cultural differences between their home culture and the host culture in which they find themselves. This Disorientation stage is represented in one drawing (Figure 4.3) by a steeply declining line and in another (Figure 4.4) by a jagged red line with the word 'anxiety' written above it. Student D commented: 'The first half of the year is just like a mess because I have to adapt to everything. The red pen just like the anxiety of how I feel because I have to adapt to the new situation.'

Student A represented this stage as chaotic lines with no pattern at all and like the previous student observed that 'life really is a mess'. Similar feelings were expressed by Student C when she commented on the impact of 'the complete change of cultural environment. I cannot totally understand so I think the culture I can't really enjoy it'.

The Yoshikawa stage of Disintegration is clearly close to the depictions above, taking account of the sojourner 'being overwhelmed by cultural difference' (Yoshikawa, 1988: 142) in a way which Bennett's (1993) denial and defence stages fail to do. However, Disintegration is too strong a concept implying as it does a breakdown, whether mentally or physically. Our data suggests that this stage is more of a Disorientation, away from the predicted or expected circumstances to a situation in which the host culture members fail to react as expected and a degree of confusion sets in. Oberg (1960: 177) contends that 'culture shock is precipitated by the anxiety that results from losing all our familiar signs and symbols of social intercourse'. The students had arrived in Britain with their own cultural scripts which were no longer applicable in the new environment. Life suddenly lost its predictability and was described by the students as 'a mess'. They felt that they had lost control of their lives as all their cultural points of reference disappeared. Perhaps this is why the students, and indeed sojourners in general, tend to over-attribute their problems in the host culture to language difficulties. Everyone they encounter is speaking a different language from them, not only verbally but at a deeper level. Language difficulties can thus be seen as a metaphor to account for the perplexity and confusion of their Disorientation.

Stage 3: Reaction

In the third stage in the experience of the Chinese students, they began to make adjustments to better cope with the new culture. Prior experience had shown that their normal strategies were inappropriate in the new environment and so they had to learn new behaviours if they were to be successful. This was termed by two of the students as 'becoming more active' and Student A represented this by four bold arrows coming out of the chaos.

For us, the data suggested that this stage is substantively different from Yoshikawa's stage of Reintegration, which is typified by rejection of cultural similarities and difference. Kim (1997) argues that the previous stressful stage of disequilibrium, due to the struggle between the sojourner's original identity and the need to adopt a new identity, acts as an impetus for adaptation in what Chen and Starosta (1998) called the 'adjustment period'. We feel this notion of a 'more active' response to the environment, the Reaction stage, is more appropriate to the stage that our students described. By this point in their sojourn, the students were beginning to appreciate the cultural perspective of the host culture and were learning to act in culturally appropriate ways. However, they spoke of the great effort required for this process, echoing the words of Bond (1996: xii): 'I am forced into cultural mindfulness on a regular basis, since I can rarely relax into a world of familiar faces, forms, and formulas.'

The new environment still surprised the students at times, portrayed by Student A as triangles depicting strange or unexpected experiences.

Stage 4: Independence

Much energy and effort was required by the students in the Reaction stage, as they sought to interact in ways appropriate to the new culture.

Gradually, however, they began to master the new cultural patterns and found life becoming easier to cope with and more predictable. They became more independent. The students' sense of identity had changed as, to some degree, they absorbed the perspectives of the new culture. Each of them mentioned the new sense of Independence that they had, not only in the practical aspects of their lives, but in thinking independently and constructing their own opinions and viewpoints. They no longer felt that they were 'children' as they had been in China but saw themselves as independent young women, thus taking on the host culture perception of them rather than that of their home culture. Yoshikawa (1988) describes this stage in a similar fashion as Autonomy and Chen and Starosta (1998: 174) comment that the rise in self-efficacy accompanying this period 'marks a growth in personal flexibility'. The students described this stage as the relative calm after the storm, with two of them depicting it in gentle undulations following on from the previous extreme highs and lows. This section in Student A's drawing had finally regained some of the rhythm and pattern of the beginning of her sojourn, on which she commented: 'I have probably sorted out something ... that is why these waves are in order.'

Stage 5: Internalisation

Both the Yoshikawa and Bennett models propose an end point of acculturation (Double-swing and Integration, respectively) for which we were unable to find any evidence from the comments of the undergraduate students and only the slightest evidence from the longer-term sojourners in the spontaneous drawing group. In essence, both models predict an end-stage during which the sojourner transcends their own culture and adopts some form of inter-cultural identity. Yoshikawa's (1987) final stage is Double-swing or *dynamic in-betweenness*, with the sojourner being able to move comfortably between cultural identities. Yoshikawa sees the individual as interdependent as well as independent. He illustrates this by referring to the Chinese characters for 'human being', which are:

$$人 間$$

The first character means 'person' and the second 'in-betweenness' leading to the comment that 'one becomes a human being only in relation to another person' (Yoshikawa, 1988: 143). His concept of dynamic in-betweenness has been much quoted by authors but often without proper attention to its relational aspect. The concept is similar to, but distinct from Bennett's Integration, which aims to construct a new identity that is culturally unaffiliated, the ultimate stage in ethnorelativism. Bennett's approach with its view of the individual as an entirely free agent arises, we have argued, from a Western individualist perspective and consequently would appear to be less relevant to the experiences of those sojourners who come, like our Chinese students, from a collectivist culture.

While the students in the spontaneous drawing group had not reached a final stage described by these models, the different cultural perspectives of their home and new cultures had undergone a process of Internalisation. They were able to 'draw nourishment from both cultural similarities and differences' (Yoshikawa, 1988: 142). They spoke very positively, for example, of the independent approach to learning they had experienced in Britain, with one student stating, '...if I just go back to China, I have to take this strategy with me'. Another student commented that though she could 'enter the culture here' when it came to dealing with deeper personal relationships 'I still [work] in my Chinese way'. This clearly demonstrates the increased levels of intercultural sensitivity and ethnorelativism developed by the students, without necessarily experiencing the deep transformation implied for this stage by both Yoshikawa and Bennett.

On the basis of our findings, then, we argue that sojourners do not inevitably change their cultural identity to one of in-betweenness (Double-swing or Integration) but do internalise differences sufficiently so that they react as appropriate to the cultural context or situation in which they find themselves at any particular time. It is likely that the sojourner is unaware of the extent of such Internalisation and the realisation of the impact of the new culture may only occur on return to the home culture, a sort of 're-entry shock'. We believe that this stage points more to the ability of the individual to internalise the experience of cultural differences within their sense of identity rather than to transcend it as others would suggest.

Acculturation: A Recursive Process

The model we have laid out above is similar to the others in many ways but is in our view more appropriate in explaining the experiences of the students with whom we worked. Whether it would explain other students' sojourning experiences better than the other models we have considered is not something on which we could make a firm pronouncement. However, regardless of whether one model or another is best, there are probably two main riders to the arguments presented. First it must be recognised that acculturation, as in any progressive process, will likely proceed in a recursive fashion, i.e. with all stages in the process being revisited at different times as the sojourner encounters new experiences. Second, it must be recognised that any model can only offer a simplification of the individual complexities that constitute any sojourner's path of acculturation and we accept that our model inevitably suffers from this limitation. In the special case of university students studying overseas, the findings arising from the research with the students at Queen's throw some light on one such complexity. Not only must they cope with a very different culture, they must also meet the challenges involved in successfully studying for a qualification in that culture. As a final comment we offer the following poignant description of the profound impact of moving as a student from one culture to another (Wierzbicka, 1997: 118):

> It wasn't just in my life that the two cultures [Polish and Australian] . . . met, it was also in my 'psyche', in my 'self', in my 'mind', my emotions, my personal relations, my daily interactions. I had to start learning new 'cultural scripts' to live by, and in the process I became aware of the old 'cultural scripts' which had governed my life hitherto. I also became aware, in the process, of the reality of 'cultural scripts' and their importance to the way one lives one's life, to the image one projects, and even to one's personal identity.

Notes

1. Within the same research project, data were also gathered to assess the intercultural sensitivity of all of the Chinese students and the attitudes of local students to these students, but the analysis of these is not reported here.
2. Clearly we must be cautious about drawing conclusions from data produced by just four students. However, such a basis for our analysis is not without celebrated precedent, as we should recall that the work of Adler (1977: 32) on 'multicultural man', which underlies both the models of Bennett and Yoshikawa, arose from the intercultural experiences of just four men!

Chapter 5

Reciprocal Adjustment by Host and Sojourning Groups: Mainland Chinese Students in Hong Kong

CAROL MING-HUNG LAM

Introduction

The present study originated from the Policy Address 1997 in which the Chief Executive Officer of the Hong Kong Special Administrative Region proposed that the local universities 'should be places for cross cultural learning and exchange' (Tung, 1997: para. 95). In the Policy Address 1998, this proposal was further specified to recruit 150 outstanding Mainland Chinese students annually into undergraduate programmes from 1999 to 2000 academic year in the hope that 'the admission of non-local students facilitates the cross-fertilisation of skills and ideas, injects an element of healthy competition for local students and broadens our students' outlook on the Mainland and the region as a whole' (Tung, 1998: para. 103). Though Chinese students have a long history of studying abroad since the Tsing Dynasty, which began in 1636, this was the very first time that a larger group of Mainland students crossed the border to undertake their undergraduate studies in Hong Kong. This ethnographic study, therefore, attempted to examine the adjustment experience of a group of 11 Mainland students from the first cohort who were introduced to the undergraduate programmes in a university in Hong Kong in 1999. The study also produced evidence of corresponding adjustment of the host group which was unexpectedly found to be not less than the sojourning group.

Setting the Scene

The case used in the present study is the first batch of Mainland students studying in the undergraduate programmes at a local university in Hong Kong. These 11 students aged 18–20 first arrived in mid-January 1999, after their one semester's study of English and computer studies in Beijing. Then, they received another semester's foundation courses, namely English, Hong Kong culture and society, mathematics, physics and computer studies at the local university. All together they had one year's preparatory courses before entering their major study, which takes another three years. Upon graduation, they would receive the Bachelor degree granted by the local university that they attended instead of the one from the Chinese university they originally enrolled in. They were first supposed to return to Mainland according to the agreement made at the beginning of the scheme, but later in March 2001 when they entered their second year of study, the policy was changed and they were granted the opportunity to work in Hong Kong after their graduation. In order to enhance the cultural exchange and mutual understanding, each of them stayed in the university hostel with one local or foreign student as his/her roommate. Described as 'the cream of the crop' among all university students in China (since the university they originally enrolled in is one of the top universities in China), this group of students sparked interest from various levels, including both the on-campus and outside media. One of the first questions the press usually asked is 'What made these students give up their place at the top Chinese university and choose to come study in Hong Kong?' A more fascinating and noteworthy question for researchers will be 'What kind of difficulties might they encounter when adjusting to this similar yet different Chinese culture in Hong Kong and how will their Hong Kong counterparts react to their presence?'

Other than the 11 Mainland informants, the key informants also consist of 15 local students in the different classes that the Mainland students attended, and a few individuals related to the Mainland group. Like many of their peers, the two groups of students were all strangers to the University where they started their brand new journey of university life. Yet, unlike others, these two particular groups not only embarked on their transition into university life, but also their transition to study in a multicultural and academically multi-level environment with their Mainland and Hong Kong peers, respectively. As Spradley (1979: 25) puts it, they were the 'ordinary people with ordinary knowledge', yet 'excellent informants' about their own culture and their own experience.

In order to keep the informants' identity confidential, their real names were replaced by a number based on the alphabetic order of their last name with 'HK' or 'ML' in front of the number showing whether they are from the Hong Kong group or the Mainland one. The class observation data were divided into two sets with the first round of observation numbered from 'Observation A' to 'Observation E', and the second round of observation 'Observation 1' to 'Observation 6' according to the order of observation.

Findings

The findings showed that the Mainland students experienced some initial culture shock, loneliness, anxiety and a communication barrier derived from the different spoken languages used by the Mainland students and their Hong Kong counterparts. These adjustment issues, however, were not as significant as their difficulties when trying to immerse themselves into the local Hong Kong network where they met major setbacks due to their social and cultural diversity, and most importantly, the different perception of their identity. What is probably more surprising is that the Hong Kong counterparts seemed to have encountered equal or more adjustment problems than the Mainland sojourners.

Social and cultural diversity

When talking about receiving and adjusting to each other's social group, many informants of both groups acknowledged that language was a problem, but not the most important one. What really hindered their communication was their social and cultural diversity, which brought them into contact with different worldviews, values and life goals, and thus different preferences of topics for conversations.

Growing up in two totally different parts of China not only gave them two different languages, but also two different cultures which governed the way they spoke, the genre they used and the subjects they preferred to talk about in their communication. As HK1 said, 'Sometimes when we meet each other, we don't know what to say.' HK6 also shared a similar thought by describing their topics of conversation as very trivial.

Later HK1 also compared the Manland students' acquaintance with them and with the international students by saying, 'Last semester there was an international girl in our class. Those Mainland students seemed more familiar to her than to us. Obviously, they had something to say when they bumped into each other. But, with us, they simply gave a glance.'

From this we can see what was lacking in the communication between students of the two groups was not actually the spoken language, but a common language – the common theme for their conversations.

Simultaneously, similar responses were given by the Mainland informants. Doubtfully, ML10 said, 'Maybe it's really the different family and cultural backgrounds, sometimes I do find it hard to associate with the Hong Kong born and raised Chinese in our communication. That is to say that maybe I'm not interested in what they say.' Another Mainland informant, ML5, also emphasised the cultural aspect as a key stumbling block in their communication. What was also put forward by ML5 was the different mindset of the science students or the local students in general compared with that of the Mainland students. As ML5 illustrated this by saying, 'to put it straight, if you talk about things like history, they don't know much, nor do they show any interests or opinions. I think this is a main difference.' To phrase it in another way, although all of the informants of the both groups except for one were science-major students, they held very different views about the importance of art for science people. For most of the informants from universities in Mainland, literature, history and art play an essential role in shaping their personality, directing their decisions and moulding the way they see the world. They need the arts to balance and monitor what they do with what they learn. This is, however, not usually how the local students think. Surrounded by the commercial and financial centres in Hong Kong and educated under an exam-oriented system, very few of them can see the value of arts in their world. In the same way, the Mainland informants could not respond to the local students when they talked about local affairs, movie stars, singers, clothing and shopping in Hong Kong. Gradually, the students of the two groups came to the conclusion that they did not have a common language that could facilitate their communication and further their relationship. That is often perceived as the vital difference between the Mainland informants and their local counterparts, and what really matters when delving into the intercultural communication and relationship between the two groups.

Holding the same view, HK1, HK4 and HK6 all believed that 'in fact the biggest problem is the different cultures'. The different background of the two groups actually made HK6 feel that the Mainland students in his class were totally detached from them (the local counterparts).

Other than the general cultural difference, what lay behind the different preference of topic for conversation in this particular case was the informants' different pursuit of life goals stemming from their different values:

> Our different mindset can very largely affect the effectiveness of our communication. For example, what we aim to achieve through the university schooling is very different, which became a barrier in our communication. For me, I simply want to finish my three years study and go find a job afterwards, while they (the Mainland counterparts) may want to obtain an excellent academic result, and accomplish something great in a certain field afterwards. Our purposes are totally different. (HK8)

Another Mainland informant, ML6 also confirmed the above thought about their plan of further study in a follow-up conversation which took place after the Hong Kong government announced the possibility of allowing the Mainland students to stay and work after graduation. With a vision of their future in other foreign countries, they were very eager to learn as much as possible at this moment, which was different from most of the local students, especially science major students who actually found little interest in science but wanted to secure a job with their degree.

Some Mainland informants were also found to fall short of cultural sensitivity in their social interaction and communication. They failed to do as the Romans do when in Rome, and therefore were not able to either maintain a successful intercultural communication or establish a close relationship with their Hong Kong counterparts. For example, in class the Mainland informants often started their lengthy querying and opinion sharing, which appeared 'different' to their local counterparts. ML8 was one of the typical ones. His enthusiasm about sharing in class has caused his classmates to 'compete' for the chance to speak because the in-class opinion sharing was marked as part of their final assessment.

Such initiative to contribute and boldness to be involved, as ML8 showed, was found very common in class across most subjects as seen in the first round of classroom observation. For example, during the Mathematics lesson in Observation 5, students were asked to solve some Mathematics problems that the teacher set on the board. Very quickly two of the Mainland students, ML8 and ML4 raised their hands and made their way to the board. After the teacher corrected one of those who finished first, some students in the class started negotiating with the teacher right away, trying to see whether there were other alternatives to this solution. Before long, ML1 went to work on her correction by doing it the way she found more appropriate. At the end, ML4 was negotiating and discussing a better solution to the mathematics problem by working together with the teacher on the board, while ML1 who had finished her solution, later again explained and discussed her solution with the teacher on the board. What was unusual in this scenario was that the Mainland students challenged not only their peers' work, but also their teacher's work and confronted each other with no hesitation, being also very open to others' challenges and willing to be corrected. No wonder one of the Mainland informants' teachers in one observation commented, 'The problem with this group of students is how to stop them from speaking instead of arousing them to speak.'

What triggered the analysis of this aspect is the fascinating association between what was observed above and what was said by HK2 earlier in this section about her Mainland counterparts. Since the frequent sharing and candid challenge in class were considered perfectly 'normal' when the Mainland informants had classes with their own group, they naturally did not see its peculiarity in the eyes of their local counterparts when having class together. Such lack of awareness among some Mainland students of the different and subtle social rules was also further confirmed in findings in one of the class observations when the Mainland informants had classes with their Hong Kong counterparts. What happened between ML3 and his local group mates can best illustrate how the dominance of the discussion by some Mainland students annoyed some of their group members.

Since the main venue where the Hong Kong informants and their Mainland counterparts mixed was the classroom, the Mainland informants' classroom behaviour became an important indicator to show the Hong Kong informants who they are, what they will and will not do. Both the enthusiasm about asking questions and sharing in class of some of the Mainland informants reported by HK2 above, and others, impressed their local counterparts on the one hand, yet stopped them from getting close to them on the other hand since they were found to be very different from the other local students.

Different perceptions of identity

A trace of the spontaneous perceptual division of the two groups in the students' responses further reveals the deep-rooted perception of the two groups' rather distant identity and this can be seen in four facets: the self-identity as a person from a different place, a different culture, a different socioeconomic status, and most important, a different level of academic group.

First of all, Hong Kong students had a very obvious regional identity, while their Mainland counterparts had an even stronger national identity.

This can be indicated by the way the local students addressed their Mainland counterparts. Regarding the Mainland counterparts respectively as *keui dei* (they), *an dei* (others), *oi an* (outsiders), and *dai yi dao di an* (people from another place), and *sheung min di an* (people up there) since China is located to the north of Hong Kong, some local students seemed to have drawn a clear boundary between the two groups. While *keui dei* (they) versus *ngo dei* (we) in Cantonese referring to two different groups might sound neutral, *an dei* ('others') or *oi an* (outsiders) sounded less friendly.

Discussing the same issue, HK5 later acknowledged that they regarded both the international and the Mainland students as 'others' or 'outsiders'. This was explicitly stated by HK2, another local informant, who had ML7, a Mainland informant, in her class throughout the semesters. She said, '[If ML7 was a local student], I would feel closer, but now it feels like there is an outsider coming in.'

Coincidently, this sense of 'outsider' was also perceived by ML10, a Mainland informant from Guangzhou who speaks Cantonese as the local students do. As she realised,

> When they did not know you are not local people, everything is normal. But once they found out that you're from Mainland, they became very surprised and excited. It's good and bad because they would ask you all kinds of questions like where you're from, and what you're doing in Hong Kong, yet that kind of, my original feeling of closeness between Hong Kong people and Mainland Chinese would disappear right away.

Another Mainland informant, ML7 put it more directly and felt that they were seen as 'aliens'. 'Alien' had two senses: those who got extremely good academic results and those from another place.

Simultaneously, born and raised in Mainland, the Mainland informants also bore a clear and strong national and social identity as Mainland Chinese. Findings in the class observation showed that many of them had a great passion for China, felt proud of being Chinese, and determined to contribute to their country in future. This was also noted by some of their Hong Kong counterparts. The national or regional identity of the two groups was such a core and fundamental identity that it embodied the essential difference of individuals of the two groups.

Second, what lies behind this classification of different territories is the different socioeconomic status of the two groups. As revealed by, for example, Saddlemire's (1996) studies on how white undergraduates viewed their African American counterparts, the perceived gap between the two racial groups may be more truthfully identified as a gap of socioeconomic status instead of that of racial status. At the time when the study was conducted, Hong Kong still enjoyed a relatively higher socioeconomic status than Mainland. It was not uncommon to hear that the local students would not like to be misrecognised as Mainland Chinese as the living standard of the two places was perceived as very different, which gave them a different level of socioeconomic identity.

The third more visible identity difference that affected the communication between the two groups is their distinct cultural identity. Defined as 'the emotional significance that we attach to our sense of belonging or affiliation with the larger culture', Ting-Toomey (1999: 30–31) ranks 'cultural identity' as the very first of the four important primary identity domains that requires our mindfulness and understanding when communicating across cultures. Although members of both groups were ethnically Chinese, they bore very different cultural values. This has been maintained by Vasil and Yoon (1996) who found a significant difference among Chinese immigrants from Hong Kong, Taiwan, China and Malaysia and therefore reminded us not to over-generalise them as a homogeneous group. As can be seen in the findings, the different cultural identity of the Hong Kong students and their Mainland counterparts can be noted ranging from areas as practical as the different food they liked and as abstract as the different values and beliefs they held towards study and life. This drove them to have very different expectations of themes in their daily conversations and an 'incompatible' feeling in their communication. As described above, this view was found highly emphasised by both the Mainland and the Hong Kong groups in the interviews. As Berry *et al.* (1987) realise, this incompatibility in behaviour, attitudes and values between the two cultures may result in psychological distress. Gudykunst (1998) also reminds us how immensely these cultural identities influence our daily communication, and how often we tend to take them for granted and fail to be aware of this constant influence.

The last but probably the most prominent identity difference between the two groups in this particular context is the Hong Kong students' self-definition as the lower academic group in contrast to the exceptionally high academic level of their Mainland counterparts. This strong and ingrained self-image was partly built by their personal actualisation and partly through the media's overwhelming publicity. This was clearly mirrored by the way they contrasted their academic results to those of their Mainland counterparts, with the Mainland group reaching an average grade point average (GPA) of '3.5' to '3.95', whereas most local counterparts have barely '2.5' and at best '3'.

In fact, because of the fear of the impact of the Mainland counterparts' bright academic results on those of the local students, ML1 disclosed that in an orientation meeting for the new students at the beginning of the semester, quite a few local students raised the same question: 'The academic results of the Mainland students are a lot better than ours. Then, the GPA average will definitely be raised because of that. Does it mean that there will be a higher possibility for us to get a lower grade or even fail?' We can see how the Hong Kong students set themselves apart from their Mainland counterparts through this type of concern.

Another voice that reinforced this distinction of the two groups was the message in the mass media through which the students were told which group they belonged to and this social climate in the society largely influenced the social climate inside the university. Identified as 'outstanding' in the Chief Executive Policy Address 1998, the Mainland group's arrival and stupendous academic performance still caught major attention in the mass media after almost two years into their stay ('Excellent students' _Ming Pao Newspaper_, 20 December 2000). Conversely, local Hong Kong students were often criticised for their declining academic competence especially in language competence in comparison with that of their Mainland counterparts (_Ming Pao Newspaper_, 20 April 2001). Early in 1994 or 1995, the English and the Chinese language standards of graduates in Shanghai outperformed those from the Hong Kong local universities ('Mainland students' _Sing Dao Daily_, 9 April 2001). Both their self-stereotyping and the media's constant comparison of the academic standard of the two groups put students of the two groups consciously and unconsciously through a group separation. This contextual group division was also surprisingly found among the Mainland informants as one of the Mainland informants shared the following insight:

> I think the key to our adjustment lies in our mindset. We (the Mainland students) must first forget that we came from a top [University] in Mainland if we want to communicate with the local students. The wall between us can be removed if we are willing to put ourselves in the local group. For example, when positioning myself into the present context, I would think of 'we' Accountancy students, instead of 'I' a Mainland student. I think the problem with some Mainland students is that they often view the local students as 'you' Hong Kong students. (ML10)

This means that ML10 has put aside her original identity. Instead of regarding herself as a Mainland student, she adopted the Major faculty she belonged to as her new identity in this contextual environment. Unlike most of her Mainland counterparts, ML10 was able to put herself into the local group using their Majors as an identity marker rather than 'Hong Kong students' and 'Mainland students'. Instead of applying her 'primary identities' (cultural identity, ethnic identity, gender identity and personal identity), ML10 put on her 'situational identities' (role identity, relational identity, facework identity and symbolic interaction identity) (Ting-Toomey, 1999: 29) in her intercultural communication. This change of mindset, a crucial step that breaks the ice of intercultural communication between the two different cultural groups discovered by ML10, truly manifested what Ting-Toomey (1999: 26) coined as the identity negotiation theory in her recent work. By acknowledging the common situational identity with her local counterparts, ML10 made the intention of her message the same as her local counterparts, and therefore ascertained a higher degree of 'shared meanings' in her intercultural communication process (1999: 19). By a high level of 'shared meanings', Ting-Toomey refers to the accurate understanding of the message in three aspects: the decoding of the verbal 'content meaning', the mastery of 'identity meaning' that shows hidden messages like respect or polite rejection, and the comprehension of the nonverbal 'relational meaning' that indicates the power distance and relational distance between two interlocutors.

ML10 seemed to be the only one among the Mainland informants who was willing to initiate this internal change to reach for external intercultural relationship and communication. What has to be made clear here is that ML10 was the only native Cantonese speaker in the Mainland group. Comparing her with the other 10 Mainland students, it was evident that she could alter her situational identity more easily since many of her local counterparts could not differentiate her from other local students.

In brief, the above findings on the identity perception of the Hong Kong students and their Mainland counterparts has articulated a series of particular perceptual barriers behind their adjustment and intercultural communication. They are the different and rather exclusive identities, from the national, cultural, socioeconomic to academic perspectives. What reinforced this gap is the competition at school and at the workplace they perceived between the two groups. Only with one of the Mainland informants who was able to put aside her original academic label in particular and put on a new group identity in association with her local counterparts was the communication gap alleviated.

Methodology

In order to truly mirror the reality of the intercultural communication between the Mainland students and their Hong Kong counterparts, it seemed that the issues could be better revealed by a study of the classroom behaviour, interactive communication and contextual influences involved when the two groups were placed together in their everyday classroom. That is why an ethnographic study approach was developed as it emphasises the examination of 'social and cultural patterns and meaning in communities, institutions, and other social settings' (Hammersley & Atkinson, 1983; Schensul *et al.*, 1999b: 1; also see Agar, 1980). It aims to understand parts of the world by looking at the way people experience and interpret life in their everyday lives (Cook & Crang, 1995). This prominence of comprehending the social, cultural, and meaning in the life of a group of people was exactly what the study aimed to bring out. Different from other qualitative research like semiotics and analytic induction, it sheds special light on the holistic orientation and cultural essence when analyzing the data (Watson-Gegeo, 1988).

Having placed the ethnographic study under the interpretive paradigm did not mean that quantitative methods would not be applied in the study. As the issue of whether to include quantitative research in ethnographic study has been constantly pondered by many ethnographers throughout the years (Bernard, 1995; Clifford, 1988; Pelto & Pelto, 1978), Schensul *et al.* (1999b) argue that both qualitative and quantitative data are crucial to ethnographic research since the former elicit the textual phenomena, while the latter present the numerical measurement to ensure validity. With an endeavour of encompassing both intensive and extensive data, my initial attempt consisted of both the qualitative and quantitative search to discover data from various perspectives and to form triangulation. A combination of ethnographic interviews, questionnaires, class observation, participant observation, journal writing and collection of their schoolwork were applied. However, not all these attempts proved successful after their first trial. The ethnographic interviews, class observations and participant observations proved to be feasible and suitable, but not the questionnaire and journal writing unfortunately. The informants seemed particularly hesitant whenever they were asked to put down their ideas in black and white. This could be respectively attributed to a general reason and a contextual one. Being bombarded by various surveys in their daily life in the institution and/or other settings, the local students seemed especially impatient when responding to questionnaires in general. For the Mainland students, being brand new to the Hong Kong society with a typical social Mainland background, they appeared very open to many new things, but remained sceptical and careful with things they had to jot down on paper.

This early tryout told me that practically, the use of qualitative methods was more possible and appropriate for two reasons. First, the number of people involved in this study was limited to the 11 Mainland students and their 15 counterparts at the local university. Second and more importantly, the mainland students were found to be a lot more willing to tell their stories verbally than in writing. Theoretically, the qualitative approach was needed since the study aimed to delve into the complex interaction and communication between the two groups through which the academic exchange, healthy competition and cultural exchange took place in this particular context. In order to unearth not only what happened, but also how, why and what it means in reality, qualitative methods were found more apposite.

The arranged ethnographic interviews

As one of the frequently quoted definitions of ethnographic interview goes, 'an ethnographic interview is a particular kind of speech event' (Spradley, 1979: 55). It differs from ordinary interviews both in terms of its structure and its rationale. Unlike the structured (or formal), semi-structured, or unstructured (or informal) interview, the ethnographic interview acts just like a series of 'friendly conversations' in which informants disclose information naturally, spontaneously and almost unconsciously without noticing that they are being interviewed (Spradley, 1979). It can take place any time and anywhere when a researcher comes across his/her informants. Certainly, what alters is that the researcher plays more an inquisitive role in the conversation than the informants, always asking, repeating and expanding questions, while the informants tend to be surprised about the curiosity that the researcher casts on them. In addition to the structural difference, the ethnographic interview also differs from the regular interview in terms of its primary goal and rationale. When conducting ethnographic interviews, rather than drawing out the informants to find out what is on the interview question list, the researcher aims to be led by the informants to seek much more than what is on his/her agenda in order to reveal the real picture of the ways the informants interpret and understand the world. 'Instead of collecting "data" about people, the ethnographer seeks to learn from people...' (Spradley, 1979: 4). With this distinct underlying principle in mind, the researcher adopts a very different approach to setting, asking, responding to and following up his/her questions derived from the response of the informants.

In the present study, a preliminary formal ethnographic interview was arranged between mid-March 1999 to mid-April 1999, three months after the China informants arrived to find out the social, cultural and academic background that they brought with them before they joined the scheme and their initial adjustment. As Cook and Crang (1995: 7) argue, simply knowing 'where people are (socially and spatially)' is not adequate, what is also important is to find out 'where they/we are coming from, going to, and where on this path the research encounter has occurred'. This is because people's identities and memories are shaped by their everyday experience and actions that respond to the world at manifold points, times and places and are tangled together throughout their course of life. To understand the background of the Mainland informants could help to trace back why they felt how they felt. The interview with the Mainland informants was conducted individually since it involved a large amount of private narration. During the interview, for the most part the informants were encouraged to tell their life stories at different stages in chronological order freely because what they spontaneously brought up on their own seemed likely to be most important to them. However, in order to cover several variables that may have influenced the way they were and the way they would be, the informants were asked about such things as parents' expectations, teachers' influence, learning strategies, learning motivation, personal goals and reasons to come to Hong Kong, if these had not come up casually. All interviews were tape-recorded except for one informant who did not like to have a record of any kind throughout the research period. With that informant, I jotted notes and key phrases mentioned.

Between early-February 2000 to early-April 2000, the second round of ethnographic interviews was respectively conducted among the Mainland informants and their local counterparts. Some were done individually, while some in pairs since they tended to respond more actively and naturally when triggered by their peers who shared the same experience. During the interview, attention was turned to the Mainland informants' life after they arrived in Hong Kong and in particular, their life with the local students and some international students at the university. With the local counterparts, focus was put on the way they felt about their Mainland counterparts, their reaction to their presence, the occurrence of their communication and interaction and the impact that the Mainland students made on them. 'Grand-tour' questions (Spradley, 1979) were used to start the informants looking back, recalling and describing their being together. Information on two areas was especially gathered in depth. They were the Mainland informants' cultural and academic interaction with the local students and their cultural and learning adjustment at the university. To fully understand the meaning of what they said, I often encouraged the informants to provide concrete examples, in which they sometimes disclosed more extensive and decisive information.

Other 'friendly conversations': Informal ethnographic interviews

Since research interviews are considered unnatural no matter how one tries to make them casual, other 'friendly conversations' with the informants of both groups were adopted to seek their spontaneous and unconscious utterances, which proved to be incredibly useful and important to disclose what they really meant by what they said. These 'friendly conversations' took place almost anywhere on or off campus whenever I had a chance to meet the informants. They lasted as short as five minutes to as long as 45 minutes depending on each particular situation. I often started with the general questions about their study and life in Hong Kong and tried to get into the areas that were worth prompting based on what the informants had mentioned in the arranged ethnographic interviews. In a way these 'friendly conversations' acted like a series of follow-up interviews. Based on an increasing mutual trust, respect and the relationship built, these 'friendly conversations' were often surprisingly fruitful and truthful, providing information to answer the questions, which arose from the previous formal interviews. At times they became the best tool to reveal the informants' 'undecided, ambiguous, and contradictory feelings' about what they have said before and what they have not mentioned previously (Cook & Crang, 1995: 46).

Participant and non-participant observation

Participant observation, one of the key characteristics of an ethnographic study (Stewart, 1998), was also employed in the present study, but to a limited extent, unfortunately. Since I needed to fulfil my duties during my regular working hours, most of the participant observations made took place off campus when opportunities were generated for the informants to expose their interactions and performances. These included some social gatherings during various festivals or occasions in which, together with the informants, I participated actively as a complete member researcher (CMR) (Adler & Adler, 1987). Unlike the classroom observation, I was an entire insider in the cases just mentioned, trying to watch the informants in natural settings from an outsider's perspective.

From the very beginning when the Mainland students were first introduced to me till the end of the study, a total of about 18 hours' participant
observations that occurred in some social parties arranged by teachers
and the 'gatekeeper' (the administrator who took care of this batch of
Mainland students), some social gatherings for festivals organized by
myself, the English lunch gathering at the student canteen, and some
lunch gatherings at a hospital canteen nearby.

Two rounds of class observations were conducted respectively during
the first semester when the Mainland students had classes by themselves,
and during the second semester when they joined the classes with the
local students. In both rounds of observation, I acted as Peripheral
Member Researcher (PMR) (Adler & Adler, 1987), observing what took
place from the side. The first round of class observation aimed at observing the more original 'self' of the Mainland informants, finding out how
they behaved and interacted in class when they were with their own
group. A total of eight hours' class observation in which I was completely
an outsider was made between late-April 1999 and early-May 1999. Since
the whole class had only 11 students, the classes were all conducted in
tutorial mode mixed with some teacher's lectures. The classes lasted 50
minutes to 100 minutes with English as the main medium of instruction.
The teachers were from Australia, Mainland and Hong Kong.

The second round of class observation took place during early-
November 1999 to early-December 1999, before the second round of interviews were conducted with both groups. In an attempt to find out more
about the interaction between teachers and students, and in particular,
the Mainland students and their Hong Kong counterparts, classes
selected to observe in this study were mostly tutorials which lasted 50
minutes per session with 15–20 students in each class. Furthermore, a
total of seven hours' class observation were made in this round as the
Mainland students were situated in six classes according to their different
majors. Since tutorials are not provided in every course due to the nature
of each subject, except for the English courses for Year 1 students, most of
the classes observed were the English classes in which English was the
medium of instruction, where students might utter some Cantonese if
they could not express themselves. These EAP (English for Academic
Purpose) courses, which last from one to two semesters according to
different majors, are compulsory for all Year 1 full-time non-English
speaking students. They aim to prepare the students with the necessary
English writing skills to cope with the English academic writing tasks
in their major studies. Unlike the lectures, the teaching and learning in
the tutorials were usually carried out through group discussions and

other task-oriented activities to provide students with more opportunities to practice in small groups what they were instructed in their lectures and these were found especially helpful to discover how the local students' reacted to their Mainland counterparts' presence and in particular, how they interacted and communicated with each other that reflected the academic exchange and competition among them.

Conclusion

With the extensive accounts and collective stories of the participants, the present study displayed an in-depth picture of the underlying adjustment difficulties encountered by the first batch of Mainland Chinese students in the undergraduate programmes in one of the universities in Hong Kong. Instead of looking into the commonly addressed difficulties in adjusting to the different diet, geographic environment and different spoken language, which did not appear to be major difficulties for most Mainland students, the present chapter has delved into the adjustment problems derived from their different cultural, social and self perception. Without the mindfulness of adjusting their primary identity to situational identity in academic contexts, both groups of students met some difficulties when adjusting to each other's presence.

From the cultural adjustment perspective, what appeared more an issue in this particular case was the reciprocal adjustment of the Hong Kong counterparts. Studying with this unexpected first group of Mainland undergraduate students coming from a high-sounding status, the local counterparts demonstrated their initial excitement, welcoming, curiosity and surprise, but for some this was followed by a certain anticlimax afterwards as they faced each other in their everyday class; just like what was experienced by their Mainland counterparts. Without the assistance of an intermediary to overcome the inherent difficulties, most members of both groups by and large still remained socially distant from each other at the final stage of the present study (two years after the study was begun).

Regarding the methodological strategies applied, the study proved the significance of examining the host students' reaction and attitudes toward their sojourning counterparts when discovering the sojourners' adjustment experience, as pointed out by Furnham and Bochner (1986). With the wide-ranging accounts presented not only by the sojourners, but also by their hosts, the study attained more plausible and comprehensive results to unearth the inner structure of the intercultural interpersonal communication and relationship among students of the two parties that show more diverse perspectives when looking at the issue, and enriched the relatively inadequate work done with the other approaches in this field which tend to focus only on the 'strangers'. By studying the sojourners as was originally planned, I learned more about the home students by including their voices. Retrospectively, I found the entire process a difficult, but rewarding and enjoyable one. Confusion, mess and frustration were definitely there especially during the process of negotiating access. All the network set-up, negotiation of access, direct observation, face-to-face interviewing and elicitation, social gatherings and daily conversing considerably expanded and strengthened my workplace relations, and most important, personal friendship. Through all these I personally experienced the blockage of our mindset derived from our self-identity in communication, and witnessed the significance of culture in our communication and conversely, communication in our culture.

Chapter 6

Study Abroad and Experiences of Cultural Distance and Proximity: French Erasmus Students

VASSILIKI PAPATSIBA

Introduction

This study explores the specifics of study abroad with the EU Erasmus/ Socrates student exchange programme and seeks to analyse the way students perceived and dealt with cultural difference, and interacted with others. Beyond recurring assumptions and assertive statements about the cultural benefits that European student mobility is supposed to bring about, how did students perceive otherness and deal with change, difference or unfamiliarity? Did this cultural experience succeed to bring closer and to increase common references among young European neighbours, nevertheless foreigners to each other?

The assumption can be made that for the majority of individuals who deliberately decide to experience a stay abroad, a certain curiosity and desire of encounter with the culturally different Other exist. However, the experience *in situ* proves to be more complex and demanding, requiring individual adjustment and capacity to tolerate change, uncertainty and difference. The intercultural approach has traditionally given an important place to the investigation of cultural shock and individual adjustment in intercultural encounters entailing a high degree of cultural distance (Furnham & Bochner, 1986; Gudykunst & Kim, 1997; Oberg, 1960). Yet, in the case of student mobility within Europe, the specific nature of the intercultural experience has not attracted intensive research interest, possibly because dissimilarity within European cultures has been thought to be less pronounced, thus preventing individuals from experiencing massive confrontation with difference and change.

At the same time, European student mobility, especially when promoted through large-scale schemes, as for instance the EU Erasmus/ Socrates student exchange programme, has not distinctly aimed at the acquisition of intercultural competence, even though enabling young Europeans to internalise a 'European consciousness' has been a hoped-for outcome. However, without specific and systematic action to support intercultural learning, acquiring a feeling of belonging in an enlarged Europe, enriching national identities with the desired European dimension, seems to be a random outcome of individual experiential learning (Papatsiba, 2003). It is worth highlighting that from a political and institutional point of view, the priority has been given to academic aspects and future professional benefits of Erasmus mobility. In the view of the political actors who initiated this scheme (i.e. the European Commission) and the academic community which supported it, student mobility was seen as a means to promote cooperation between higher education institutions and to support the development of the European labour market (Papatsiba, 2005).

Investigation of French Erasmus Students' Cultural Experiences Through Student Reports

Context of the study and corpus

A set of 80 texts giving accounts of 'Erasmus' periods abroad was randomly selected from the institutional archives of the French Regional Council of the Rhone-Alps in order to empirically investigate the above mentioned questions. This regional (local) government was the first in France to set up an active policy for supporting studies and training abroad for HE students in 1987. The regional scheme of relatively generous student grants and the EU Erasmus grants appeared almost simultaneously, but the former had an international scope, and had a second characteristic of particular interest. For 10 years (1987–1997), a personal account of personal experiences of 'studying and living abroad' was requested from those students who benefited from the regional financial support. These texts of approximately 10 pages each were written by French Erasmus students who reported on their stay abroad to the above-mentioned local authorities. Despite the instruction to produce a ten-page typed text, the number of words per text varies between 819 and 7551 words. The mean value is 3117 words and the median is 2932. The total number of words in the corpus is 249,750.

The authorities had insisted on the personal character of the account which was meant to holistically embrace students' experiences. The instructions for the reports were formulated as follows: 'Personal report of ten typed pages, in French, recounting your experience and life abroad (Practical information: life in the institution, social life, knowledge of the country, advice to your "successors")'. Students who received the regional grant signed a contract with the Regional Council stipulating that they would provide this report at the end of their stay abroad in order to receive the last instalment of the grant (25% of the total amount).

Sample

A large variety of subjects (e.g. sciences, medical studies, business studies, human sciences, language studies, vocational HE training, etc.) and types of higher education institution (university, *grandes ecoles*, technological institutes) were represented in the sample of 80 reports. Thirty-seven students were male and 43 female. The students were in their third, fourth and fifth year of studies, with the majority in their third year. Eleven European countries (Austria, Denmark, Germany, Great Britain, Greece, Italy, Ireland, Netherlands, Portugal, Spain and Sweden) constituted the host country for the temporary stay.

Researching Subjective Positioning of Cultural Distance or Proximity

The various topics developed by students were categorised for purposes of content analysis, in order to examine systematically students' perceptions of the Erasmus stay and ways to deal with difference. For the purpose of this chapter, I will focus on a part of the findings showing two main types of approach regarding students' relationship to the host culture and experiences of otherness and strangeness. The first approach was distilled from students' utterances about the background picture of the host country or the city of stay and its landmarks, and their encyclopaedic knowledge (see second-order Category A 'Background context', in methodology section). It was interpreted as showing distant positioning to the host culture and society. Within this approach, descriptions of contemporary society, especially condensed in the Category A3 'Cultural characteristics of people', evoked a rather stereotypical perception of 'people' as a homogeneous group of 'others', sited at some distance from the student-observer. The second type of approach (see second-order Category D 'Sociability and Interpersonal relations', in methodology section) was devised based on more detailed comments on students' encounters and personal interactions, thus providing evidence of attitudes of proximity, and attempts to understand the culture from the inside. In particular, through the analysis of the Category D.2 'Encounters', experiences of solidarity and empathy but also misconceptions and adverse difference were revealed.

A Distant Approach to the Foreign Culture and the Other

Conventional descriptions of culture: Inheritance and encyclopaedic knowledge

Students devoted a part of their account to tourist-guide type of information about the host country, or city and places visited. They described their visits to various famous sites and exhibited encyclopaedic knowledge about the cultural inheritance, the history, geography and sometimes the economic or political situation of the country. Thus, it seems that an initial contact with the host culture was made through cultural tourism activities and reading. In these parts of the reports, students positioned themselves as cultured visitors and observers in search of aesthetic experience. It is possible to deduct that the written form of these accounts and their public dimension incited students to have recourse to conventional presentations, inspired by the model of tourist guides. The latter favoured an aspect of the 'cultural experience' as description and admiration of sites, concealing a timeless and motionless image of the culture. The students, facing the vague and perhaps intrusive request from the local authorities to account for their experiences, would have reproduced this model which enabled them to partly fulfil their duty of writing without involving themselves in a genuine personal writing. However personal or not these presentations may be, students' insistence on describing places and sites also signals that, at some level, culture was seen as inheritance and was approached through the observation of codes and conventions about what constitutes a *high culture*.

Whatever the nature of these texts, the fact that the register of cultural tourism is present in nearly all reports tends to suggest that it represented a stage of French Erasmus students' approach to the foreign country and its inhabitants. When this approach to the host culture remained the only one, it raises questions about the challenge of encountering a different culture and the effects of Erasmus stay. For more than one-third of students in fact, it was the *sole* approach to the host culture and summarised what students identified as 'cultural dimension of the stay' or 'cultural benefit'.

Some textual and content indicators signal that students did not aim at interacting with the natives through tourism. First of all, the structure of the texts: tourism and various trips are separated from the parts devoted to encounters. Second, students themselves underlined the difference between tourism and integration in the student and local life. Finally, more evidence that trips and visits were important as entertainment but somewhat limited in providing students with opportunities to create contacts with natives is that these were generally organised among French or sometimes with other Erasmus students. In other words, during these short escapades, sociability within national groups or between foreigners prevailed.

National portraits: Determinism and generalisations

Students dwelled on the presentation of inhabitants as a single 'cultural type', perceiving and emphasising their supposedly common traits and features. In the presentation of the cultural characteristics of natives, students sought to capture these attributes which supposedly defined inhabitants' specificity, what supposedly made them similar and different from others. By trying to designate the collective dimension of individuals, as totally forged by the culture, students smoothed out all social and interpersonal differences. Furthermore, the simple assertion of a specificity, without attaching to it any value judgement and implicit hierarchy, is an extremely difficult operation, especially for these young people who arrived in a foreign country, generally without having been mentally prepared to encounter and to deal with otherness. The impartial assertion of a neutral difference, or peculiarity, is difficult to realise in a social world that constantly treats difference on a hierarchical basis. Independently of positive or negative judgements concealed in these presentations, the latter contained generalisations and expressed a 'static' view of the foreign culture, signalling a distant look at the foreign society.

Attempting to determine the 'cultural characteristics of the inhabitants' led students to draw up presentations of national portraits. They endeavoured to focus on the psychosocial dimensions of a 'specific people', supposed to be completely forged by the culture. They aimed at capturing a kind of 'human essence' which, however, was particular to a given cultural context and marked thereafter every individual raised within it. Any individual thus appeared as a *representative* of his/her culture and as such became interchangeable. What marked this approach, is the reduction of complexity of cultural contents that vary according to social backgrounds, gender differences, professional cultures, locations of residence, and so on. In the same way, the individual diversity that may lead individuals to differently convey their culture, and in various degrees, was neglected. Thus there emerges a general national portrait, a national 'temperament', a dominant 'character' culturally defined. Unsurprisingly, these generalisations resulted in stereotypical (positive or negative) views of societies.

> Ireland is a country where people live one day at time, without really worrying about the following day. There, one takes the time to listen to others, to talk, to have fun and to laugh, and it is surely what makes Irishmen so accessible and such cordial people. (Report 62)

Despite students' contentions about refraining from generalisations, sweeping statements and simplifications were produced, resulting sometimes in less positive or even negative conclusions. For instance, the following provides an interesting example of an unsuccessful attempt to avoid stereotyping. This writer started by affirming that common beliefs are invalid, but he/she ended up generalising and confirming, as the use of the adverb 'certainly' signals, national characteristics supposedly captured by his/her direct experience.

> Contrary to what is commonly believed, the Germans do not lack humour. However, there is something in which they are certainly deficient: it is the detachment *vis-à-vis* life, because their thirst for the absolute prevents them from joking about serious events. [...] The Swabians (inhabitants of Baden-Wurtemberg) are also characterised by their severity and their avarice, but ... one cannot make general statements ... (Report 16)

These statements are characterised by a common syntactic feature. The subject of the sentence is collective: 'the Germans', 'Londoners', 'Irishmen', 'British society', 'the Swabians', 'the inhabitant of Heilbronn'. Generalising usually conveys simplified perceptions that may lead to judgements, likely to persist through time. Research on students' perceptions of inhabitants' variability showed that perceptions shaped during the stay abroad did not evolve later on, or at least during the first year after students' return to their home countries (Stangor *et al.*, 1996). Despite researchers' expectations about a possible selection and recollection by students of the most positive elements of their experience, the conclusion drawn was that the only malleability of perceptions could occur during the stay abroad and thanks to intensive interactions and ties with groups of natives. The latter are valuable and it is not a simple coincidence or a peculiarity of these French student reports that accounts of generalising impressions, extrapolated to the whole population, existed alongside the accounts of fleeting contacts and instrumental communication. Indeed, in those text sections, where the validity of a statement was hardly relativised and delimited, no close relationships with 'representatives' of the host country and culture were reported.

Inhabitants' disposition towards foreigners: Xenophilia versus xenophobia

Once the first traits of national portraits were depicted, students commented on natives' behaviour and disposition with regard to foreigners in general. Developing this dimension enabled student to implicitly tackle the attitude of the inhabitants towards them, which was regarded by them as the main reason for successful or failed contacts. But how did students understand this self-disclosure of the locals, favourable to foreigners? On the one hand, it was seen as curiosity, as interest in the difference enabling natives to approach foreigners. On the other, xenophilia was considered as a positive *a priori* disposition regarding foreigners who had an advantage or a worthy position.

Here also, students claimed to be objective and impartial, yet the inhabitants were judged through the relations that they established or the interest that they expressed for the French student, as a foreigner. At the heart of these accounts, one finds a unilateral approach to the situation of interaction, which seems to result only from the attitude of the natives, whereas student's attitude or behaviour was minimised or simply not mentioned.

> Moreover, people in Great Britain are open-minded enough and thus like to encounter foreigners visiting their country... The inhabitants of Swansea created a group which is used to organising a small festival (and prepares good Welsh cakes!) and connects the 'locals' with the foreign students. I find that it is a revealing initiative of the Welsh mentality. (Report 7)

This alleged disposition towards foreigners is expressed either as openness, or as withdrawal. It is apprehended either in a political dimension, as cosmopolitanism versus nationalism – regionalism, or in its socio-emotional dimension, expressed by adjectives of temperature: warm or cold. Within the interpretative limits of these texts, the combination of socio-emotional and political or rational dimensions was used as an argumentation device aimed to convince the reader of the soundness of the student's perceptions and hence enabling the latter to put forth apparently 'grounded' judgements.

Concerning the cosmopolitanism of the inhabitants, it seems, in a somewhat naive approach, to result from opportunities to encounter foreigners visiting the country or communities of migrants.

The 'Santiaguans' are accustomed and prepared to receive people coming from all over the world. This is what makes them very open and hospitable. (Report 77)

Moreover, the Dutch people express a large broadmindedness. So the essence of Dutch culture is made up of different other cultures, such as Indonesian, or Pakistani culture (in particular in the field of cuisine). This fact gives to this country this characteristic cosmopolitan aspect. (Report 31)

In these quotes, it is interesting to underline the causal relationship that the structure of the argumentation reveals. In the first one (No. 77), we can see the presence of 'this is what makes them' and in the second (No. 31), 'this fact', which are argumentative transitions expressing deduction and certainty. The positive disposition of openness toward foreigners, xenophilia, was explained as being the natural result of encounters between different communities. One can then raise the question about students' perception of French society, which is far from being culturally homogeneous and contains indeed inter-breeding. Thus, it seems that the distance from the familiar environment sharpened students' perception of culturally mix societies. However, the advantage gained in perception was not necessarily accompanied by a more complex treatment of the issue of interaction between various communities.

Attempting to summarise this distant approach to the host culture and the other, we can highlight the following elements. First, this approach contains a high degree of determinism. Culture seems as if it has the strength to inextricably mark all its members and constantly be reflected by them, ensuring thus stability and invariance. Second and as a consequence, it seems as if all individuals who belong to the foreign culture formed a *uniform group*, and are also distinct from every other. Third, students' comments on the cultural peculiarities of the host society and people were given as *truth statements*, as evidence. In other words, students who favoured these descriptions claimed to be objective and impartial in their presentations and did not acknowledge any element of subjective or truncated perception and influence of individual judgement. Finally, the *insider's* comments, understanding or interpretations were not considered in these sections. For these reasons, what students expressed here signals a distant viewpoint on the culture. These statements also appear to be connected with occasional interactions and encounters and constantly presented through the lens of cultural difference. Generally, it seems that the majority of students, if not all, experienced this phase, at least at the beginning of their stay. However, their approach can later evolve differently. For some students, this mode of apprehension of the other remained the only one, for others closer relationships were created during the stay.

Insights Into the Culture Through Interpersonal Communication and Relationships

As we have already mentioned, the majority of students developed this distant approach, but it was exclusively adopted by one third of the writers. Another third provided more information about the relational aspect of their experience abroad that will be presented in this section. The 'culturally different others' were presented as individuals not entirely determined by their national cultural belonging, but as partners with whom students communicated, interacted and finally gained a reciprocal knowledge, even if differences were finally insuperable for some of them. These interactions evolved beyond anonymous and fleeting contacts and reveal attitudes of narrowing the gap between partners. They signal the step taken towards the other which did not stop merely at the identification of different customs, lifestyles and behaviours.

Even if the interpersonal bonds did not directly lead to intercultural learning, they nevertheless supplemented the newcomer's global relationship to the new setting, and increased his/her perception of variability and complexity. Thus, the new context was not approached like inanimate space, or 'virgin' ground, but like a 'sphere' inhabited socially and emotionally by others. Hence, the analysis of interpersonal relationships constitutes an indispensable element in the understanding of residence abroad, especially regarding the issue of the confrontation with otherness, and we shall analyse the way students experienced their fellows and also themselves as strangers and the extent to which this was defined by proximity or distance, by congruence or divergence, identification or contrast. Were relationships marked by difference or were grounds for resemblance found?

From strangeness to familiarity: Intercultural experiences and interpersonal contacts

Since bonds forged between the stranger and the natives can facilitate the overall adjustment of the former (Furnham & Bochner, 1982, 1986; Furnham, & Erdmann, 1995), stimulate change in international images (Yum, 1988) and also become a vehicle for acquiring intercultural competence (Carlson & Widaman, 1988; Stier, 2003; Volet & Ang, 1998), the field of interpersonal relations is of particular relevance to the understanding of the dynamics of the Erasmus sojourn. Indeed, affective ties, such as close relationships and friendship among student-sojourners and host nationals have been regarded as the nodal point of the success of an expatriation experience (Carlson & Widaman, 1998; Gareis, 2000; Kelman, 1975; Klineberg, 1981; Murphy-Lejeune, 2003; Stangor *et al.*, 1996). The precise nature of the contact (superficial, acquaintance, friendship, partnership, enemies, etc.) between sojourners and natives has been investigated by various researchers (e.g. Cook, 1984; Rothbart & John, 1985; Stephan, 1985; Stroebe *et al.*, 1988). The interest in (and preoccupation with) interactions between mobile students and host nationals originates in the search for evidence confirming that the objective of international understanding (Carlson & Widaman, 1998; Klineberg, 1981), inherent in student exchanges programmes, is fulfilled.

It can be claimed that the idea underlying the assumption that relationships are beneficial to intercultural communication derives from the contact hypothesis concept (Allport, 1954). According to this well-established but also much debated psycho-social concept, stereotypes are born out of social isolation and broken by personal acquaintance. Therefore, proximity would encourage personal contact and in turn would reduce cultural distance, prejudice, and so on. However, this proposition does not enjoy universal and unconditional validity, since conditions have been attached to it, from its very introduction. Alongside the need for contact to be personal and sustained (Brewer, 1996), four core requisites have been reported as crucial determinants of successful contact: status (equality versus inequality) of the different groups in contact; co-operative interdependence in the pursuit of common goals; absence of competition; legitimacy offered by institutional support or presence of social norms supporting inter-group contact (Amir, 1969; Forbes, 2004; Pettigrew, 1971). Consequently, superficial and intermittent acquaintance does not necessarily bring about understanding and tolerance and this is particularly relevant to students on temporary stay abroad.

Researchers with particular interest in student intercultural experience have also emphasised the importance of intimate rather than casual contact for attitudinal change (Gudykunst, 1979) and change of cognitive maps (Yum, 1988) and from the middle of the 1970s, empirical results pointed in this direction. Kelman (1975) stressed that the extent and the quality of contacts between host nationals and sojourners had a significant impact on the latter, in developing positive attitudes regarding the former. Stroebe *et al.* (1988) strongly supported the idea that in the absence of contacts, students' attitudes did not evolve, whereas the intensity of interactions with the local community influenced positive cultural experience. Stangor *et al.* (1996) equally stressed that communication and relationships between students and members of the host society were of crucial importance. The quantity and the quality of contacts that American students reported having created with natives during their year abroad in Germany and England, influenced the extent to which students expressed sustained positive attitudes towards natives. The researchers supported, in accordance with the Contact Hypothesis, the view that the most important aspect in the success of an exchange programme is whether or not, and the extent to which, students entered significant relationships with members of the host country. In this respect, Stangor *et al.*, 1996 pointed to the fact that not a single student had reported having established 'too many' contacts with natives, whereas more than 55% of students reported having had too few. This result is not surprising. It is consistent with other findings in the literature on mobility and temporary stay abroad. Two large-scale studies have shown that students' relationships with natives are not to be taken for granted. In a survey contacted at a British university, McKinlay *et al.* (1996) found that the closest friends of international students were their co-nationals or students with a shared linguistic background rather than the host nationals (i.e. British students). The results of Nesdale and Todd's (1993) study of 2000 students in Australia showed that three-quarters of them had only superficial contact with Australians.

To sum up, research has raised caveats and revealed difficulties students face in developing any kind of close relationship with natives (Kudo & Simkin, 2003).

Students' awareness

As for students' views regarding the relational aspect, their comments acknowledged its importance. However, the fact that the issue was explicitly tackled by approximately one-third of students can imply that a substantial number did not engage in significant social intercourse. This seems to be in line with the aforementioned studies, showing that between over half and three-quarters of surveyed students reported weak interaction with natives. However, such an outcome would contradict students' initial wish for encounters, openness to others and understanding of a different culture.

> I arrived full of desire to encounter new people, to discover the way of life of English, to immerse myself in their culture. (Report 36)

The issue of the nature of relationships developed during the stay comes to the surface in the accounts, pointing to the role these can play in structuring students' experience. Indeed, students put it directly in relation to the objective, and the hoped-for benefits of a stay abroad. However, the introspective tone of the following extract, as well as the direct address to the sponsors of the reports (the Regional Council), stress the magnitude of the challenge these bonds present for students.

To bind contact: With whom? How?

Will the stranger be able to constitute this minimum human entourage? Among the foreigners that I could meet, I did not see anyone who did not manage in one way or another. However, it would be interesting to look closer at the precise type of these bonds. For the Rhône-Alpes Region, which must ensure that the sponsored stays are the most beneficial possible, such a study would seem to me of a great interest. Are the bonds made rather with 'natives', other foreigners, or with compatriots? Are bonds of friendship, professional friendship or simple contact? Many questions whose answers would allow a concrete evaluation of the nature of immersion in the host country and the way it evolved. (Report 80)

Generally, it appears that students who engaged in the process of communication usually succeeded in creating relationships, despite possible initial difficulties and misunderstandings. They seemed to have acted towards reduction of both interpersonal and intercultural distance: the transition from the phase of strangeness towards a feeling of familiarity resulted from the interface offered by relationships and interpersonal bonds. Students encountered cultural differences which finally became less important in their eyes, because of the emergence of similarities linked to age and student status, between initially culturally different partners.

A new departure and new ties

The initial situation is common: by leaving a familiar setting, students leave also their family, friendship networks and acquaintances built up over time. Even if the departure does not necessary imply an affective rupture, it does introduce a physical distance which has a direct influence on the immediacy and availability of these relationships. The need to create a new entourage, to interact with the others, is then felt and pushes the newcomer to seek contact.

Once abroad, one goes right back to square one and strongly feels the need to get to know people. (Report 37)

Students' accounts for making acquaintances and creating a relational network present some common features. Initially, it seems that bonds were forged between foreign students, and in particular between 'Erasmus' students, or between compatriots. For a smaller proportion of students, friendships can be also formed with local students, and later on, eventually with natives outside student groups.

Being a foreigner brings closer: Affinities between foreigners

Being a foreigner seems to bring closer individuals who share this temporary condition or 'status'. Generally the first relationships were formed within groups of foreigners, composed either of various foreigners or fellow citizens. Hence, initial affinities were formed based on the contrast between foreigners and locals. These entailed feelings of solidarity which emanated from the shared situation of being a foreigner. Foreign students confronted with the conjunction of circumstances, which created challenges and difficulties, came closer and developed ties, supportive networks and friendship.

The following day, I went to the university to meet my new professors, and had the astonishing surprise to meet other 'Erasmus' like me. There were students from Vigo, Barcelona, Italy, Paris and Lyon. From this moment on, I felt by no means abandoned anymore, since we were several students in the same situation. (Report 34)

Alongside the support and solidarity in order to overcome various challenges, students evoked another reason which pushed them to approach other foreign students. The latter, deprived of their familiar networks and eager to become acquainted with culturally different people, adopted a more pronounced self-disclosure attitude than local students.

The Erasmus 'cocoon'

After an initial stage of excitement, with a mixture of new encounters but also feelings of loneliness, the community of foreigners seems to break down into different sub-groups. The situation of being a foreign student varies according to the duration of studies in the host country and that can influence students' strategies of adjustment and relational dynamics. As students explained, complicity developed more easily between students coming for a temporary stay and bonds developed between Erasmus students. Students agreed that the latter formed a united group. An important number reported having remained within the network of Erasmus students where there were possibilities of encounters, acquaintances and friendship.

Studying in an Italian academic context, I participated in the Erasmus community, like any other student from the EU. The expression 'Erasmus community' has its name justifiably. Indeed, since their arrival in the host town, students who participate in the Erasmus exchange programme have formed a compact and united group, of which many friendships are born. (Report 4)

It can be argued that the 'Erasmus community' provided students with opportunities to capture European diversity through acquaintance, relationships and affinities between young Europeans. In turn, this can also be seen as a way of apprehending Europe at the individual level and developing a sense of European belonging that may impact on the process of European integration.

Naturally, I met a lot of students participating in the Erasmus student exchange framework and studying at the TU Wien. We formed a group of people coming from very diverse national backgrounds and I think that these bonds are very important for European integration. (Report 29)

However the problem arises from the moment when the grouping of 'Erasmus' students isolates them from the reality of the host country and prevents students from engaging with the host culture and interacting with natives.

From the very beginning, the 'ERASMUS' students find themselves confined together: they have their own rhythm of life which is different from that of the Danes, they have their own parties... The result is that as June arrives, the foreign student commonly does not really know any Dane. (Report 59)

Although the importance of having relationships with European students, coming from various national backgrounds, cannot be underestimated, it also seems crucial to enter in communication with the natives. The latter, living in the natural setting of the host culture, represent the concrete and multi-dimensional challenge of confronting otherness. Thus confining oneself to merely interacting with other Erasmus students can affect the process of intercultural learning. The latter is more complex than learning about customs and lifestyles of students' respective home countries. In addition groupings of foreign students can reinforce the formation of defensive attitudes and delay, or even prevent, engagement in mutual understanding and empathy with the culturally different other, 'representing' the culture which students are immersed in and confronted with.

The following writer alerts us to the importance of better supporting ties between local and Erasmus students.

> In order to improve this action [Erasmus exchanges], it would be simply necessary to try to go further in the bonds than the Erasmus initiative supports between foreigners and autochthons. On the one hand, concerning foreign students, they mix well together, thanks to this action, I believe. But on the other, the bonds between foreigners and Germans seem to me to need to be consolidated. To create bonds is one of the necessary conditions for a successful stay. However, this is not always simple. (Report 80)

With time, networks shaped between foreigners on the basis of common projects of activities and discoveries, but also for escaping from loneliness, did not remain stable. They gave way to networks of co-nationals or mixed with natives.

From the pursuit of otherness to its encounter: A national pause...

Although students were cautious in publicly acknowledging the reinforcement of their bonds with other French students, since the report was supposed to witness beneficial outcomes of a stay of abroad, and not least linguistic learning, several signs of this national sociability were found. Sometimes students knew each other before leaving the home country, but generally they met in the new setting. In this respect, the 'weak links' of the reception have to be highlighted: language courses for co-nationals, reserved rooms in the same residence, societies mainly offering activities to foreign students and so on. All these initiatives aiming to provide support can result in favouring 'national pockets' and groups of foreigners that hardly mix with local students.

These contextual reasons should not be neglected or underestimated. However they should not hide the deeper reasons involved in a situation of confrontation with otherness and its various phases. The recourse to compatriots may prevent from one feeling left to one's own resources during inevitable moments of cultural fatigue, inherent in the immersion in a different language and culture.

I admit that almost inevitably much of my time was spent with other French people. Some were already my friends and others became.

I believe that it is natural to mix with people having the same national-ity; the language and the culture bring us closer. If this is somewhat regrettable with regard to the learning of German, it is however a good support during difficult moments. (Report 29)

The communication with co-nationals, resting on the identity of language and culture, provided a basis for emotional closeness and support. To a certain extent, fellow citizens replaced the family left behind.

I went through a bad patch, especially at the beginning, when every-thing was evolving so quickly with the feeling of being abandoned, because of the difference of customs and language, and left to my own resources in an unknown country and with the friends and my family far away. (Report 64)

A comforting break for a new impetus?

Research on the systems of social support while abroad has shown that national solidarity is not to be spurned; on the contrary it can facilitate a smoother transition and protect against exposure to situations of great acculturative stress (Adelman, 1988; Furnham & Bochner, 1986; Torbiorn, 1982). Alptekin (1983) considers the recourse to compatriots as a necess-ary stage towards integration in the foreign society. He stresses that it is psychologically preferable to receive this type of support than experien-cing loneliness which may lead to depressive reactions.

Thanks to the support of friends, I do not have to admit to any depression, as I was warned. At the end of my stay, I bring back [...] many very good French friends with whom I am very close [...] and with whom we shared moments of mutual support. (Report 36)

Hence at the beginning, solidarity between co-nationals appears desir-able, not to confine the student to homogeneous and familiar networks, but to provide confidence for encounters and interactions that are felt less reassuring and require more initiative and personal effort. However, in many cases the initial motivation of encounter with the culturally different other can crumble through reality testing. Research has informed about this discrepancy between the initial appeal of cultural difference and the possibilities of dealing *in situ* with cultural shock. Students' unrealistic expectations and lack of awareness about the process of confrontation with a different cultural reality and integration into a different setting were considered by Lillie (1994) to trigger withdra-wal attitudes. The resulting disillusion led them to self and group

enclosure and to develop a position of 'we against others', often legiti-
mated by their common national identity. A similar conclusion was
reached by Stangor *et al.* (1996). In their study, American students, enrolling in a study abroad programme, were compared with a control group,
before their departure. The results showed that they were significantly
more positively predisposed towards the future host country than the
control group. To some extent, this overly positive disposition was seen
as a sign of idealisation. The latter did not however ensure that students
would gain a rich intercultural experience, but on the contrary, and along
with the lack of contacts later on in the host country, it was interpreted as
an important reason for the disenchantment experienced by the majority
of students.

Successful Relational Experiences

By way of discussion, some interesting dimensions of the expatriation
experience can be highlighted at this stage, in order to draw attention to
key elements involved in the experience of confrontation with otherness
and its successful negotiation.

Positive perception of double strangeness

Developing an intensive pro-social activity seems to rest on a double
positive perception: of the other as a stranger, and of oneself as a foreigner.
In the following report, the student underlines the gratifying reaction of
people he/she encountered, the latter having adopted an encouraging
and accessible attitude to his/her extrovert outlook.

> I had the opportunity to have many encounters with people from all
> socio-professional milieux and age groups. The common point of all
> these encounters is that, all were very friendly and very open. On
> this occasion, I think the fact of being a foreigner does not create gaps
> between us, but on the contrary makes it possible to cross the barriers
> more easily. (Report 72)

This quote reveals an important element regarding successful relational experiences: being a stranger is not felt to be an experience of dis-
possession or loss of one's entourage but an opportunity to expand and to
diversify it. This attitude leads to new encounters which in turn are
experienced as enrichment.

In these cases, being a foreigner proves to be an asset. It arouses curiosity towards others, who are approached without (or with less) prior
socio-cultural assumptions and tacit knowledge, usually operating in

familiar contexts. This can result in reduction of distance often created by rapid and also rigid classifications of people and settings.

Suspension of pre-constructed categorisations

In one's familiar environment, precise views and fixed opinion about categories of people with whom one can interact and develop contact are commonly held. Familiar signs of belonging and other social attributes are more easily identified and interpreted compared to these, characterising individuals in a foreign society. The tacit socio-cultural knowledge along with the command of social codes and conventions often guides one's behaviour in a familiar setting, and thus, interactions and reactions regarding new encounters can evolve following patterns within a known repertory of individual behaviours and attitudes.

This is not to imply that during a stay abroad, one's perception and categorisations become bias-free. We have already examined students' perceptions and interpretations underlying a fragmented and especially a deterministic conception of culture. The latter usually leads to stereotypical judgements and prevents students from discovery. However, for those students who developed a relational approach to the culture, their perception was not pre-determined and their interpretative schemes were progressively formed following the acquisition of new socio-cultural competences.

I enjoyed going out with friends and mixing with people of my parents' age. At the begging, it felt quite inappropriate to see these fifty-year-olds enjoying the nightlife, but later I finally thought that it was good to continue being able to enjoy and to dance despite the years and the time passing. (Report 63)

Weakening of projective explanations

In students' view, the contacts and ties (or their absence) forged during their stay abroad seem to result, in the first instance, from the behaviour and the availability of others and only secondly from one's own behaviour and attitude vis-à-vis others. Similarly, students' comments aiming to explain distances and misunderstandings had a pronounced projective character: the natives did not make the first step, or were not easy to approach or not willing to invest in temporary bonds; the conditions at the host institution or residence hall did not promote intergroup contact; leisure activities did not provide exchange students with opportunities for sustained relationships, and so on. However students who aimed at creating interpersonal bonds and apparently succeeded in doing so, highlighted their own personal involvement and responsibility regarding their relationships to others.

> But when one tries to fit into a group of Swedes, the possibilities for new acquaintances become unlimited (one meets new people every evening). Once again, I think that my behaviour *vis-à-vis* the Swedes is mainly the reason of my successful integration. (Report 35)

Another common point of great importance is the expression of a positive perception of the culturally different other. The latter was presented as a partner within a relationship and not as *a representative of one's culture*. The interaction became first and foremost interindividual and interpersonal.

Negotiating the image of 'the French'

Developing relationships on the basis of interactions between peers involves going past the stage of communication through stereotypical images. However, the latter were proven to resist and to substantially influence the communication. If on the one hand the positive stereotypes facilitated the contact (Report 68), the negative and reductionist ones compromised, to a large extent, the interaction (Reports 19, 42).

> In general, if you like contacts, you will not be disappointed. The Germans are very sociable and sympathetic. They have a very refined image of France and French and everything that comes from our home country inspires them with good taste. (Report 68)

> In any case, all foreigners, and particularly the French, are regarded as potentially hypochondriac. (Report 19)

> French! After a few weeks this word resounds almost like an insult, so hard are the stereotypes to bear. (Report 42)

Endorsing a single-component image allotted by the outside, or accepting these stereotypical definitions of one's identity often resulted either in personal unease or even in identity polarisations. Many students confronted with a mono-dimensional facet of perception (i.e. above all being French) expressed signs of national identity reinforcement. They seemed to have internalised stereotyped, generalising and even negative judgements, without being able to negotiate these attributions differently and to bring the interaction onto richer grounds. This difficulty essentially resulted from having to behave as 'the ambassador' of one's country. Some students felt they did not have any choice than to defend their national identity by expressing opinions in line with actions of national governments and policies.

> Abroad, one is regarded as the representative of one's own country and thus is led to justify or explain certain political, economical or even historical aspects. (Report 74)

To hold this position, without being able to express a personal view, leads to the reception of judgements that are not normally directly addressed to the specific individual. However, the person finally becomes their recipient and ends up feeling affected.

> Fateful questions: What do you think of Chirac? When one has been a voter for a couple of years, then perhaps it is not too difficult to pull through. However the problem is not necessarily in the answer, but in the question. Continuously confronted by this kind of question, you end up feeling attacked and despised. They did not really understand the necessity of this [a particular policy], how could we explain to them that we don't agree either? (Report 75)

However, some students succeeded in negotiating an identity defined by multiple senses of belonging (national, social, cultural, professional, etc.) and in which the national culture did not become the sole quality of an individual. Similarly these students reached a level of recognition of one's values without placing them in an absolute hierarchy. A certain hierarchy appeared legitimate however, but from an individual perspective, since it can be connected with cherished situations, objects and memories.

> What differentiates my world from that of the Other in another country, is that it belongs to me, that I know it well, but this sense of familiarity should not delude us by creating an absolute hierarchy. It is proper that there is a hierarchy if it is based on an honest feeling: this house, this landscape linked to my childhood are particularly dear to me, more than this foreign landscape, because it did not witness me crying as a small child because I had grazed my knee. But it is just as dear to others who filled it with their childhood and fill it today with their memories.

At the end of this analysis, it can be noted that achieving a degree of intercultural understanding during a temporary stay abroad cannot be a secondary objective or a side-effect of an individual action primarily focusing on other goals. One does not forge relational ties, as one learns to use the transport system or to discover new areas and various tourist attractions. To develop deep relationships is not an imperative need either. Indeed, being satisfied with some contacts, relationships with compatriots, visits of the family or friends and then some trips to the home country can be enough for some months. For many students, the experience of cultural difference was treated less as a source of knowledge itself, enabling the individual to decentre from national norms and to acquire tolerance towards otherness, and more like a situation enabling, above all, the enhancement of the individual's potential. Living abroad was seen as a major opportunity to prove to themselves and others their capacities to undertake unusual activities and to achieve autonomy. However, students who developed the relational aspect of the stay did not only seek the adventurous and initiatory aspect of living abroad as a simple confrontation with the unknown and as adaptation to difference. They tried to understand the culturally different other and also themselves in an interdependence, and within a more complex and less predetermined view of otherness. To sum up, the major outcome for those who explored cultural difference by adopting a relational approach was not only the awareness of cultural difference, but also its recognition and acceptance without hierarchy and favouritism: societies continue to evolve 'successfully' while being organised differently, with other ways of thinking and living, with different values and sensitivities. In our sample, this approach was adopted by approximately one-third of students.

Methodology

The chosen texts constitute what historians would identify as a 'primary source': they were not produced as a response to specific research questions or a predetermined research design. Therefore, if the risk of bias relating to research design and researcher's assumptions was somewhat reduced, analysing these existing reports in a promising way was still an important challenge of this study (Papatsiba, 2003).

The corpus of 80 texts was analysed at four levels using various techniques:

(1) content analysis (e.g. L'Ecuyer, 1987) and grounded theory (Glaser & Strauss, 1967);
(2) lexico-analysis (e.g. Benzécri, 1981; Bolden & Moscarola, 2000) supported by data-analysis software;
(3) critical discourse analysis (e.g. Benveniste, 1966; Kerbrat-Orrecchioni, 1999; Magri, 1995; Perelman & Olbrechts-Tyteca, 1970); and

(4) in-depth qualitative analysis based on concepts drawn from social psychology and intercultural studies (e.g. Byram, 1997; Kaës *et al.*, 1998; Schutz, 1987; Simmel, 1979; Todorov, 1986; Wagner & Magistrale, 1997).

The research methodology focused on systematic analysis of three types of elements and indicators: the categories that students used to recount their experience, indications of linguistic subjectivity versus neutrality (or involvement versus distance), and communication with the recipient as named in the texts (e.g. administration, peers and oneself) where rhetorical strategies containing truth claims or relativisations were made. Triangulation with results of quantitative analysis confirmed the validity of the initial qualitative design and subsequent results and interpretation.

A general underlying principle in all the analyses was that the texts under scrutiny were revealing more about the reactions, stances, attitudes, representations and stereotypes of their writers than they did about the settings they encountered. In other words, the analyses did not aim to establish any truth statement about the host country, culture, people, academic system and so on, or whether students accurately observed and 'objectively' reported the various situations. On the contrary, we were interested in the relationship that students developed with the contexts encountered and not in the peculiar 'reality' of these contexts. The various methodological stages are reported below.

At the first stage of research, the aim was to make the dimensions of the Erasmus experience intelligible. Many have suspected it to be a period of 'academic tourism' entailing a kind of 'entertaining parenthesis' that in the final analysis provides opportunities for personal development. Beyond these presuppositions, (a) how did students comprehend their residence abroad with the Erasmus programme and (b) how did they account for their immersion in a foreign academic and social context? Which categories did they construct, and in which registers of meaning can these categories be incorporated? To answer these questions, the corpus was initially treated as a 'single' text in order to detect regularities and to identify the constant fields of Erasmus experience. This approach sought to capture the invariant characteristics of the Erasmus stay independently of the infinitely unique ways of dealing with the experience, which were examined at a later stage of the analysis.

Two techniques were used here: content analysis and lexico-analysis, both assisted by data-analysis software (Alcest and Sphinx Lexica for French language). The first one was used in an exploratory way at a stage that comprised 53 texts out of 80; the second was applied to the whole corpus. With regard to the content analysis, it was conducted on the whole content of the corpus following an inductive approach. It was based on two conceptually close approaches: (a) an 'open model' of category-building (L'Ecuyer, 1987), according to which the researcher neither applies pre-existing categories to the data, nor favours certain topics; (b) a 'grounded approach' (Glaser & Strauss, 1967) that developed a 43 unit taxonomy based on topics emanating from the data itself, without being guided by any hypothesis that would have required the selection of discrete units of the discourse. Coding all the data provided a grid of analysis grouping the 43 sub-categories in 12 categories and in five second-order categories.

Concretely, the grouping of items (at the level of the student texts) resulted in sub-categories (e.g. monuments, collective celebrations and customs, house market and prices, student behaviour in the lecture rooms, teachers' authority, sports, encounters, etc.) which in their turn were gathered in further categories (e.g. cultural inheritance, housing, studies, leisure, relationships), then, more synthetically, in second-order categories (e.g. landmarks and their functionality, sphere of individual action, images and traces of the subject) which indicated the main dimensions of the Erasmus experience. The categories remained close to rationales of natural categorisation, that people make spontaneously without any conceptual aim. These are indicated by terms 'borrowed' from the vocabulary of the corpus, or if they were re-phrased, it was without introducing a real change in the semantic level of the vocabulary used by students (e.g. cultural characteristics of people, housing, studies, practical environment of everyday life, etc.).

On the other hand, the second-order categories constituted an attempt at conceptualisation. As such, they *introduced* a break with ordinary categorisations spontaneously composed by individuals in their effort to classify and understand the world. For instance, the second-order category 'sphere of individual action' is not a spontaneous definition of an explicit phenomenon immediately available to the individual perception, but a proposition that reflects a certain analytical effort based on acquaintance with that phenomenon and its systematic exploration.

Although the whole design was intended to make the dimensions of the Erasmus experience intelligible, it was not confined to the descriptive level only. Indeed, it allowed a progression towards a conceptual construction that had as its objective the elaboration of the type of relationship that students developed with their new settings, the host society and the 'others'. Thus, the panorama of situations exposed in the texts was organised on a continuum that aimed at presenting the students' approaches to these situations: from an external or 'outsider' positioning expressing cultural distance (second-order categories A – background context and B – first landmarks and their functionality), towards a quasi-insider positioning expressing acquaintance and attitudes of proximity and understanding (second-order categories D – sociability and interpersonal relations and E – images and traces of the subject). The findings presented earlier exemplified this tension in students' positioning, by focusing on representations and attitudes relating to the *culturally different other*, which is at the heart of the issues that a period of study abroad raises.

In addition to the qualitative analysis based on quotes from student texts, a quantitative lexical analysis (although not presented here), assisted by software, was used for the content analysis. The purpose was to measure the presence of each category in the texts and, therefore, the (quantitative) importance of each second-order category. It involved a first stage requiring the construction of lexical sets, named 'dictionaries'. This consisted in choosing words from the items, at the level of the student texts. These words were connected with a certain theme and were likely to represent this theme in the various measurements. Eleven dictionaries, of 19 to 88 words specific to the categories (A.1, A.2, etc., with the exception of the categories E1 and E2 that were represented by one common dictionary), were built, with a total of more than 600 words.

To avoid the superposition of the categories, all the selected words were systematically examined to verify their semantic context. Several words were rejected because of their multi-semantic use. For instance, the word 'cuisine' in French means 'kitchen' and 'culinary tradition'. According to our grid of analysis, the utterances relative to the 'kitchen' were classified in a different category to the category including utterances related to 'culinary tradition'. These lexical sets then represented the categories (A1, A2, etc.) of the categorisation, and after grouping them the five second-order categories (A, B, C, etc.) during the various measurements. The latter were measurements of intensity (i.e. total number of words of a dictionary found in the corpus divided by the total number of words in the corpus), and can be interpreted as follows: during the utterance, the writers consciously or not decide to use one word or another while drawing from the various repertories available to them that correspond to the dimensions they want to express. Measuring the intensity gives us an indication of the relative weight of these dimensions in the discourse analysed. In addition, a factor analysis enabled us to gain insight into the way these categories and second-order categories were related to each other.

If working on all eighty texts proved to be essential to make the dimensions of the Erasmus experience intelligible, there remained nevertheless insufficient evidence to understand the disparities in the attitudes and positioning of students. More precisely, since it was the varying degree of personal versus impersonal writing which led to contrasting impressions concerning the intensity and depth of the experience, a third level of analysis, comprising elements of discourse analysis, appeared useful. In concrete terms, we proceeded to identify systematically the markers of subjectivity in the texts. Among various indicators, the extent to which the personal pronoun 'I' was present proved to be an important indicator. It highlighted divergences which were not organised and could not be elucidated through traditional sociological characteristics – such as sex, discipline, type of establishment or country of destination. The operation consisted in measuring the intensity of the pronoun 'I' in each report and resulted in the formation of three groups of texts: (a) 27 reports were classified in the group of 'impersonal' style texts (I < 0.50%); (b) 26 in the 'median' group (I = 0.50% and <1.39%) and (c) 27 reports in the 'personal' style group (I > 1.39%). The two subcorpora of 27 texts, consisting of the most impersonal and the most personal texts, were chosen for further analysis as they represented the two poles of the discourse. This operation aimed at targeting the texts which, because they used a particular type of discourse, (i.e. one indicating involvement as against distance), highlighted the differences between major discourse strategies which in their turn were seen as tangible traces of latent processes. In the case of linguistic involvement, expressed here by a strong use of the marker 'I', the writer adopted the position named 'ego'. In the opposite case, the position of maximal distance was named 'universal subject'. The term 'universal subject' was borrowed from Culioli, according to whom the position of 'universal subject' is what allows the inter-exchange of the subject holding a certain statement, or in other words when 'any subject is presumed to be able to take the place of the subject of the utterance' (Culioli et al., 1970: 47). As to the term 'ego', it has been used by Benveniste (1966) to conceptualise the base of subjectivity in the language.

In the final stage, we arrived at the hypothesis, drawn from the data, that personalisation or neutralisation of subjectivity in the writing reflected the extent to which the various dimensions of the stay (general descriptions revealing distance versus reflective statements revealing change and value of diversity), as represented by the grid of analysis, were evident for each student. Two measurements were used: the intensity of the 'dictionaries' (the 11 lexical sets built for each category) with the intensity of the marker 'I', and then with the two sub-corpora of 27 texts expressing the subjectivity or neutrality of the discourse. To put it differently, we examined the extent to which the different dimensions of the Erasmus stay were reflected differently in the two contrasting corpora by their style sub-corpora. Finally, the prevalence of one mode of expression, that indicating either distance or implication in the discourse, was shown to relate to topics students have favoured. These topics in turn revealed the various ways in which the students had dealt with the strangeness (closeness versus distance to the host culture).

Chapter 7
Ethnographic Pedagogy and Evaluation in Short-Term Study Abroad

JANE JACKSON

Introduction

It has long been assumed that immersion in the target culture coupled with formal classroom learning will result in significant linguistic and cultural gains for foreign language students. As a result, the number of study and residence abroad programmes has mushroomed in recent years. While in some contexts, students routinely participate in 'year abroad' sojourns (Alred & Byram, 2002 and this volume; Coleman, 1997, 2002), a growing number of universities in Asia are now sponsoring students on short-term study abroad programmes (e.g. four to 10 weeks) to provide them with the opportunity to experience the target culture and speech community firsthand (Crew & Bodycott, 2001; Jackson, 2004a, b).

While much research has explored the language acquisition of long-term sojourners (e.g. 10 weeks to a year or more) (e.g. Coleman, 1995, 1997, 2002; Freed, 1995; Jordan & Barro, 1995; Parker & Rouxeville, 1995), few studies (e.g. Brecht & Robinson, 1995; Freed, 1995, 1998; Laubscher, 1994; Pellegrino, 1998) have investigated the experiences of students within the context of their sojourn. Furthermore, despite the growing popularity of programmes that involve shorter stays, they have largely been ignored by researchers. What impact can a short-term sojourn have on foreign language students? Realistically, what can they learn in only four to 10 weeks in the target culture? What approach should be used to gauge the effects of the various elements of the sojourn on the students' learning?

Within the context of study abroad programmes, traditional forms of educational research and programme evaluation consist of experimental designs (pre- and post-tests) and quantitative-dependent measures of linguistic attainment or psychological states (Ginsberg & Miller, 2000; Ward *et al.*, 2001). This product-oriented approach tends to overlook the processes of language and cultural learning and how these relate to broader cultural contexts. Quantitative measures simply cannot capture many of the complexities of language and cultural learning.

Mixed-method, process-oriented approaches to research and programme evaluation, which employ both qualitative and quantitative modes of data collection, offer an alternative means of investigating the impact of the sojourn experience. This chapter reports on a small-scale ethnographic study, which investigated the experiences and perspectives of students in a short-term study and residence abroad programme. Before focusing on the findings, the underpinnings of an ethnographic approach to research and programme evaluation are discussed to provide a framework for the present study. I then outline the various elements of the programme, the goals of my investigation, the context and the findings. The analysis of the data centres on the language and cultural learning of the sojourners and their personal growth. In the second part of the chapter I discuss in more detail the research methodology and the advantages and disadvantages of using an ethnographic approach to demystify the learning processes of student sojourners.

The Roots of Ethnography

Ethnography is a behavioural science, which is deeply rooted in sociology and cultural/social anthropology (Agar, 1996; Atkinson, 1994; Geertz, 1973; Hammersley & Atkinson, 1995; Heath, 1982; Hymes, 1974; Kottak, 2002; Watson-Gegeo, 1988).

Ethnography is the study of people in naturally occurring settings or 'fields' by means of methods which capture their social meanings and ordinary activities, involving the researcher participating directly in the setting, if not also the activities, in order to collect data in a systematic manner but without meaning being imposed on them externally. (Brewer, 2000: 9)

The primary goal of this mode of research is to develop a deeper understanding of the meanings that behavioural practices and beliefs hold for a particular group of people at a particular time. Thus, ethnographers collect their primary data by becoming immersed in the culture they are investigating (e.g. through observing and participating in a group's activities). Besides participant observation, they rely on interviewing and informal conversations to gather data from participants in the cultural scene under study (Ferraro, 2001; Rossman & Rallis, 2003;

Spradley, 1979, 1980). Ethnographers may also make use of quantitative measures (e.g. surveys) and such techniques as mapping (e.g. illustrations of the cultural scene) and photography (e.g. digital images or videotapes) to gather additional information about the area under investigation (Ferraro, 2001). Through naturalistic, systematic observation and inter-action with informants, the researchers build up a 'thick, rich description' of cultures or aspects of a culture from an 'emic' or insider's perspective. In the process, ethnography 'generates or builds theories of cultures – or explanations of how people think, believe, and behave – that are situated in local time and space' (Lecompte & Schensul, 1999: 8).

An Ethnographic, Interpretive Approach to Programme Evaluation

Evaluation researchers have begun to employ ethnographic fieldwork in educational contexts where the primary aim is to better understand the learning processes of participants in a particular programme (Fetterman, 2001; Knapp, 1999; Royse *et al.*, 2001). This process-oriented form of evalu-ation is preoccupied with 'answering a "how?" or "what is going on?" question. It concerns the systematic observation and study of what actually occurs in the programme, intervention, or whatever is being evaluated' (Robson, 2002: 208). In particular, ethnographic data collection methods have been found to enhance the researcher's understanding of 'the process of knowledge, cognitive, attitudinal, and behavior change' (Schensul *et al.*, 1999: 36). This mode of evaluation is in line with a constructivist or interpretivist stance.

> Proponents of these persuasions share the goal of understanding the complex world of lived experience from the point of view of those who live it. This goal is variously spoken of as an abiding concern for the life world, for the emic point of view, for understanding meaning, for grasping the actor's definition of a situation, for *Verstehen*. (Schwandt, 1994: 118)

In practice, this marriage of ethnographic research and process evalu-ation is characterised by an 'emphasis on developing adequate rapport with programme participants, the descriptive emphasis of data-collection and interpretation, and the focus of fieldworkers on understanding what the programme meant to the participants' (Knapp, 1999: 172). As such, it involves intensive, naturalistic inquiry on site, a reliance on the ethnogra-pher as the principal data collector and analyst, and the subsequent prep-aration of evaluative reports that emphasise a detailed narrative account over statistics.

This approach is especially useful in small programmes or single institutions in which the ethnographer has the capacity to gather ethnographic data while developing a close relationship with the participants (Brown, 1995; Fetterman, 2001; Royse *et al.*, 2001). In the process of carrying out investigations of this nature, educators can identify subtle aspects of programmes that would have been missed by traditional forms of evaluation that focus exclusively on outcomes.

Ethnography is critical to describing and monitoring the process of change. It is also an approach that is useful in studying natural phenomena. Thus, it can provide the methodology for describing the evolution of the intervention process and its effects on individual and environmental factors. Using ethnography involves an iterative or recursive process of continuous data collection, analysis, and reflection that results in changes in intervention. (Schensul *et al.*, 1999: 44–45)

Within the context of study and residence abroad, ethnography can identify the individual, contextual and cultural factors that influence language and cultural learning by capturing the sojourners' views about their goals and experiences (e.g. their intercultural contact, attitudes towards members of the target culture). An ethnographic approach can monitor changes in the sojourners (e.g. their intercultural adjustment, the development of their intercultural communicative competence) and ascertain how the various elements of the study and residence abroad have or have not influenced their thinking and/or behaviour. The resulting detailed description and analysis can play a critical role in improving the design and delivery of study abroad programmes, including such aspects as their objectives, materials, curriculum, teaching, organisation and learning (Brown, 1995; Greene, 2003; Lynch, 1996; Posavac & Carey, 2003; Royse *et al.*, 2001).

A Short-Term Study and Residence Abroad Programme

The English Department at the Chinese University of Hong Kong recently established the Special English Stream (SES) to challenge and enhance the education of English majors. The first offering consisted of seminars in literature and applied linguistics (ethnographic research), summer fieldwork in England, debriefing sessions, and a research report-writing course related to the experience abroad. The coursework and sojourn were credit bearing and fully integrated into the BA (Bachelor of Arts) curriculum.

Participants

Fifteen English majors in the second year of a three-year BA programme were selected for the first offering of the SES based on their grade point average in their first year of university studies (3.3 or higher) and performance in an oral interview. All of the participants were Chinese Hong Kongers (12 females and three males) with an average age of 20.8 years on entry into the programme. They spoke Cantonese as a first language; their proficiency level in English was advanced with an average of B on the 'Use of English' A-level exam taken at the end of their secondary schooling. The students used the language in formal classroom situations but tended to rely on their mother tongue in social situations.

Only five of the students had ever visited an English-speaking country before entering the SES; three had studied English for one month in Canada, the US, or Britain. For most, personal contact with people from other cultures was very limited. The majority of the students who had ventured outside Hong Kong had made brief visits to other Asian countries. For most, the sojourn coincided with their first trip away from their parents.

Programme aims and objectives

The SES was designed to enhance the overall English language proficiency of the students in both academic and social situations. Since the programme centred on a period of residence in an English-speaking setting, a key aim was the development of their intercultural communicative competence (Byram, 1997; Byram & Zarate, 1997; Murphy-Lejeune, 2003; Roberts *et al.*, 2001). The following framework, adapted from Byram (1997), helped set specific competencies for the SES sojourners:

Attitude shift – Abandon ethnocentric attitudes towards other cultures, and heighten their awareness and understanding of the differences and relationships between their own (Hong Kong Chinese) and a foreign culture (English).

Skills of observation and discovery – Observe and analyse how people of another language and culture (English) perceive and experience their world; become aware of the beliefs, values and meanings they share.

Cultural knowledge – Become aware of aspects of English culture (e.g. beliefs, values and meanings) which help natives of that culture to communicate without making these assumptions explicit.

Skills of interaction – Draw upon the previous three areas in real time to interact successfully with English people in England.

Critical cultural awareness – Make use of specific criteria to critically evaluate perspectives, practices and products in both their culture (Hong Kong Chinese) and English culture.

The sojourn aimed to enhance the students' intellectual growth (e.g. to synthesize and solve problems) and interpersonal and social skills so they would become more independent, self-confident, and, willing to take the initiative to interact in English in a wide range of settings.

Programme Components

Literary and ethnographic studies

Before the sojourn, in the literary studies seminar, the students discussed readings that were related to the plays and cultural visits that they would experience in England. In the applied English linguistics seminar, with my assistance, the students honed the skills necessary to carry out ethnographic research in England (e.g. participant observation, note-taking, diary-keeping, reflexive interviewing, the recording of field notes, the audio-recording and analysis of discourse). Through weekly tasks outside of class, they were encouraged 'to make the familiar strange' and become more aware of aspects of their culture that they took for granted. After they had developed basic ethnographic research skills and begun to move from description to analysis and interpretation, they undertook a small scale ethnography project to explore their own cultural world using the tools of ethnographic research (Barro *et al.*, 1998; Jackson, 2004a, c, d; Jordan & Roberts, 2000; Jurasek, 1995; Jurasek *et al.*, 1996; Kelleher, 1996; Roberts, 1995, 1997; Roberts *et al.*, 2001; Rossman & Rallis, 1998). For example, one student explored the discourse and culture of a group of mah-jong players, while another focused on the life of a Filipino maid who worked for a Chinese family. The ethnographic project was intended to foster a systematic approach to cultural and intercultural learning in preparation for the sojourn in an English-speaking country (Jackson, 2004a, d).

Sojourn in England

For five weeks, each student lived with an English family (homestay) to more fully experience the local culture. At an English language centre in Oxford, on weekdays, they took literary, language, and current affairs courses as an intact group due to the specialised nature of their studies. Arrangements were made to give them the opportunity to interact with other international students during informal activities and outings. In addition, they attended local cultural events (e.g. Shakespearean plays) and visited literary sites. Under my guidance, they also conducted ethnographic research on a cultural scene of their choice (Jackson, 2004a, d).

As the sojourn was fully funded by a language enhancement grant to the department, there was an 'English only' policy for the sojourn. When the students entered the programme, the department head explained that it was intended to encourage them to become fully immersed in the English-speaking environment and maximise the opportunity provided by the grant.

Throughout the sojourn, the students were required to keep a detailed fieldwork diary to record their observations and reactions to each day's activities, including their homestay experience, excursions, research and lessons (Berwick & Whalley, 2000; Jackson, 2004c; Kohononen *et al.*, 2001). They were encouraged to describe confusing or disturbing intercultural experiences (Arthur, 2001) as well as encounters that were particularly rewarding. They were also asked to describe and reflect on their use of English and steps they were taking to enhance their communication across cultures.

Debriefing

Back in Hong Kong they emailed their diary entries to me and, at the beginning of the next semester, six weeks later, we met together for several three-hour long debriefing sessions. In small groups they discussed the 'English only' policy and identified the most stressful aspects of their sojourn as well as their coping strategies. Their findings were shared with the full group and excerpts from their diaries (e.g. critical incidents) were discussed and analysed. After the debriefing, the students began to write up their ethnographic report, using the data that they had collected in England. This stimulated further reflection on their sojourn.

Findings

Pre-sojourn aspirations

By way of a survey and interview, the students were prompted to set personal goals for the sojourn. The following were typical:

> I hope I can learn more about British people. It seems to me that many are very proud. It may be my prejudice. I would like to see if there are many nice people. I want to introduce China and Hong Kong to people from other countries, at least to the host family. I want to behave well before foreigners so they will not think that Chinese people are bad. (Pre-sojourn survey, female, 8)

I want to be more independent and get immersed in the British culture (e.g. have conversations in English with native speakers, lead a "British" way of life), widen my horizon, and interact with foreigners. (Pre-sojourn interview, male, 10)

Most expressed the desire to enhance their oral English and intercultural communication skills and learn more about the local culture. Since most would be away from their parents for the first time, they expected to become more independent. It was interesting to note that several revealed that they harboured negative views about the host culture.

Pre-sojourn anxieties

In the pre-departure survey, the students assessed their readiness for the sojourn by way of a series of statements using a five-point Likert scale. They provided further insight into their concerns by way of open-ended questions on the survey as well as a follow-up interview. While very excited about the prospect of travelling abroad, not surprisingly, most were apprehensive about living with strangers from another culture and had doubts about their ability to cope in an unfamiliar environment. Even though their proficiency level in English was advanced, many were apprehensive about the need to communicate entirely in this language with native speakers who, they feared, might not be welcoming to them. The following comments were typical:

I worry I might not be able to adapt to the life there as I am very reliant on my family. (Pre-sojourn interview, female, 5)

I'm worried about the medium of communication because I'm used to talking in Cantonese but in the UK I'm supposed to deliver all my thoughts in English. And I wonder how friendly the foreigners will be. (Pre-sojourn survey, male, 10)

I'm afraid I'll get lost. I'm also afraid that the English people are not nice. I do not know if they will discriminate against Chinese people. It will be terrible if I cannot communicate with them effectively. (Pre-sojourn survey, female, 8)

Reactions to The 'English only' policy

Before leaving for England, the students were invited to express their views about the policy in both a survey and interview. While, the majority felt that it would be a good idea, many conceded that it would be difficult to adhere to because they lacked sufficient vocabulary to convey all of their ideas.

> I think the policy is appropriate. Of course, it will be more difficult for me to use only English as compared to Chinese but I think I can handle it. Although I've learned English for more than 20 years, it's not my mother tongue, and it would be hard for me to explain or express some complicated concepts in English. (Pre-sojourn interview, male, 7)

Others felt that it would be unnatural to communicate with each other in English, noting that they would have ample opportunity to converse with local people in the language.

> I think it'll be hard to carry out because in private we would all use Cantonese. Using Cantonese is the best way to make my friends understand me so why should I use English? (Pre-sojourn interview, female, 13)

The Sojourn Experience

During the five-week sojourn, I observed and documented the students' attempts to adapt to their new surroundings and communicate across cultures. Later, back in Hong Kong, their diary entries, the post-sojourn interview transcripts and surveys, and my field notes were analysed with the help of NVivo. This facilitated my identification of the most common issues that the students found difficult to cope with during their stay in England and provided insight into their language and cultural learning processes outside the classroom. The following section highlights some of the most frequently cited stressors.

Initial culture shock

Since most of the students had not been away from home before, not surprisingly, most were homesick and doubted their ability to cope early in the sojourn (Adler, 1975; Oberg, 1960; Pedersen, 1995; Ward *et al.*, 2001). They were apprehensive about living with 'strangers' and used avoidance strategies to reduce contact with their hosts and their pets (e.g. going home late, hiding out in bookstores).

> Homesickness was quite serious at the very beginning of the trip. I had not left my home for so long a time. I can still remember, at midnight, I was weeping in my bedroom in my host family. After a week, however, my homesickness suddenly went away. I don't know why actually. Perhaps, I started to get acquainted with Oxford … Also, I could

hang around in the bookstores; I could read whatever I wanted without disturbance. (Post-sojourn survey, female, 6)

I am very reluctant to go home after school. My friends all have the same feelings and so we hang around together until dinnertime. This may be because I am living in an unfamiliar environment and feel like an outsider intruding in a stranger's family. I feel quite uncomfortable at home and I go upstairs immediately after I have dinner every night because I do not know how to start conversations with them. I am not a shy person but I just don't know how to deal with this situation. When I open the door and go home the dog always barks at me. I begin to miss my family in Hong Kong a little. (Sojourn diary, female, 14)

Attitude towards unfamiliar diet

During the sojourn, many students found it difficult to adjust to the English diet and, on excursions, they frequently talked about how much they missed Hong Kong style Chinese food. Initially, many were not willing to try foods that were new to them, vividly describing the 'torture' and 'agony' they faced each night at the dinner table.

The food was the most difficult thing to adjust to. I myself dislike a lot of dairy products such as eggs, milk, yoghurt, cheese, butter, etc. Therefore, it was a kind of torture that I needed to face every day and night in the U.K. I missed Hong Kong foods a lot. (Post-sojourn survey, female, 11)

I did not expect to have difficulty with Western food. It was quite an agony not having rice as dinner for almost a week! (Post-sojourn survey, female, 6)

Differing medical beliefs and practices

Some of the students discovered that their ideas about health and medicine were quite different from those of their English hosts. In the following excerpt, for example, this young sojourner revealed how difficult and frustrating it was to explain her dietary concerns and health beliefs to her host family.

At the very beginning, the only impression I got from the British food is 'hot air'; it is a Chinese concept, which shows the interior unbalanced body situation, symptoms like sore throat, bleeding gum ... I explained to my host mum that I felt awful when I eat too much fish'n chips but she doesn't understand what I mean. It's the first time I felt that I couldn't quite communicate with her because of our cultural difference. Although she said she understood what I was saying, what she answered is to let it be; she said it would pass very soon. However, I want to tell her that in Chinese concept, it could not be combated; it is about one's inborn body; different people are genetically destined the amount they could accept before irritating the natural balance. I felt bad to explain all this to her as she doesn't even understand. (Sojourn diary, female, 15)

Unfamiliar routines

Along with a different diet, the students discovered that the daily routines of their host families deviated from what they were used to. For example, in Oxford, their host families had their main meal around 5 or 6 pm; in Hong Kong the students usually ate much later and it was not unusual for them to stay up till one or two in the morning or even later. This difference was another source of friction early on.

The most difficult thing was to adapt to my host family's schedule, like having dinner really early in the evening and sleeping early at night. Because my host parents went to bed very early, I couldn't make any noise after 10 pm, the time when I am most energetic and productive. (Post-sojourn survey, female, 13)

Pace of life

Early in the sojourn, another frequent complaint was the much slower pace of life. Some revealed that they felt as if everything around them was happening in slow motion and 'boring' was by far the most frequent adjective used to describe Oxford. At this stage, their discourse was full of comparisons between England and Hong Kong with the latter depicted in a much more favourable light.

The slow pace of life was the most difficult thing to adjust to because I'm used to the faster pace of life in Hong Kong. I was impatient in the McDonalds in Oxford because I could not get my food fast even in a fast food restaurant! (Post-sojourn survey, female, 12)

Hong Kong people can be regarded as very efficient people but people in Oxford were totally different. I had to leave home early cause things just went late but in Hong Kong you have a better control of time. And, I think this is a major thing to adjust to. (Post-sojourn interview, female, 11)

Displays of affection

Another aspect of English culture that proved disquieting for the students was the frequent and open display of emotions by their host families. While recognising that their hosts were trying to make them feel at ease, the students were still uncomfortable with the expressions of affection, both verbal and physical.

People in the UK are very friendly; sometimes, to me they were too friendly and I was not very comfortable with it. I was quite embarrassed when I was hugged or kissed by my host mum. I think this is just the difference in the ways Chinese and Western people behave. (Sojourn diary, female, 15)

Perceptions of discrimination

The most troubling aspect of the sojourn related to their response to intercultural encounters that did not go well. As in the following incident, when they experienced difficulty communicating across cultures, they attributed it to prejudice against their ethnic group.

We went to a travel agency to purchase boarding tickets for the train. The agent showed her prejudice towards Chinese since she showed us a grave face and was very impatient about our questions and advice. We thought that it was very unfair for her to treat us this way. For the first time in my life I have been discriminated against and I think that is not a pleasant experience at all. (Sojourn diary, female, 13)

While it is conceivable that the ticket agent was prejudiced against the students because of their ethnicity (or youth), there are other possibilities. For example, she may simply have been annoyed because they had unwittingly broken some of the 'rules' for communicative events of this nature in this context. Early in the sojourn, I observed that the students rarely said 'please' or 'thank you' in intercultural transactions. In the exchange with the ticket agent they may have seemed rude and overly aggressive. At this stage of the sojourn, they did not consider that differing communication styles and politeness norms might have played a role in their disappointing encounters with people from other cultures.

Intercultural contact in social situations

In the first half of the sojourn, on informal outings, most of the students found it difficult to initiate and sustain conversations with non-Chinese international students. When encounters were not satisfactory, again, the first reaction of many was to regard their interlocutors as prejudiced against the Chinese, as in the following encounter that took place in a pub midway through the third week of the sojourn.

> At the pub the attitude of the international students towards us was rather apathetic. I felt quite uncomfortable because they seemed to be quite cold to me. I just stopped trying to blend into their group and became close with three Chinese students who came from Beijing. Chinese could always accept Chinese! Actually, the problem is the prejudice the international students had towards Chinese. I do not know what images we had given to them but I just sometimes find them particularly cold to Chinese and this hurt me because it was a kind of discrimination. (Sojourn diary, female, 11)

Confounding English humour

The frequent use of sarcasm and other forms of humour (e.g. self-deprecation) was another area that proved challenging for the students who felt bored and irritated when they did not understand why their hosts were laughing. Due to insufficient background knowledge and lack of familiarity with this type of discourse, the Hong Kong students found it difficult to join in, and this created further distance between them and their hosts.

> My host father's jokes were not always interesting enough to laugh at. Some of them I found boring and I can hardly laugh... The English are used to these kinds of jokes and they will respond by a laugh spontaneously. However, Chinese people seldom make jokes within the family and we all talk seriously in front of the family. (Sojourn diary, female, 1)

> I just don't understand why the English laugh and what is so funny. Perhaps this is due to the differences in cultures. We can learn the English language but we can't easily understand their culture. What they find ridiculous may appear to be nothing wrong to us. Sometimes when my host mum and dad laugh, I don't quite understand what the matter is in the television programme. I think 'learning to laugh' is not an easy task. (Sojourn diary, female, 5)

Sitting on the sidelines

In their diaries, interviews and surveys, the students disclosed how uncomfortable they had felt when invited to take part in activities with strangers. At the first karaoke event at the language centre, for example, they huddled together on the sidelines and watched as the teachers and other international students got up to sing, dance and enjoy themselves. Many of the Hong Kong students were acutely aware of their reticence; in their diaries they revealed that they were concerned about 'losing face' in front of people they did not know well. This fear and the belief, by some, that their lack of participation was part of the 'character of the Chinese' kept them from fully participating, especially in the early stages of the sojourn.

> After the performance of the teachers, it was the turn of the students. First, an Italian went up to sing a song. Then the social coordinator asked us SES students to sing. All of us were reluctant to sing so we didn't give him any response... It is embarrassing for us to be listened to by strangers because we are worried they may criticize how we sing. (Sojourn diary, female, 12)

> We were inactive in the karaoke time tonight. Although we watched the performances happily, we did not sing in spite of the repeated invitation and many of us left early. Some of the staff was nice and they cared about us. They asked for the reason of our inactivity and I think that they would like to try their best to improve the situation. One of our teachers asked us which foreign singers we are more familiar to. But I think even if he has got some music videos that we know, we may still refuse to sing. That is the character of Chinese, I think. (Sojourn diary, female, 9)

Use of Cantonese

While they lived with local families and had the opportunity to interact with international students during frequent informal activities and excursions, due to the specialised nature of their programme, they also spent much of their time with their Chinese classmates. While they used English with me, they frequently lapsed into Cantonese on outings (Jackson, 2004b).

Based on their diary entries and post-sojourn interview and survey, I discovered that most regretted that they had not made the most of the opportunity to become fully immersed in English. A variety of explanations was given for the failure of the language policy: comfort in using their mother tongue, peer pressure, lack of familiarity with informal/social English, habit, the fear of being labelled a 'show-off' or 'teacher's pet' by their peers, and the difficulty in conveying emotions in English.

The following diary entry provided insight into the complexity of this phenomenon:

> My SES classmates and I did not speak English in Oxford as frequently as we expected. At the beginning of the trip, we would speak English among ourselves actively. But gradually, we spoke English less. To me, one of the problems of speaking English among friends is the English I learnt at school is formal English. Speaking formally with my friends appears quite awkward to me. Moreover, I am not familiar with English slang and it is not easy for me to speak informal English. There are also some particular Cantonese to vent my emotion and I can hardly find any English expression to replace it. Sometimes, a slow conversation can be boring among friends. When speaking with friends, I am used to speak fast without many pauses. English cannot let me express myself as fast as Cantonese. So these are why I spoke English less frequently in Oxford. (Sojourn diary, female, 12)

> A great barrier is that students have associated speaking English with pleasing teachers so those who speak it are teased by others... Another barrier is that we are not used to speaking English when we are chatting with friends. In Hong Kong, we speak English only when we deal with something serious like presentations, interviews and examinations. (Sojourn diary, female, 8)

Evidence of Gains During the Sojourn

As well as awkward moments and unsettling intercultural encounters, the students also experienced personal achievements, which they discussed with me with during the sojourn as well as in reflective moments back in Hong Kong. Since I had observed them and become close to them in the months prior to the trip, I was more attuned to changes in their linguistic, personal, and communicative behaviour and attitudes. The analysis of their diaries, pre- and post-sojourn interviews/surveys (both open and closed questions), and our debriefing sessions provided tangible evidence that they had met some of the personal and institutional goals set prior to the sojourn.

Linguistic improvement

Student opinions varied widely about whether or not their command of English had improved during their residence in England. The diaries of those who were the most satisfied with the sojourn contained significantly more comments about positive exchanges with both locals and international students. It appears that these students had made more of an effort to build a relationship with their host family; during informal activities, they were also observed to initiate conversations with people outside their group. In the process, they had become much more confident when conversing with native speakers and more at ease using English in informal situations.

> Though I could not manage to speak English the whole time, I still tried very hard to do so and I can feel that my willingness to speak the language has increased and my ability to listen to native speakers of English has improved quite a lot. I feel more confident to speak English in front of them now because I know we can understand each other. In Oxford, I loved watching the news on BBC and ITV because I liked to see how much my listening skills had improved. (Sojourn diary, female, 13)

> Concerning my oral English, I improved a lot, especially the articulation of words and intonation. Moreover, I have a deeper understanding of some daily expressions, for example, 'of course,' 'sure,' 'sorry', 'it's okay', etc. I was worried about the listening before I went to Oxford. Through more than a month's training, I can now listen and understand more than 95% of the speech. I now have more courage and confidence to speak English. (Sojourn diary, female, 15)

Making connections across cultures through social discourse

The observation techniques developed in the pre-sojourn ethnography course fostered the habit of careful observation and reflection on cultural scenes. For example, after several weeks in Oxford, many of the students became aware that it is common for locals to make a remark about the weather to initiate conversations. With this knowledge, some began to try this communication strategy when interacting with locals.

> There was a heavy pouring of rain .... And the headmaster (of the language centre) asked me humorously, 'Did you bring the rain to Oxford? Weather again!' Sometimes I find it boring to talk about the weather all the time but I understand it is an art to talk about the weather in Britain. It is necessary to master this skill if you want to have good communication with the British. (Sojourn diary, female, 3)

Most of the students also came to realise that humour (e.g. self-deprecation) is a common form of discourse in England. For many, initial frustration was gradually replaced by a genuine desire to better understand this style of communication in order to develop a better relationship with their hosts.

The situation is getting better: I can sort of sense my host parents are making a joke, and, no matter if I understand it or not, I will say 'you funny guys', 'you are incredible', 'you are wild, man', 'you crazy couples'. It seems that all these expressions satisfy and please them. They may even think that I am really amused by what they have said. Indeed, I still cannot catch their English humour even the last day. This embarrassing experience makes me realize that a difference in cultural background can create lots of misunderstanding . . . . Besides trying to adapt to foreign culture, we must learn several rhetoric expressions to respond, or more exactly, to pretend we understand what the speakers try to say. This technique is a social skill which makes us much more sociable and adaptable to different environment. (Sojourn diary, female, 6)

Shift in attitude and appreciation of differences

Early in the sojourn, many of the students were easily irritated and constantly compared everything around them to Hong Kong, noting how much better life was back home. As they became more comfortable in their new surroundings, however, most began to see the world around them in a more positive light.

On the first few days after my arrival, I found the ticketing system on the bus not very efficient. People queued up at the door and the passengers on the bus kept waiting for the bus to go on. As a Hong Kong citizen, I was not very satisfied with that. I kept protesting that this system doubled the time that I spent on transportation. However, this shortcoming gradually becomes a treasure in my eyes. I find that the Oxford people interact with the bus driver in a very friendly and polite way when dealing with the tickets. In this way, people become refreshed at the beginning of the day. I love this kind of interaction and so I join the English people to say 'Good Morning' to the bus driver when I get on and 'Cheers' when I get off. (Sojourn diary, female, 11)

And, back in Hong Kong, after they had had some time to reflect on the sojourn, many commented that it was important for sojourners to have a positive attitude to overcome obstacles that are a normal part of adjusting to an unfamiliar culture.

Growth in independence, self-confidence and a sense of adventure

In the beginning, most students had been quite anxious and reluctant to spend time with their host parents; some had even been afraid to go 'home' at the end of the day. By the end of the five weeks, however, most were talking more positively about their homestay experience and were no longer hiding out in bookstores after class.

I have gained more than I expected. Before I arrived, I used to be very frightened because I did not want to live with strangers; I was afraid that I would be too shy to talk. However, this trip has made me even more outgoing and independent. I no longer have to depend on others to start conversations for me, nor do I stay quiet during a gathering. (Sojourn diary, female, 13)

I also observed that many of the students seemed more confident in intercultural encounters and a few initiated conversations with 'outsiders' (e.g. international students) in social situations instead of waiting to be approached. And, in the last evening together, several of the SES students volunteered to sing at the farewell party, much to the delight of their classmates and teachers.

Last night, we attended the farewell barbecue and karaoke. This time we were more active . . . . One of our classmates represented us in the competition. I felt really happy about that. This can show to the others that we are not timid and can actually sing very well. (Sojourn diary, female, 9)

I have gained a lot in this trip and I feel very happy and glad that I have this chance to go to Oxford. As well as the enhancement of my oral English, literary and linguistics ability, I noticed my personal growth. I have become more independent and confident. (Sojourn diary, female, 1)

Gradually most of the students became more adventurous and less concerned about what people would think. While in some cases they took very small steps forward, nonetheless they were positive developments. Like the following female student, most took pride in becoming more courageous, independent and self-confident.

My personality and independence were further developed from this trip to Oxford. I had to take care of myself in this unfamiliar place. It boosted up my confidence to ask strangers the direction of the roads in English. Even in Hong Kong, using Cantonese, I dared not to initiate conversations with strangers. I must admit that I was rather shy. But after going to Britain, I am more courageous to ask questions and satisfy my curiosity. (Post-sojourn survey, female, 6)

More curiosity and openness

The analysis of the diaries and post-sojourn surveys (which were compared with their responses in the pre-departure surveys) provided evidence that many of the students had become more curious about the world around them and more accepting of differences. In her own words, the experiences of the following sojourner helped to 'transform' her, opening her eyes to new ways of being in the world.

My host family has transformed me into a person who likes to try out new things since I have contributed a lot of 'firsts' in Oxford. In the past I hated animals a lot; I stayed away from dogs and cats most of the time because I was afraid. After living with three young boys, two cats and one dog, I have become comfortable with animals; I even want to have a cat at home now! As for the food, to me yoghurt was the only thing that I would not eat as the texture was very strange. However, under my host mother's strong urging, I tried it for the first time and it was great! This trip taught me not to be afraid of trying new stuff and only by trying would you able to gain more. First impressions are never the real judgment of things. (Post-sojourn interview, female, 13)

Evaluative, Ethnographic Case Study

Rationale

As the SES was fully funded by a language enhancement grant, it was necessary to prepare an evaluative report about the sojourn. Since I taught the pre-sojourn applied linguistics and report-writing seminars and accompanied the students on the sojourn, I employed an ethnographic approach to programme evaluation, which was in line with the experiential nature of the SES and my philosophy of education. Ultimately, I hoped to understand the sojourn from the students' perspectives and be in a better position to recommend improvements. Rather than limit myself to pre- and post-tests of their linguistic proficiency, which would have been inadequate, I broadened the scope of my investigation. With the support of a research grant, I focused on their language and cultural learning processes to deepen my understanding of the factors affecting their attitudes towards English and the host culture and their emerging intercultural communicative competence.

Data collection

Using an ethnographic approach to programme research and evaluation, my longitudinal case study followed the SES students from the selection process to the report-writing course that followed their sojourn, eighteen months later. This allowed me to measure changes in their attitudes and behaviour as they progressed through the programme (Saldana, 2003). Efforts were continually made to gain an emic (insider's) perspective of the sojourn experience, an essential element in research of this nature (Agar, 1996; Atkinson, 1994; Spradley & McCurdy, 1988; Watson-Gegeo, 1988).

The investigation and evaluation of the various stages of the SES made use of both quantitative (pre- and post-sojourn surveys, evaluation forms) and qualitative data (participant observation, reflective diary entries, open-ended responses in surveys, critical incident reports, individual and group semi-structured interviews (in both Cantonese and English), informal ethnographic discussions, photographs/videotapes (e.g. a visual record of the sojourn), field notes, open-ended questions on surveys, research portfolios/reports) to document the students' experiences and their reactions to them. Triangulation of the data figured prominently in the collection and analysis of the data, which was facilitated by the use of QSR NVivo, a qualitative software programme (Gibbs, 2002; Richards, 2002).

Data analysis

To gain an insider's perspective and better understand their language and cultural learning processes, I adopted an ethnographic, culturally-oriented model of narrative analysis (Cortazzi, 2001; Reissman, 2002a, b). I hoped to discover how the students made sense of experiences during the sojourn (e.g. how they grappled with situations that differed from their expectations). In my investigation of their 'versions of reality' (Ochs & Caps, 1996), I examined how their intercultural stories were constructed, mindful of the elements of narrative context (e.g. the purpose of their diary entries or ethnographic conversations, the cultural context and time frame in which they occurred). Since all of the data was dated, it was possible to track their learning throughout the programme.

In my analysis, I examined the expressions the students used to convey their ideas and emotions and noted repetitions in their narratives, the ordering and sequencing of their accounts, and the issues and themes that caught their attention (Bailey & Ochsner, 1983). I then compared their personal accounts with their pre-departure concerns and expectations and the goals of the SES. To facilitate my analysis, I used QSR NVivo, a qualitative software programme, (Gibbs, 2002; Richards, 2002) to code and triangulate data.

Benefits of an ethnographic approach

Due to the holistic, complex nature of learning on study abroad programmes, traditional reductionistic approaches to programme evaluation are inadequate. While the students in my study could simply have been given pre- and post-surveys and language proficiency tests, this would not have enhanced my understanding of their language and cultural learning processes. 'Study abroad challenges educators and researchers to discover new ways to explain and measure the process of change that is the essence of education' (Kauffmann *et al.*, 1992: 144–45).

The observation of the students from their entry into the SES until their exit 18 months later allowed me to become aware of changes in their perceptions, attitudes and behaviour. My analysis of their diaries, surveys, interviews, conversations and debriefing sessions provided evidence of their personal growth and emerging intercultural communicative competence; most had become more self-confident during the sojourn and more at ease when using English during informal encounters. They had also become more aware of the uniqueness of their own culture and the possible impact of differing values and beliefs when communicating across cultures.

The findings shed light on the 'culture bumps' or critical incidents that the students experienced as they grappled with this unfamiliar cultural setting. In particular, their personal accounts revealed their lack of familiarity with social discourse conventions in English (e.g. ways to initiate and sustain informal conversations with strangers). The data also highlighted variations in the coping mechanisms, degree of adjustment, personal growth and self-confidence of the student sojourners. These discoveries helped to define competence empirically in terms of future students' ability to cope with problematic intercultural situations in this context.

My investigation also highlighted the difficulties that the students encountered when trying to adhere to the 'English only' policy during the sojourn. This knowledge helped me to better understand the complex and sensitive nature of this issue and highlighted the need to provide ample opportunities for future SES students to openly discuss the policy before and during the sojourn.

By carrying out an intensive, ethnographic investigation of the students' experiences, a much more accurate and richer picture of the learning situation emerged. This enabled me to provide tangible evidence of progress that was comprehensible to the programme donors. It also facilitated the identification of aspects of the programme that had worked well along with those that needed improvement. In particular, it underscored the need for well-designed pre-departure workshops, on-going support during the sojourn, and thorough, systematic debriefing sessions. It provided justification for the offering of a credit-bearing course in intercultural communication that would address the most typical problems that Hong Kong students may face in England. While the ethnography course had helped the students to become more observant, they needed more knowledge about factors that could impact on communication between people from different cultures and more specific information about English culture (e.g. typical politeness markers in social situations).

By adopting an ethnographic approach to programme evaluation, educators can enhance their understanding of how sojourners develop linguistic and cultural competence. This information can lead to improvements in programmes in terms of objectives, materials, syllabi, pre-sojourn preparation, sojourn support, debriefing and modes of assessment. Ethnographic evaluation can be particularly useful when the primary audience of the study is the programme itself – that is, when ethnographic fieldwork can be put to formative as well as summative ends (Knapp, 1999: 170).

Another significant advantage of this process form of evaluation is that the students are continually encouraged to reflect on their language and cultural learning, including both positive and negative elements. This can heighten their awareness of their strengths and weaknesses as intercultural communicators and motivate them to reflect on ways they might improve future encounters across cultures.

Limitations of an ethnographic approach

Ethnographic approaches to programme evaluation are not without their limitations and constraints. They are very labour intensive and costly; lengthy immersion in the field setting coupled with close contact with the participants also means that ethnographers face a rapport-building task far greater than that in other forms of evaluation. 'The success of the qualitative evaluator depends upon a degree of sensitivity, a tough hide that can withstand rejection and even hostility, and a sense of humour to carry the evaluator through the awkward initial phase of getting acquainted' (Royse *et al.*, 2001: 90). Much depends on the willingness of the participants to openly disclose their views throughout the study so that enough data can be gathered to offer sound analytic or interpretive insights.

Along with maintaining rapport and adequate confidentiality, the multiplicity of roles required (e.g. participant observer, interviewer, evaluator, confident) can also be daunting for ethnographers (Denscombe, 2003; Knapp, 1999: 171). There is also a greater potential of ethical problems associated with intrusions upon privacy and the gaining of informed consent from the sojourners. Moreover, while qualitative methods (e.g. participant observation, interviewing, making inferences) may appear simple, this is deceptive. In reality, they are quite complex; researchers must continually integrate the data they gather and make inferences. Without adequate skills and a coherent theoretical framework, educators may end up with a string of isolated narratives.

Conclusion

While this chapter focused on a short-term English language study and residence abroad programme for Hong Kong Chinese students, this holistic, process approach to evaluation could certainly be adapted in immersion programmes in other settings and with other target populations/languages. Ethnography has a vital role to play in demystifying the language and cultural learning experiences of student sojourners. If used appropriately, it can have a significant impact on the quality of programmes of this nature by providing essential direction for their refinement and revision.

Acknowledgements

My investigations of the sojourn experience have been generously supported by Direct Grants from the Chinese University of Hong Kong: *Crossing Cultures: English Majors at Home and Abroad* (CU2081008) and *Linguistic and Cultural Immersion: Perceived Stressors and Coping Strategies* (CU2010244). I would like to thank the Special English Stream (SES) students who openly shared their thoughts and feelings with me.

Chapter 8

Student Perspectives in Short-Term Study Programmes Abroad: A Grounded Theory Study

GERTRUD TARP

Introduction

Internationalisation has become important in a society with increasing globalisation. In this study internationalisation is to be understood as international initiatives taken by educational institutions to increase the students' intercultural understanding and competence. Internationalisation initiatives will often appear in terms of intercultural teaching/learning programmes and contact with foreign countries through visits and correspondence. The study focuses on 17–21-year-old Danish business school students on short-stay programmes abroad. The stay takes place in groups of about 20 students and is organised according to European Union and local school requirements depending on the way it is funded. At the same time it is integrated in the school's internationalisation programme. The number of students involved in these European Union programmes[1] and similar initiatives is very large, and yet the ways in which students experience and perceive these programmes is not well understood. One of the purposes of this project is thus to provide an approach to evaluation of their outcomes, as well as to suggest ways in which similar short-stay programmes might be researched.

The findings focus on student outcome seen from a student perspective, and recommendations are made on the basis of the findings. The method applied is grounded theory, which is empirically agency focused. It offers specific tools to collect and analyse data and to generate a theory grounded in the data. Since grounded theory is a theory building method, existing theory will not be defined or discussed in connection with the research question and the analysis but in connection with the method applied and as a comparative element when the theory has been generated. The chapter presents the case and the approach taken and then, in the second part, discusses the method in more detail.

Case Study: Rationale

The study focuses on Danish upper-secondary students' short-term stays in England/Wales, France, Ireland, Scotland and Spain, respectively. The concern of the school system is that students do not achieve sufficient intercultural understanding and competence in the classroom. The initiatives recommended for students to achieve intercultural understanding and competence include short-term student stays abroad. The purpose of the study is to find out how students experience these initiatives. The linguistic aspect and the preparation and follow-up procedures are only included in the research when appearing from the data. The study covers the following short stay programmes, which in this study are referred to as student exchanges:

- Socrates Lingua^2 exchanges, with or without private accommodation, duration two weeks.
- Local school, student exchanges without EU funding, and with private accommodation, duration one to two weeks.
- School visits, a Danish school class pays a visit to a foreign school, without EU funding and without private accommodation, duration one week.

A student exchange is to be understood as a short journey made for a particular purpose to a foreign country. An exchange includes a cross-cultural meeting with a specific purpose and is planned in advance by schools in two or more countries, i.e. a meeting between Danish students and foreign students with a specific purpose in mind. All the exchanges mentioned in this study are between Denmark and one foreign country. Business schools also organise study tours, in which case a group/class of Danish students pay a visit to a foreign country. Study tours are not included in the study because they do not include the element of a cross-cultural meeting between students planned in advance.

The data originate from four Socrates Lingua exchanges between Denmark and England/Wales, France and Scotland, respectively. In addition, data come from three local school exchanges between Denmark and France, Ireland and Spain, respectively.[3] The reason for including local school exchanges is that they are more widespread in the business school system than Socrates Lingua exchanges. In addition it is possible to compare the findings in order to examine which factors influence the outcome. For each exchange there is a specific programme according to either the local school requirements or the EU requirements. In the case of Socrates Lingua exchanges, the programme includes a joint educational project (JEP). Some of the priority objectives in Socrates Lingua activities focus on:

- encouraging the acquisition of new knowledge;
- bringing the school and the world of work closer;
- fighting against social exclusion and marginalization;
- promoting proficiency in several community languages;
- increasing investment in human resources. (European Commission, *Socrates Guidelines for Applicants 1997*, 1996: Preface.)

Some of the priority objectives in local school programmes focus on:

- communicating in a foreign language or communicating with people whose language you do not know;
- understanding foreign and own culture;
- reducing prejudices concerning foreign cultures;
- developing students' independence;
- increasing young people's mobility in Europe.
  (Translated from: local school programmes.)

The following is an example of a two-week Socrates Lingua exchange with private accommodation between Denmark and Scotland. The topic of the joint educational project is marketing, and according to the Lingua application, the description of the exchange is:

Development of a number of skills within marketing, technology and languages through a transnational exchange of students from a Danish business school and a Scottish college. Marketing and IT skills are main pillars in the curricula of both groups of students. These subject fields will be the main basis in order to develop the students' linguistic skills and at the same time increase their understanding of languages and cultures within the European Union.

The purpose of the project is to apply marketing theories and marketing strategies on the market of the foreign country, to increase the technological and linguistic skills of the Danish students and to give the Scottish students a thorough introduction to the Danish language. In addition the purpose is to develop the use of electronic communication. Keywords in the project are:

- a pre-exchange of marketing information on video and in text;
- the exchange will focus on the development of linguistic and marketing skills through company visits;
- each visit will result in a video section about the company visit and the company's marketing strategies. The video is produced by the students.

The produced material (video and project material) will be integrated in the daily education at the domestic school in the subjects English, Marketing and Economics. (Translated from: lingua project summary.)

Not all the Socrates Lingua exchanges and the private school exchanges had private accommodation. This was apparently due to various factors such as students not living with their parents, parents not having space enough to host a foreign student or students living far away from the school. The groups of students going abroad were either a class of students or students from different classes who had chosen to participate in a mixed-class group. The teachers in charge of the exchanges state that many students would probably not have participated in a two-week exchange if they had not received financial aid from the European Union. It is difficult for exchanges to compete with ordinary study tours. An exchange has to be cheaper than an ordinary study tour or at the same price level. If not, students choose an ordinary study tour often because study tours are regarded as a holiday and consequently not so stressful as an exchange. In some cases the exchange group consists of interested students, who have chosen to participate in a mixed-class group because not enough students from the same class were interested in participating in a two-week exchange with private accommodation. In other cases the students are enrolled in an international class at a Danish business school with the purpose of increasing their intercultural understanding and competence through student exchanges. These students have chosen exchanges when enrolling in the business school.

Findings: Student Agendas

The findings show that when students participate in an exchange, they have specific expectations concerning the outcome. The students do not seem to be passive recipients, but they make active decisions both about the programme they are told to follow and about what is not on the programme. They all make judgements about the right thing to do to fulfil their expectations, and the student expectations or student agendas do not always correspond to those of the school system. Class solidarity seems to be an essential purpose for some students:

> My primary purpose is to improve the feeling of solidarity in class, to experience the Scottish everyday life and to meet new people. My secondary purpose is to experience Scotland and to have fun with the Danish and the Scottish students. (Translated: Marie, Lingua exchange, hotel accommodation, Scotland.)

Student expectations or student agendas focus on four major elements:

- To learn a foreign language, i.e. communication in the host country language or in English as a lingua franca.
- To experience otherness, i.e. all kinds of experiences related to the foreign culture at all levels from sightseeing to experiencing everyday life.
- To experience class solidarity, i.e. socialisation with the Danish group of students.
- To develop oneself, i.e. the students' wish to develop, apart from linguistic skills, their own awareness, knowledge and skills, which are included in language learning.

Besides student expectations, there are external factors which influence the student outcome. Depending on their expectations, the students deal with the external factors in different ways. The external factors comprise causal and intervening conditions and context, which will be further defined below.

The causal conditions are embodied in the terms of an exchange programme set up by the school according to specific requirements from the local schools and the European Union; they include destination, length of stay, accommodation, language and planned activities.

Intervening conditions are the general conditions bearing upon what the students do during the exchange. From the students' perspective these conditions work to either facilitate or constrain what they do:

> I was annoyed that the Scottish students were not interested in cooperating. What I especially liked about the exchange was to get away from my mother and to have to take care of myself. The greatest advantage was that I got to know my classmates and had the possibility to look at them in a different way. I did not have to do anything to adapt to the Scottish culture. (Translated. Marie, Lingua exchange, hotel accommodation, Scotland.)

The students react in different ways:

In advance I would like to know that the French did not prepare the exchange well enough. Some Danish students complained that the French student were too young (14), but I got the best out of it and enjoyed having a younger brother. I would give the following advice to future exchange students: Imagine the worst, buy a phrase book, you will need it, write a diary, take one day at a time, it can only become better if you imagine the worst. After the exchange you will be happy about getting through. (Translated: Louise, Lingua exchange, private accommodation, France.)

I would like the Scottish students to be better prepared for the exchange. I would advise future exchange students to talk to the Scottish students because they do not do anything special to talk to the Danish students. (Translated: Jens, Lingua exchange, hotel accommodation, Scotland.)

The facilitating and constraining conditions relate to:

- 'planning', which covers the preparation stage and the exchange programme;
- 'the others', which is related to the foreign culture;
- 'the Danes', which is related to the Danish students' behaviour while being abroad;
- 'accommodation', which is related to hotel and private accommodation;
- 'self', which is related to what the student regards as being facilitating/constraining about herself/himself in the interaction with the foreigners.

The conditions relating to the students' age, gender, former travel experiences and family relatives abroad can be facilitating or constraining depending on each individual student. The research does not show any clear pattern as to the influence of these factors. With respect to grounded theory, Strauss and Corbin (1990) emphasise that only factors grounded in the data can be seen as determining factors for agent behaviour. This means it cannot be taken for granted that factors such as age and gender are determining for student behaviour.

Context is where the students get the experiences to fulfil their expectations. The contexts mentioned by the students are:

- sights, i.e. all kinds of sightseeing;
- entertainment, i.e. visits to pubs, discos, bars and shopping;

- host family, i.e. all kinds of experiences related to the host family;
- education, i.e. experiences related to the joint educational project, school and company visits.

For some students the host family became an essential factor:

What meant something to me during the exchange was the host family and the farewell ceremony with the family where I did not know what to say. I was surprised by the Scottish attitude to time, always having time enough. I would advise future exchange students to be kind, if so the Scots will do everything for you. (Translated: Per, Lingua exchange, private accommodation, Scotland.)

Some students realised that they had to adapt to the foreign culture and to be open:

I realised that I needed to adapt to be accepted; a crazy tourist from Denmark will not be accepted. When I went to discos I had to wear the right clothes to be accepted by the Scottish students. I would advise future exchange students to be open in order to be able to cope with the situation. (Translated: Katrine, Lingua exchange, hotel accommodation, Scotland.)

The students use different strategies to fulfil their expectations such as:

- to adapt;
- to compare;
- to cooperate;
- to learn;
- to go sightseeing;
- to socialise.

The students' expectations and the fulfilment of their expectations are like a mosaic. The students have different expectations, and by means of different strategies applied in specific contexts they fulfil their expectations in different ways. The findings show that all the students benefit from the exchange, but the student gain does not always correspond to the students' expectations and/or to the school system's requirements. Some students are disappointed although their expectations are fulfilled, and others fulfil their expectations in spite of constraining intervening conditions:

I especially enjoyed the trip to Edinburgh where the Danish students could be together, and I especially benefited from marketing, language and culture. I learnt that I have problems adapting to a family. I think the exchange was good but also very disappointing. The Danish students stayed too far away from each other. Besides I would like the Scottish students to show more interest, for instance by going to class when the Danes were there. (Translated: Michael, Lingua exchange, private accommodation, Scotland.)

A student going to France emphasises that she learnt to manage on her own:

I learnt about myself that I am more able to manage in a different environment than I expected, and that I can do more than I expected. The result of the exchange is that I am not so nervous about going to a foreign country. (Translated. Ane, Lingua exchange, private accommodation, France.)

Some students increased their awareness:

I became aware of my own communication problems and my own values. I have a better feeling of what to do in my future career. I would advise future exchange students to become familiar with their own culture before leaving. (Translated: Lars, Lingua exchange, private accommodation, Scotland.)

When comparing student expectations with EU and local school requirements, it appears that the administrative requirements especially focus on:

- learning a foreign language;
- experiencing otherness in terms of a foreign culture.

The student expectations also focus on:

- experiencing class solidarity;
- developing oneself.

The students' outcome depends on the individual student's expectations and the causal and intervening conditions. If the students participate in a Socrates Lingua exchange with private accommodation, they experience a higher degree of otherness than if they participate in one-week local school exchanges without private accommodation. However, the students play an important role in dealing with the causal and intervening conditions. Consequently, if the school forces the students to participate in a two-week Socrates Lingua exchange with private accommodation, the students' outcome will not necessarily correspond to the school requirements. If the students' expectations are focused on class solidarity, they will deal with the causal and intervening conditions in such a way that they fulfil their expectation of class solidarity. On the other hand, if students participate in a one-week local school exchange without private accommodation, they only get limited access to the foreign culture and tend to focus on class solidarity.

The context of experience is crucial to the outcome of the exchange. For some students, interaction with foreign students especially takes place at bars and discos because in that context, they feel free to interact with each other. According to the students' advice, certain tools can improve their access to the foreign culture. The tools include joint activities such as a joint project, sports and games and activities involving the students in interaction with the foreign culture. What especially turned out to be successful was the application of participant observation techniques and questionnaires that trained the students as 'ethnographers'. These techniques can be applied to exchanges with and without private accommodation and thus also involve students who are not interested in private accommodation.

Although the students' access to the foreign culture can be improved, it is still important to pay attention to different student expectations. From their point of view, mixing students with different expectations is not satisfactory. If students who focus on self development, language learning and access to the foreign culture are mixed with students who focus on class solidarity and an entertainment/sightseeing access to the foreign culture, the latter group might to some extent prevent the former group from realising their expectations. This is especially the case in connection with two-week Socrates Lingua exchanges with private accommodation. The difference between student expectations is less noticeable in case of one-week local school exchanges without private accommodation since the demands on the students' self is much lower, and since class solidarity and a certain degree of otherness are on most students' agenda of expectations.

The findings show that if student exchanges are to be successful in accordance with the institutional requirements, there are two principal parameters, which have to be optimised at the same time:

- causal conditions;
- student expectation/agenda.

There are the following two possibilities:

- If the student has optimal causal conditions, little or nothing might happen if the student has a non-optimal agenda.
- If the student has an optimal agenda, something might happen if the causal conditions are non-optimal.

Optimal causal conditions, i.e. private accommodation and successful school cooperation do not necessarily result in a successful student outcome in accordance with the institutional requirements. If the causal conditions are optimal and the student agenda non-optimal, i.e. a student agenda focusing on class solidarity, the student outcome may be non-successful. If the causal conditions are non-optimal, e.g. in terms of hotel accommodation and non-successful school cooperation, the students lack access and interaction possibilities which are crucial to their agenda. However, in that case an optimal student agenda, i.e. a student agenda focusing on language learning and experiencing otherness, may lead to a successful student outcome despite the limited access and interaction possibilities.

In short, the essence of the study is that the students have certain expectations and purposes when participating in an exchange; they have an agenda. Causal and intervening conditions play an important role for the students' outcome. However, the students' agenda plays an even greater role. The students' agenda is what influences intervening conditions, student access to and interaction with the foreign culture, and student outcome.

A comparison between the findings and existing institutional studies carried out in Denmark shows that most of the institutional reports focus on administrative aspects of student exchanges. However, some reports mention the division of student expectations indicating that some students lack interest in international activities. The aspect of class solidarity is sparsely represented in the reports although class solidarity seems fairly important as an outcome of student exchanges.

Existing theoretical studies by Herbert Christ (1993), James A. Coleman (1995–1998, 2002), Carol Morgan (1993) and Elizabeth Murphy-Lejeune (2002, 2003) show that the outcome of student sojourns abroad varies depending on both internal and external factors. Christ draws attention to the aspects of understanding and misunderstanding and the complexity of learning outside the classroom. Coleman mentions that the linguistic outcome of residence abroad has a high level of variation depending on each individual student. Coleman's study shows that residence abroad may result in organisational problems, and that it is connected both with positive and negative outcomes. Morgan emphasises that students are not tabula rasa when going abroad, but they have formed specific schemata in advance, which are often confirmed instead of changed. Murphy-Lejeune's study raises questions as to the differences between short, medium and long-term sojourns. The study outlines the students' somewhat privileged circumstances and attribute of youth compared with other migrant groups (Tarp, 2004).

The findings of this study show that the causal conditions can be influenced by the schools involved while the student expectations and the intervening conditions can be influenced by both the students themselves and the schools through different techniques. Important aspects when dealing with student exchanges are therefore: .

- student agenda;
- student access to foreign culture;
- student interaction with foreign culture.

If exchanges are going to be successful in accordance with the EU and local school requirements, a greater degree of student involvement is necessary. In their research Jeffrey and Craft (2003, 2004) talk about the inclusion of the learner in decisions about what knowledge is to be investigated, about how to investigate it and how to evaluate the learning process. Learner inclusion makes students more creative and responsible. Transferred to student exchanges this means focus on:

- what to investigate about the foreign culture;
- how to investigate it;
- how to evaluate the exchange.

Jeffrey and Craft state that a learner inclusive approach

> highlights and prioritizes the 'agency' of the learner in the teaching and learning process and might be contrasted with a 'child considerate' approach (Jeffrey, 2001) that views the child as an organism that needs nurturing rather than being democratically included. (Jeffrey & Craft, 2004: 84)

Student inclusion is the condition of deeper student involvement and of encouraging collaboration with the foreign culture. With the purpose of including the students in the exchange process, of accepting them as autonomous subjects and of making them responsible, four methods of awareness tools and instrumental tools were developed (Tarp, 2004). The methods focus on:

(1) The application of different kinds of questionnaires with the purpose of:

- improving teacher access to students to learn about student exchange agendas;
- increasing students' awareness of the exchange process;
- increasing the involvement of students in the exchange planning.

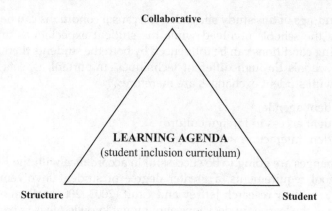

Figure 8.1 Student inclusion curriculum

(2)   The application of ethnographic methods with the purpose of:

- improving student access to the foreign culture;
- improving student interaction with the foreign culture;
- increasing students' intercultural awareness.

Applying the methods should result in negotiation and collaboration between the school system's learning agenda and the students' learning agenda with the purpose of making a student inclusion curriculum as illustrated in Figure 8.1. In that way the student agendas are influenced and modelled by the school system through an agency-focused perspective. The development of the four methods is an attempt to bridge the gap between the school system/teachers and the students and between theory and the empirical world, as will be discussed in the following section.

Research Method: Agency/Structure Perspectives

One of the choices to make when choosing a research method is the choice between a theoretically based and an empirically based method. In the case of a theoretically based method, it is a question of choosing one or several theories as the basis of a hypothesis, which has to be operationalised in order to create a connection between the hypothesis and the empirical world. In the case of an empirically based method, it is a question of generating a theory on the basis of empirical data. The grounded theory approach is an attempt to develop theories grounded in the data by means of constantly comparative techniques, and not until the theory has been generated, will it be related to existing theory (Tarp, 2004).

To understand the basic idea behind grounded theory, it is important to be aware of its history and the development of the agency/structure perspective. Grounded theory was originally developed in order to legitimate qualitative research in relation to quantitative research. In addition, grounded theory is based upon respect for the agent and the agency perspective contrary to viewing agents as 'judgmental dopes' (Ritzer, 1996: 236) controlled by the structure above.

Within the framework of sociology, the emphasis on structure and large-scale issues is anchored in Durkheim's, Marx's and Weber's theories in Europe and was further developed by Parsons at Harvard University, USA. More recent contributions have been made by for example Habermas and Luhmann. The focus on structure is based on the belief that there are metaphysical laws also in the social world; that there is a metaphysical structure controlling physical objects both in nature and society.

The opposite attitude is especially seen in the USA within the Chicago school and symbolic interactionism. The Chicago school is regarded as urban ethnography and as the main force behind sociological fieldwork. It started after the Great Depression at the University of Chicago as an attempt to explore the city. The German sociologist Georg Simmel helped shape the development of American sociology and was one of the dominant figures behind symbolic interactionism. Simmel focused on small-scale issues, individual action and different forms of interaction, and he saw the understanding of interaction among people as one of the major tasks of sociology.

Symbolic interactionism was further developed by the American sociologist, Herbert Blumer, who is seen as the dominant founder of symbolic interactionism. Blumer was in favour of a 'softer' method such as sympathetic introspection and participant observation, contrary to other sociologists who thought that agents should be studied more scientifically, for instance by using questionnaires and statistical data. Blumer focuses on respecting the nature of the empirical world and on finding a methodology to reflect the empirical world (Blumer, 1998: 60). This is different from Durkheim's understanding of social facts as being external to and coercive of individuals. Durkheim sees actors as constrained or determined by social structures and institutions and able to exercise little or no independent judgement.

An attempt to bridge the gap between agency and structure was made by Peter Berger and Thomas Luckmann (1966). They deal with the question of how groups and individuals know things and perceive things in the social world. Their work focuses on everyday knowledge such as how to conduct oneself in social situations and the problems of identity that arise during adolescence.

Anthony Giddens also tries to bridge the gap between agency and structure and to link the American and the European agency/structure discourse in a theory on social conduct. Giddens is inspired by ethnomethodology (Giddens & Pierson, 1998) in his structuration theory (Giddens, 1997). He talks about the agency/structure duality, i.e. the duality of structure, whereby social actions both create and are constrained by social structures. Through their actions, human agents may either transform or reproduce such structures. According to Giddens the difference between dualism and duality is that duality is a mutual influence or recursiveness in social life whereas dualism is the contrast for example between individual/society and subject/object (Giddens, 1979: 4–5). Thus some theories within sociology focus on external and coercive social factors and view agents as not being able to judge. Other theories see agents as being able to judge although they do not believe that agents are endlessly reflexive, self-conscious, calculative and rational.

Agency-focused sociology provided a basis for grounded theory, which is particularly rooted in American symbolic interactionism and was developed in the 1960s during a field observational study at an American hospital. Grounded theory was developed by the sociologist Glaser, a student of Lazersfeld at Colombia University, and by the sociologist Strauss, a student of Blumer, at the University of Chicago (Glaser, 1978, 1992, 2002; Glaser & Strauss, 1999). The theory was later influenced by the cooperation between Corbin and Strauss (Corbin & Strauss, 1990; Strauss, 1996; Strauss & Corbin, 1990, 1994). It is a methodology focusing on qualitative research, exploration, induction, analytical and interpretative procedures and theory building. Grounded theory was developed to help qualitative research in the USA in the 1960s. As Strauss and Corbin put it:

> To legitimate careful qualitative research, as by the 1960s this had sunk to a low status among an increasing number of sociologists because it was not believed capable of adequate verification. (Strauss & Corbin, 1994: 275)

The development of grounded theory is an attempt to close the gap between theoretically based and empirically based research. Glaser and Strauss argued against dominant functionalist and structuralist theories developed by Parsons, Merton and Blau. Within the framework of grounded theory it is emphasised that actors are seen as having, though not always utilising, the means of controlling their destinies by their responses to conditions. They are able to make choices according to their perceptions, which are often accurate, about the options they encounter. Both pragmatism and symbolic interactionism share this stance. Thus, grounded theory seeks not only to uncover relevant conditions, but also to determine how the actors respond to changing conditions and to the consequences of their actions.

The grounded theory approach and the ethnographic approach are often seen as interrelated although ethnography grew out of a structure-focused tradition. Ethnography means writing about people; it is written representation of a culture or selected aspects of a culture, and it was inspired by Durkheim's functionalism. According to Durkheim (Layton, 1998: 25) social facts cannot be studied by armchair introspection; he emphasised the importance of participant observation. The researcher must go into the field to discover how a society conceives of its own institutions. The evidence will be found in the external, objective signs provided by patterns of behaviour.

Within ethnography Geertz talks about 'thin and thick description'. In his opinion the difference between 'thick description' and 'thin description' is that 'thick description' catches what is behind what is happening or behind what the agent is doing. The ethnographer is able to grasp what is behind the action, i.e. to explain the action due to his/her insight into the field achieved by being present in the field (Geertz, 2000: 30). According to Geertz, 'thin description' is when the researcher describes what the agent is doing but does not try to explain what is behind the action (Geertz, 2000: 7).

Strauss and Corbin refer to conceptual density in grounded theory and emphasise the difference between conceptualisation and description:

> *Conceptual density* refers to richness of concept development and relationships – which rest on great familiarity with associated data and are checked out systematically with these data. (This is different from Geertz' 'thick description,' where the emphasis is on description rather than conceptualisation). (Strauss & Corbin, 1994: 274)

The difference between Geertz's 'thick description' and the grounded theory approach – between description and conceptualisation – is that 'thick description' interprets what is behind or between the lines, what is invisible, whereas grounded theory methodology conceptualises on the basis of data produced by means of various approaches and coming from different sources. The conceptualisation results in patterns generating a theory constantly being checked with new data. In grounded theory the researcher does not have the same interpretive role as in case of 'thick description'. The researcher conceptualises what is in the text or in the action/interaction and not what is behind the text or behind the action. The understanding and the explanation of the empirical world is developed through conceptualisation and theory building. Grounded theory is also used to uncover and understand what lies behind any phenomenon, but the techniques to evolve the answer are different from those applied in case of 'thick description'. The grounded theory approach includes a special text-focused technique, which contributes to eliminating researcher-biased interpretations. Geertz's technique focuses on the researcher's interpretation and does not anticipate researcher-biased interpretations to the same extent as grounded theory.

Grounded theory is the method suitable in this study because it respects the agent perspective, which is the focus of the research. In addition grounded theory is not loaded with theory, and it offers techniques to anticipate researcher-biased interpretations.

Research Method: Grounded Theory

Today different versions of grounded theory are applied (Layder, 1998). This study is primarily based upon Strauss and Corbin's version but also to some extent influenced by Glaser's version. The aim of grounded theory is to develop a theory about the phenomenon studied on the basis of the empirical data collected. It is an attempt to develop categories, which illuminate the data, to 'saturate' these categories with many appropriate cases in order to demonstrate their relevance, and to develop these categories into more general analytic frameworks with relevance outside the setting.

Although the basic idea of the grounded theory approach is to respect the agents as agents having the capacity of action, it is important to be aware that agents might not always utilise the means of controlling their destinies by their responses to conditions. Grounded theory seeks not only to uncover relevant conditions, but also to determine how the agents respond to changing conditions and to the consequences of their action. It is the researcher's responsibility to catch this interplay (Corbin & Strauss, 1990: 5).

The agents may do a miserable job when responding to conditions. They might choose to act or refrain from acting in response to conditions. However, the purpose is to explore and expose the action from the point of view of the actor, and in education this can contribute to displaying the rationality of pupil conduct:

> This readiness to explore and expose social action from the point of
> view of the actor, with empathetic fidelity, stands at the root of Symbolic

Interactionism (...) In education this perspective can, as a wide range of studies illustrates, display the nature, meaning and existential rationality of pupil conduct to teachers and to others. (Hargreaves, 1994: 148)

It is not a question of proving or disproving existing theory. On the contrary, it is a question of being open to new impressions and contexts. Strauss and Corbin underline the importance of not being constrained by existing theories:

It makes no sense to start with 'received' theories or variables (categories) because these are likely to inhibit or impede the development of new theoretical formulations, unless of course your purpose is to open these up and to find new meanings in them. (Strauss & Corbin, 1990: 50)

Although Strauss and Corbin emphasise the advantage of generating theories grounded in the data, they do not totally reject opening up existing theories and finding new meanings in them. However, the latter approach will have a different perspective and a different aim.

It shall be emphasised that a grounded theory approach does not mean that the researcher does not have any theoretical knowledge. The researcher needs thorough knowledge of the grounded theory paradigm before generating theory on the basis of the inductive/deductive approach. In addition, the researcher needs theoretical sensitivity and knowledge in order to compare the generated theory with existing theories to further illuminate the findings.

The grounded theory methodology is an inductive/deductive approach, i.e. that it constantly moves from data collection to analysis and back to data collection. It is a way to interweave data collection and data analysis. The analysis moves from the broad overall perspective to a more refined, limited perspective resulting in the construction of categories and the generation of theory.

When applying a grounded theory approach, the earliest stages of the research are more 'open' than the later ones. In the early stages, a number of categories will probably be developed, and during the process these categories might be modified or further developed, and additional categories might be added. Strauss and Corbin mention that the researcher does not have to adhere rigidly to the techniques they offer. They cite Diesing (1971) stating that:

The procedures are not mechanical or automatic, nor do they constitute an algorithm guaranteed to give results. They are rather to be applied flexibly according to circumstances; their order may vary, and alternatives are available at every step. (Strauss & Corbin, 1990: 59)

Applying grounded theory is a long process developing and changing all the way through and becoming more and more explicit.

Data Collection and Modes of Analysis

When applying grounded theory, the data collection is decided by the aim of the research. It is a process continuously changing from the moment the initial data are collected till the categories are saturated. In the research described here, the data collection instruments comprised:

- Semi-open questionnaires before the student exchange. The purpose was to construct a profile of each student as to age, gender, experience with foreigners, expectations, stereotypical images of foreign culture, preparation, purpose and parents' attitude to exchanges.
- Semi-open questionnaires after the exchange. The questionnaires after the exchange illustrated what the students primarily remembered from the exchange (positive and negative experiences, events, differences), attitude to future exchanges, and changes in attitude to exchanges.
- Diaries about the students' daily experiences during the exchange.
- Semi-structured interviews focusing on the students' narratives about their experiences abroad. Although the interviewing procedure focused on narratives, an interview guide was used. The intention was to have overall and joint guidelines for the interviews and to be able to ask specific questions in case the students had little to tell. However, if the students were forthcoming on a specific issue or question, they were allowed to talk as long as it remained pertinent to the research.

In most cases a whole class/group of students were chosen as informants. In a few cases the teacher in charge of the exchange chose the informants.

The analysis includes three major stages: open, axial and selective coding. Open coding is to identify and label categories grounded in the data. The questionnaires were the first data to be coded, so they were broken down into statements consisting of words, phrases or sentences. Each statement was coded meaning that the statements were labelled and conceptualised. When looking through all the statements, it turned out that many statements could be placed under the same label. A number of statements had for instance language in common:

- improve language skills
- knowledge of the English language

- improve my English
- use my English

All the statements related to language were given the same number and the same label. In this case the label is:

- language learning

Figure 8.2 shows an extract from the open coding of questionnaires before the exchange, Question 10. It shows examples of how the data are broken down into statements, how they are numbered, and how statements relating to the same phenomenon are grouped under the same label number. The labels applied are either *in vivo* codes originating from the student statements or sociological constructs, which are codes formulated by the researcher. The intention is to choose labels, which are abstract enough to summarise the statements, and which do not refer to any specific theory.

New categories might be added when additional data are coded, but discovered categories cannot be abolished; they can only be densely described and modified. Some of the statements are deviant and can be discarded as more or less irrelevant. However, it is important to be aware that deviant statements are often interesting and essential for the analysis. The following deviating statements show the student's attitude to the exchange and what the student focuses on.

Question: How did you prepare yourself for the exchange? Student answer: I got a guarantee from my parents that I could come back if it did not work out. (Translated. Britta, Lingua exchange, private accommodation, France.)

Questionnaire before the exchange
Question 10: What is your primary purpose of going to Scotland/France?

Student no.	What is your primary purpose of going to Scotland/France?	Statement no.	Label no.
1	Improve language skills	326	326
1	Insight into the Scottish everyday life and culture	327	327
2	Good feeling of class solidarity	328	328
2	Good experience	329	327
2	To get to know new people	330	327
3	To improve language skills	331	326

Figure 8.2 Extract from open coding

Question: What did you especially like about the exchange? Student answer: That the Danish currency is strong. (Translated: Jonas, Lingua exchange, hotel accommodation, Scotland.)

The next stage is axial coding, which is to form relationships between categories and to find patterns. The basis of axial coding is the paradigm model (Strauss & Corbin, 1990) including a number of elements: causal and intervening conditions, phenomenon, context, action/interaction strategy and consequence/outcome (see Figures 8.3 and 8.4 showing the axial coding elements and an example of axial coding). An example of the paradigm features transferred to the exchange situation could be:

When I participate in an exchange (causal/intervening condition), I have certain expectations (phenomenon), to fulfil the expectations I do or do not X (action/interaction strategy) within the context of Y. After a while, I feel changed/the same, and I have experienced Z (consequence/outcome).

Causal conditions refer to 'the events or incidents that lead to the occurrence or development of a phenomenon' (Strauss & Corbin, 1990: 100). In reality, a single causal condition rarely produces a phenomenon. Therefore it is important to identify and to describe the specific properties of the causal conditions. The causal conditions are represented in terms of a student exchange programme with different properties such as accommodation, length of stay, host country and planned activities.

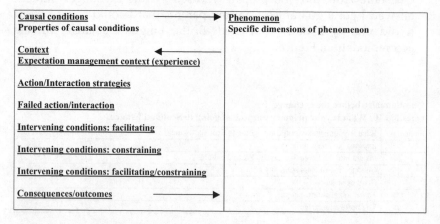

Figure 8.3 Axial coding paradigm

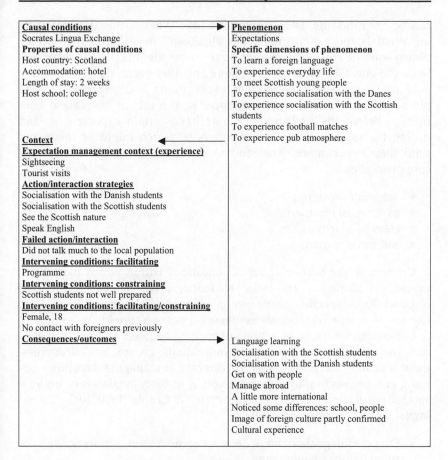

Causal conditions	Phenomenon
Socrates Lingua Exchange	Expectations
Properties of causal conditions	**Specific dimensions of phenomenon**
Host country: Scotland	To learn a foreign language
Accommodation: hotel	To experience everyday life
Length of stay: 2 weeks	To meet Scottish young people
Host school: college	To experience socialisation with the Danes
	To experience socialisation with the Scottish students
Context	To experience football matches
Expectation management context (experience)	To experience pub atmosphere
Sightseeing	
Tourist visits	
Action/interaction strategies	
Socialisation with the Danish students	
Socialisation with the Scottish students	
See the Scottish nature	
Speak English	
Failed action/interaction	
Did not talk much to the local population	
Intervening conditions: facilitating	
Programme	
Intervening conditions: constraining	
Scottish students not well prepared	
Intervening conditions: facilitating/constraining	
Female, 18	
No contact with foreigners previously	
Consequences/outcomes	Language learning
	Socialisation with the Scottish students
	Socialisation with the Danish students
	Get on with people
	Manage abroad
	A little more international
	Noticed some differences: school, people
	Image of foreign culture partly confirmed
	Cultural experience

Figure 8.4 Extract from axial coding, student number X

'Intervening conditions are the broad and general conditions bearing upon action/interactional strategies' (Strauss & Corbin, 1990: 103). From a student perspective these conditions work to either facilitate or constrain action/interaction. Facilitating conditions cover conditions, which the students regard as facilitating in the interaction process with the foreigners. Constraining conditions cover conditions which the students regard as constraining in the interaction process with the foreigners.

The phenomenon is the central idea, event or happening, about which a set of actions/interactions is directed at managing or handling it, or to which the set is related (Strauss & Corbin, 1990: 100). The phenomenon can be identified by asking questions like: What is this data referring to? What is the action/interaction all about? In addition the specific dimensions of the phenomenon have to be identified and described. Since the questionnaires cover a before and after event, the phenomenon is a unity consisting of student expectations and experiences. The phenomenon, expectations/experience, is a result of the causal conditions. Before the exchange students have certain expectations, and during the exchange they get experiences, which might or might not fulfil their expectations. The student expectations have the following core properties:

- language learning;
- experience of otherness;
- class solidarity;
- self development.

Context is 'the particular set of conditions within which the action/interaction strategies are taken to manage, handle, carry out, and respond to a specific phenomenon' (Strauss & Corbin, 1990: 101). Context is where the students get their experience abroad.

Grounded theory is an action/interaction-oriented method of theory building. Whether one is studying individuals, groups, or collectivities, there is action/interaction, which is directed at managing, handling, carrying out, responding to a phenomenon as it exists in context or under a specific set of perceived conditions (Strauss & Corbin, 1990: 104). Action/interaction has specific properties:

- Purposeful/goal oriented, done for some reason – in response to or to manage a phenomenon.
- Failed action/interaction, in this case it is important to ask why.
- Processual/evolving in nature, movement or change over time.

The question asked can be: Under conditions of private accommodation/hotel accommodation, what strategies are used? What do the students do to fulfil expectations?

Action and interaction taken in response to, or to manage, a phenomenon has certain outcomes or consequences. These might not be predictable or what was intended. The failure to take action/interaction also has outcomes or consequences. Consequences may be actual or potential, happen in the present or in the future. What are consequences of action/interaction at one point in time may become part of the conditions in another (Strauss & Corbin, 1990: 106). Consequence or outcomes cover the same categories as expectations:

- language learning;
- experience of otherness;
- class solidarity;
- self development.

This makes it possible to compare the unity expectations/experience and to look at the process from expectation to outcome. Figure 8.4 is an example of an axial coding diagram linking categories and subcategories in a set of relationships.

Selective coding is the last stage in the coding process. It is an integration procedure in order to find mechanisms or processes giving rise to a given condition. Selective coding is carried out to form a grounded theory. The integration procedure is not very different from axial coding applying the coding paradigm. It is just done at a higher, more abstract level of analysis. It pertains to coding systematically and concertedly for the core category. Selective coding is to select an abstract category to encompass all that has been described in the story. The story should indicate its properties and relate the other categories to it, making them subsidiary categories. Selective coding is to tell the story analytically. It is to write in a few sentences the essence of your story and to ask questions like: 'What about this area of study seems most striking? What do I think is the main problem?' (Strauss & Corbin, 1990: 119).

To explain how major categories are integrated and to form a total picture, the categories are grouped according to their specific location (phenomenon, context, conditions, outcome) in a conditional matrix, which is an analytic aid, a diagram, useful for considering the wide range of conditions and consequences related to the phenomenon under study. The matrix enables the researcher to both distinguish and link levels of conditions and consequences (Strauss & Corbin, 1990: 158). The conditional matrix covers each student and shows (see Figure 8.5):

- Research fulfilment of expectation: student fulfilment compared with the researcher's judgement.
- Student fulfilment of expectation: fulfilment expressed by the student.
- Structure fulfilment of expectation: student outcome compared with the EU and local school requirements (fulfilled 1; not fulfilled 0).

	Student no.1	*Student no.26*	*Student no.41*
Research fulfilment	Positive	Negative	Positive
Student fulfilment	Missing	Positive	Positive
Structure fulfilment	1 (fulfilled)	0 (not fulfilled)	1 (fulfilled)
Causal conditions	Hotel accommodation Scotland	Private accommodation Scotland	Private accommodation France
Context	Sights	Host family Education	Host family Entertainment
Failed Interaction	Lack of contact		
Constraining conditions	The others	The others Accommodation	The others
Facilitating conditions	Planning	Self The others	Self The others
Facilitating/ constraining conditions	Female 18	Female 18	Female 17 Excursion
Phenomenon: Expectations	Language learning Otherness Class solidarity	Language learning Otherness Self development	Language learning Self development
Outcomes/ consequences	Language learning Otherness Class solidarity Self development	Otherness Self development	Language learning Otherness Class solidarity Self development

Figure 8.5 Extract from conditional matrix

- causal conditions.
- context of action/interaction.
- failed interaction.
- constraining intervening conditions.
- facilitating intervening conditions.
- facilitating/constraining intervening conditions: conditions which the students do not see as facilitating or constraining.
- phenomenon: student expectations.
- consequences/outcomes.

Since the theory is grounded in the data, conditions such as age, gender, former travel experience and family background will only be included in the final theory building if the analysis reveals a pattern showing that they are either facilitating or constraining. The conditional matrix links the categories to the core category, and the pattern appearing makes it possible to tell the story and generate a theory grounded in the data, as was demonstrated in the first part of this chapter.

When applying grounded theory, it is important to be aware that 'we are never able to grasp all of it' (Strauss & Corbin, 1990: 111), but we can try to capture as much of the complexity and movement of the real world as possible. The general rule in grounded theory is to sample until theoretical saturation of each category is reached. This means until no new or relevant data seem to emerge regarding a category, the category development is dense, and the relationships between categories are well established and validated.

Effects of the Research Method

The application of grounded theory is combined with both strengths and weaknesses. The constant comparison means that the researcher continuously has to assimilate and accommodate incoming data to theory in order to develop a final theory. The recursive process between data collection and theory building – between the informants and the researcher – resonates with Piaget's definition of biological adaptation. Piaget states that:

> biological adaptation is thus a state of balance between an assimilation of the environment to the organism and an accommodation of the organism to the environment. Similarly, it is possible to say that thought is well adapted to a particular reality when it has been successful in assimilating that reality into its own framework while also accommodating that framework to the new circumstances presented by the reality (...) Generally speaking, adaptation presupposes an interaction between subject and object, such that the first can incorporate the second into itself while also taking account of its particularities; the more differentiated and the more complementary that assimilation and that accommodation are, the more thorough the adaptation. (Piaget, 1971: 153–154)

Thus grounded theory can be considered a collective, constructivist learning theory since it asks the researcher to make constant comparison enabling the categories and the theory to be adapted through assimilation and accommodation. In that way grounded theory respects Piaget's theory of constructing knowledge, and the researcher becomes a learner learning on behalf of a community.

Grounded theory is combined with participant observation. Consequently the researcher comes up against the ethnographic paradox that you can observe but only describe in your own words. In general, ethnographic studies are not without their critics. Nunan notes that:

> long-term ethnographic analyses are immensely rich in data, and their reporting therefore requires selection and interpretation. Since the data

gathered by ethnographic researchers is unique and complex, it is impossible for other researchers to check it or replicate it, and so the interpretations and conclusions of ethnographic researchers must be taken on trust. (Nunan, cited in Corbett, 2003: 98)

To allow for the above criticism I have not applied participant observation. Instead data originate from informants talking about themselves and their own experiences. The agents tell their own version of their experiences through semi-open questionnaires, diaries and semi-structured interviews. The method applied can be called 'listening' ethnography adapted to the field being studied and to the empirically, agency-focused grounded theory approach. The interpretative aspect becomes part of the analysis when the researcher develops categories on the basis of the data. However, in the case of grounded theory this process is to a greater extent based upon craftsmanship than on interpretation since grounded theory offers specific techniques to code and analyse data. Within ethnography, selection becomes essential due to the rich amount of data. Even though grounded theory requires comprehensive data materials, selection is not essential since all the data are coded and analysed. Concepts and relationships are grounded in the data and are thus born as operationalised. The researcher does not have to operationalise an existing theory before looking for examples in the world. On the contrary the researcher is sure that the categories exist in the real world since they are grounded in the data.

To some extent grounded theory imitates the scientific quantitative method, the hypothetico-deductive research method, which focuses on producing valid conclusions drawn from reliable data. Grounded theory observes these research genre demands through recursive movements between data collection, analysis and theory building. However, the attempt does not fully succeed since it is a question of words not figures. The validity criteria of grounded theory are challenged by postmodern logocentricity and scepticism asking the question whether language can represent the world, 'We can't represent others in any other terms but our own' (Van Maanen, 1988: 12).

Within qualitative research there is a tendency to discard the concepts of reliability and validity fully or partly. According to Lincoln and Guba trustworthiness is the right concept to be applied in qualitative research:

> The conventional criteria for trustworthiness are internal validity, external validity, reliability, and objectivity. Now the questions *underlying* the establishment of these criteria are also appropriate to ask of naturalistic inquiry. (Lincoln & Guba, 1985: 218)

The problem about Lincoln and Guba's definition is that they do not distinguish between data and findings, which is important when applying grounded theory. To understand the difference between reliability and validity, the laboratory (Tarp, 2004) or the court can be applied as a metaphor of comparison. In court the witnesses' statements must be reliable, which is obtained through cross- examination. The judging statement is based upon reliable witness statements, and it must be valid. If conflicting data occur, the case is reopened to allow for a different judging statement. In the case of grounded theory the data must be reliable, and the conclusions on the basis of the relationship between categories must be valid. The researcher can test whether a theory is right or wrong by validating the relationship between categories with new data. The reliability of the data is checked by asking the informants control questions as a means of cross-examination. The validity of the theory is checked by looking for new examples, which might be assimilated to the theory, or which might force the theory to be accommodated.

Some of the aspects characterising grounded theory are the way to ask questions and to collect and analyse data. Glaser's (1992: 25) statement of never asking the question directly can both be regarded as a weakness and a strength. It might mean that to some extent the researcher mistrusts the informants. However, it is important to be aware that the informants might not answer the question posed. In this connection, common criticism is that in the case of interviews, the informants' reports may be false thus not producing reliable data. In my opinion Glaser's statements emphasises the importance of listening to the informants instead of cross-questioning them by means of pre-organised questions not allowing any narratives.

However, in the case of interviews the researcher cannot be sure that the informants do not supply data with a filter in order to be politically correct. This might happen where informants are selected by the teacher. It is possible to allow for the aspect of reliability by approaching the informants by means of different research instruments, e.g. semi-open questionnaires, diaries and semi-structured interviews. The multi-strategy approach gives access to the multi-layered nature of student exchanges. When answering semi-open questionnaires, the students give information without the researcher's direct intervention, and they have the possibility to add further information. The diaries are also written without the researcher's intervention.

When interviewing the students, the interviewer's position is that of a listener instead of an interviewer. Approaching the informants in different ways increases the degree of density and reliability. Due to the comprehensive amount of data, the different data collection instruments and the cross-checking of categories against new data, the probability of political correctness in the answers is minimised. By using different sources for collecting data, the data are checked for reliability through tri-angulation (Lincoln & Guba, 1985: 283).

The pedagogic effect of being involved in research is discussed by Byram (1996), who talks about the 'pedagogical function' of the interview. Byram argues that the interview process itself helps the interviewee to develop a new understanding of the experiences which are in focus. The interview process might create reflection and reanalysis of taken-for-granted realities. Interviews can be applied both before, during and after a period of residence abroad. The pedagogic effect clearly appears from a report written by one of the teachers in charge of an exchange:

> The use of questionnaires and interviews before and after the student exchange had the effect that the students had to precisely express their expectations before the exchange and their own experiences in connection with the exchange after the exchange. This contributed to making the students more responsible for their own actions both in con-nection with the exchange and the report writing. (Teacher in charge of Lingua exchange Denmark/Scotland)

The quotation shows how the researcher influences the students by approaching them by means of semi-open questionnaires and semi-structured interviews. Consequently, in the case of student exchanges semi-open questionnaires and semi-structured interviews can be applied as a tool to get access to the students' voices and to increase the students' awareness. It can also be applied as a means of discovering another culture (Tarp, 2004).

Conclusion

The research illuminates how Danish business school students experi-ence short stays abroad in terms of EU and local school exchanges. The findings show the diversity in student agendas and gains and the import-ance of student inclusion in exchange curriculum building for student exchanges to be successful. The comparison with other studies empha-sises the importance of paying attention to both internal and external factors in student stays abroad. The method applied, grounded theory, was originally developed with the purpose of legitimating qualitative research and respecting an empirically focused agent perspective.

Different schools have developed within sociology in Europe and the USA with different attitudes to agency and structure and to empirically based and theory based research. When applying grounded theory, the research process becomes open and traceable. The data collection and modes of analysis are divided into different data collection and coding stages resulting in theory building through assimilation and accommodation, meaning that grounded theory resonates with constructivist learning theory. The authority lies in the data delivering new theory by means of specific analysing techniques, and the researcher has to respect patterns grounded in the data in order to generate a theory. The discussion of the influence of the research on the informants and the researcher demonstrates the values of the techniques inherent in grounded theory. The conclusion is that a grounded theory approach has both strengths and weaknesses to some extent depending on the researcher and the field being studied.

Notes

1. EU-funded student exchanges are organized by CIRIUS, an independent state-subsidised institution attached to the Danish Ministry of Education.
2. The research study started in 1996; for that reason the term Lingua is applied. Today the term Socrates refers to the European programme for education. Socrates consists of eight actions.
3. The total number of informants were:

   - 53 students answered questionnaires;
   - 2 exchanges classes wrote diaries;
   - 35 students were interviewed either individually or in focus groups.

Chapter 9

The Assistant Experience in Retrospect and its Educational and Professional Significance in Teachers' Biographies

SUSANNE EHRENREICH

Any discussion of the role of residence abroad in German foreign language teacher education involves grappling with a number of seeming inconsistencies. While there is a long tradition of voices recommending a compulsory period of residence abroad for future language teachers (e.g. Rossmann, 1896), more than a century later, it is still not a formal requirement at most German universities. Foreign language teacher educators never stop emphasising the need for compulsory stays abroad (e.g. Zydatiss, 1998), however, in the face of only scanty empirical research in this field, they often rely upon the myths of quasi-automatic linguistic and cultural benefits in an apparently ideal immersion situation abroad. As a result, curricular integration in terms of preparation or evaluation of student stays abroad is still rare (e.g. Woodman, 2003). In 2004/2005 the assistant exchange, often regarded as the ideal type of residence abroad for future language teachers, celebrates its centenary, looking back on an impressive overall number of participants. Again, however, empirical research investigating the experience and its actual effects is almost non-existent (Alred & Byram, 1992; Byram & Alred, 2001).

This chapter describes a study which sought to examine the effect of the year abroad experiences of German foreign language student teachers who lived and taught abroad as language assistants in English-speaking countries (Ehrenreich, 2004). The overall aim of this study was to explore, from the participants' point of view, and evaluate, with reference to teacher education, the impact of the assistantship in four domains: personal, linguistic, (inter)cultural and professional learning. In Section I of this chapter, findings of the study will be presented, Section II discusses the qualitative research design of the study, reflecting on methodological choices which had to be made in the course of the research process and describing the techniques used to collect, analyse and interpret the data.[1]

I. THE CASE STUDY – CONTEXT AND FINDINGS

Context

Reviewing the literature not only provided important insights, but also helped to identify serious gaps in research. Theoretical or programmatic literature on stays abroad almost exclusively presents a romanticised and largely uncritical picture of the experience and expresses high hopes concerning its effects. Yet, empirical studies, especially those conducted in a qualitative fashion, do not always support this optimistic stance (e.g. Coleman, 1996; Farag, 1997; Wilkinson, 1998). While studies on foreign language teacher learning and teacher knowledge suggest that residence abroad may have a significant – positive or negative – long-term impact on (student) teachers' professional identities (Appel, 2000; Caspari, 2003; Schocker-von Ditfurth, 2001), this issue has, so far, never been closely studied. An apt summary of the current state of research concerning foreign language assistants, the group of future teachers I was particularly interested in, can be found in Murphy-Lejeune's (2002: 47) recent study: 'Particularly interesting, and despite its long existence in Europe, this experience abroad remains relatively unexplored.' This need for further exploration becomes even more obvious in view of the very large number of German language assistants who have lived and taught in English-speaking countries (27,000 between 1952 and 2002; cf. Ehrenreich, 2004: 448).

For my study I conducted 22 semi-structured retrospective interviews with people who had in the past worked as language assistants, some of them being teachers already and others still in their studies but intending to be teachers. Careful sampling strategies were used so as to make visible potential continuities and discontinuities of the long-term impact of the assistant experience in teachers' biographies. In the course of my research, a multitude of possible perspectives on the phenomena under investigation emerged, making an integrative framework necessary which combined the following three conceptual models. First, an adaptation of the concept of the 'small social life-world' (Luckmann, 1970), taken from phenomenological life-world analysis, proved invaluable for an adequate understanding of the assistant experience:

> a small social life-world [...] is a *fragment* of the life-world, with its own structure, within which experiences occur in relation to a special inter-subjective reservoir of knowledge that is obligatory and pre-existent. A small social life-world is the correlate of the subjective experience of reality in a partial or temporally restricted culture [...]. A small social life-world is described as 'small' [...] because the complexity of *possible* social relevances is reduced within it to a *particular* system of relevance. (Hitzler & Eberle, 2004: 70; italics in original)

Second, while it is virtually impossible to define the concept of 'the good language teacher', a synopsis of currently discussed concepts of foreign language teachers' knowledge-base served as a useful basis for evaluating the impact of the assistantship from the point of view of foreign language teacher education (Byram, 1997; Freeman & Johnson, 1998; Terhart, 2001; Zydatiss, 1998). Third, a holistic integration of both perspectives was possible with the help of Terhart's developmental model of teachers' professional biographies. In this model, Terhart conceptualises the process and the stages of developing a professional identity as a teacher (i.e. the process of becoming and being a teacher through education, experience and reflection) as a *life-long* process of professional *and* biographical learning (Terhart, 2001: 27ff.).

For readers unfamiliar with the specifics of the German system of teacher education it might be helpful to know the following: in Germany, foreign language teacher education in most federal states consists of a four-year or five-year philology degree, which generally includes only very few methodology courses and very little teaching practice; in most cases residence abroad is not compulsory. After their university degree teacher candidates have to complete a two-year pre-service teacher education course (*Referendariat*; i.e. German equivalent to British Postgraduate Certificate of Education (PGCE) or to Irish Higher Diploma of Education).

Findings

The major findings were organised into the following five areas: the assistants' 'relevance system', personal learning, linguistic development, professional learning in schools and classrooms and (inter)cultural experiences. Due to constraints of space, I will focus here on just three areas.

The Assistants' 'Relevance System' – Changing With Time

In order to arrive at a phenomenological description of the assistant year and its educational impact it was necessary to reconstruct the 'relevance system' (Hitzler & Eberle, 2004: 70) shared by the 'small social life-world' of (former) assistants. As mentioned above, the assistant year can be conceptualised as a temporary and purposive *'fragment* of the life-world', a fragment which is both 'intentionally constituted' and 'goal-directed' (Hitzler & Eberle, 2004: 70). The intentions and goals associated with the assistantship shape both the participants' values and priorities and their perceptions and evaluation of what is important and unimportant, i.e. they frame the subjective 'relevances', according to which they interpret and assess the meaningfulness of their experiences abroad. However, assistants are not always (fully) aware of the single components of their 'relevance systems' and of the way these influence their practice of interpreting reality. One of the tasks of this study, therefore, was to reconstruct this 'relevance system', its components and its dynamics. For this, my informants were invited to tell me about their reasons for going abroad, their hopes concerning their stay, and whether or not their expectations were fulfilled.

It is important to note that the numbers given below are a result of the researcher's analysis of the *qualitative* narrative data and are used here to *illustrate* important aspects and changes in the assistants' relevance system; they should not be (mis-)read as 'statistical evidence' (see also below Research Methodology).

Motivations and expectations before the year

Language (18 of 22 informants) and culture (18 informants) were the main motives for going abroad, the latter being closely linked to a general wish for a change; the opportunity to try out one's teaching skills was an important factor for 15 informants; aspects related to personal growth and maturity were mentioned by only two informants. In a close cross-case analysis interesting characteristics of the assistants' 'relevance system' emerged: First, in most answers we find as a recurrent theme high professional ambitions, which my informants sought to realize through their stay abroad:

> Well, first of all, I am a hundred per cent certain that a foreign language teacher who can't speak the foreign language is not a good foreign language teacher. And therefore it's absolutely necessary to hear the language, to speak it, to practise it for an extended period of time. That's one of the main reasons why I decided to do it. (Frank)[2]

Sara, who had already spent a year at a high school in the US, was not the only one to express the following ideal: 'Well, I just thought if I want to teach English I need to have seen both [the US and Britain]. You need to have been there. For me that's a must.' Second, all informants remembered very clearly why they had chosen to spend a year abroad as an assistant and, interestingly, despite the retrospective nature of the interview, the accounts of their reasons for spending a year abroad were still heavily influenced by the terminology and concepts pervasive in a lot of year abroad literature assuring students of the tremendous linguistic benefits and cultural insights of such stays. Third, further analyses of the interviews underline the impact of those initial '"in-order-to" motives' (Hitzler & Eberle, 2004: 68). For the assistants, they retain a lasting importance as criteria for their personal evaluation of the 'success' of their year.

Developments during the year

Asked about the most important experiences in their year abroad, an overwhelming majority of informants (20) mentioned personal development and growth (cf. Coleman, 1996: 66). (Inter)cultural experiences also play a major role (13), but often a highly ambivalent one, as for many participants positive and negative (inter)cultural experiences during their year go hand in hand. Teaching, though still seen as an important experience, causes a lot of disappointment (15). Language learning loses its significance and is mentioned as an 'important experience' by only four informants; this is a trend which is well documented in the literature (e.g. Byram & Alred, 1993; Farag, 1997; Wilkinson, 1998). An unexpected, and again highly ambivalent, 'relevance' emerges in the course of the year: the assistants' network; which is socially important, but linguistically often regarded as counterproductive.

As we can see, what assistants rate as important changes dramatically in the course of the year. It should be kept in mind, however, that some of these reinterpretations of initial relevances are also indicative of processes of adaptation to certain non-ideal contextual factors. However, most participants are positive or even enthusiastic when it comes to an overall evaluation of their year abroad and their final verdicts cover the whole gamut of emotions from 'a wasted year' (Heike) to 'awesome' (Tim) (cf. Murphy-Lejeune, 2002: 81).

Schools and Classrooms – Professional Learning

The question of whether and how the experience of having taught as an assistant in a foreign school environment influences teachers' pedagogical knowledge, their beliefs and teaching practices has only received little attention so far (cf. Alred & Byram, 1992; Byram & Alred, 2001). Important insights, however, can be gained from research in the field of international teacher training (Block, 2001; Lawes & Barbot, 2001).

Teaching as an assistant

Looking at the interviewees' narratives about school and teaching, my analyses confirm what had already been established by Byram and Alred's (1993: 37) study more than 10 years ago: 'The only pattern in the work of an assistant which is discernible is that there is a wide variety of experience.' In my study, this variety ranges from five-minute-withdrawal sessions with a small group of pupils preparing GCSE-role play situations to fully-fledged whole-class teaching following a course book. At a second glance, however, and again in accordance with Byram and Alred's studies, assistants have a lot in common. Many of them start out highly motivated and look forward to trying out their teaching skills. Yet, some weeks into the year, they often get the impression that schools are not deploying them effectively and they therefore feel 'underused' (Byram & Alred, 1996: 278). As a result, many of them modify their priorities and turn their attention away from teaching to focus on other aspects of their stay.

Having said that, it is important to keep in mind that language assistants embark on their new task of teaching with a virtually complete lack of professional preparation in all relevant areas: Most of them have very little or no prior teaching experience, nor are they qualified to teach German as a foreign language. They have little or no understanding of the foreign education system and its underlying philosophy (cf. Rowles *et al.*, 1998: 3), and finally, they have all to come to grips with 'that awful status in-between' (Sara) of being neither pupil nor teacher (cf. Byram & Alred, 1993: 40), but rather '*Lehrer* (teacher) *light*', as one former assistant put it.

It will emerge below how the ambivalent nature of the perceived long-term professional gains of the assistant experience is, to a remarkable degree, caused by these contextual factors and challenges.

Comments on schools and teaching concepts

According to the *Pädagogische Austauschdienst* (PAD), i.e. the German programme coordinators, assistants will gain an insight into the host country's education system (KMK-PAD, 2002: 35). Merely being around in the schools, however, is not enough as my informants' accounts show. For example, many of them expressed how appalled they were at the low level of their pupils' proficiency in German: 'Well, compared to that, German pupils in eighth grade do much better' (Jan).

Obviously, this is an assessment derived from a direct comparison with German pupils' level of English at the same age. Of my 22 interviewees, only four mentioned positive observations in the language classrooms abroad and not more than two arrived at an interculturally balanced, i.e. context-sensitive assessment of the foreign concept of language teaching. Of the 19 assistants who commented on the foreign school system, 13 were prepared to make sweeping generalizations about the school systems and felt that the German school system was 'definitely better'.

This is a dilemma which has its roots in the students' national-cultural educational biographies (cf. Block, 2001; Byram & Alred, 1993: 42; Lawes & Barbot, 2001) and it draws our attention to a fact which is well-known in intercultural education. Intercultural understanding is not an automatic by-product of intercultural encounters, and, likewise, just being in a foreign school system does not automatically lead to real, in-depth understanding of that system. In order to arrive at such an understanding, integration in the school community and regular interaction with teachers and students about culture-specific aspects of educational systems (e.g. language teaching concepts, co-education, school uniforms, pastoral care) are crucial.

Professional continuities and discontinuities

In pedagogical terms, many interviewees felt that interacting with their pupils, though not always easy, was a rewarding experience, confirming their choice of career (16 informants). Back at university in Germany, however, they had to cope again with the conceptual discontinuity between their teaching realities abroad and their academic studies in a philology course which offers no opportunities for them to reflect on their professional experiences.

In terms of teaching methodology no transfer seems possible between the assistant experience and German teacher education courses (*Referendariat*). My informants' perception of the professional significance of their assistantship is shaped by a socially shared knowledge about the style of teaching required in those courses which involves teaching *whole* classes at a *German grammar school* on the basis of perfectly *thought-out and structured* lesson plans, etc. Therefore, the assistantship and teacher training are seen as 'two distinct worlds' (Uli); for Anna, the beginning of her teacher training meant 'starting from scratch again'.

Being able to establish links between the teaching experience as an assistant and one's teaching in Germany seems to be the 'privilege' of those who have already reached the status of qualified teachers. Yet, my data suggest that there is an additional conceptual prerequisite. Stories about how they benefit from their assistant year in terms of teaching ideas and methods have only been reported by those interviewees for whom the differences between their home-cultural educational concepts and those of their host country did not feature as a 'deficit', but rather as a 'complement': 'Well, it was extremely interesting, because everything is so different from what we do at our grammar schools. But (lively, fast), a lot of those ideas can be applied here, especially those for younger learners' (Katrin).

In the post-communication phase just after the interview many informants expressed their amazement at how much the interview had helped them, for the very first time, to see the wealth of links between their assistant experience and subsequent stages of their teacher education and career; a very positive pedagogical effect of the research interview (Byram, 1996)! If this is the case, we have every reason to assume that, as far as professional learning is concerned, former assistants are often not conscious of the scope of professional benefits they 'actually' derive from having taught for a year at a foreign school.

(Inter)Cultural Experiences – Ambivalences

Exploring the intercultural domain of the assistant experience proved much more difficult than analysing other aspects of the same experience. First of all I must admit that, as a teacher educator and researcher in that field, I had high hopes concerning the potential intercultural benefit of the assistantship myself. Early entries in my research diary give evidence of my initial optimism, which was – as I then thought – supported by the evidence of a first, cursory analysis of my data. This optimism, however, subsided in the course of the research process and gave way to a more realistic evaluation of the complexities of intercultural learning. The more systematically I examined my data, the more clearly the following pattern emerged: While my interviewees did not hesitate to communicate openly about positive as well as negative or even disappointing aspects of their personal lives, their linguistic development and their work as an assistant, there seemed to be a certain bias in their narratives about intercultural aspects of their stay and work. In several interviews conflicting messages and revisions could be found which needed to be (re)analysed carefully. These narratives followed a discourse which is typical of year abroad success stories in general and which therefore makes research in this area particularly difficult. However, this phenomenon was only addressed explicitly by one individual: 'I have told you some of the negative aspects now because ... these are the things you don't usually talk about (smiles). Normally, you just tell people "I spent a year in England and it was good"' (Heike).

It seems that narratives of residence abroad are bound to be positive. If yours isn't, you hide it because this is seen as a personal failure which you are not keen to display (cf. Byram & Alred, 1993: 57).

Avoiding essentialist views of culture or mere political correctness?

When asked about cultural similarities and differences between Germany and their host culture, many assistants hesitated to provide an answer. Some claimed this is a matter of mentality or intuition which cannot be defined analytically. Others seemed to be very careful not to generalise and employ stereotypes. At first this looked to me as if these interviewees displayed a high degree of cultural sensitivity – not wanting to essentialise about cultures and as if they had indeed adopted a pluralised view of culture. A second analysis of each interview text as a whole, however, revealed a whole range of inconsistencies and I finally came to the conclusion that my direct question had triggered answers which conformed to what the interviewees deemed to be politically correct. Obviously, culture-related comparisons, generalisations and stereotypes are something 'future foreign language teachers don't talk about'. The fact that stereotypes abound as soon as we leave this domain should make foreign language teacher educators think. In the previous section on 'schools and classrooms' we saw how the assistants' accounts about the target culture school systems revealed this behaviour very clearly. Caught 'off-guard', as it were, many of the former assistants were quite outspoken and did not hesitate to come up with ethnocentric judgements, making it evident that language teacher students need a great deal of conceptual support in order to be able to reflect on, conceptualise and articulate their views of cultural identity and of cultural otherness.

These observations, disillusioning as they may appear, are by no means new. In fact, they only remind us of how pervasive a 'romanticised' view of cultural understanding as an automatic by-product of exchange programs has become and how little this type of discourse is contested:

> The culture-contact hypothesis according to which frequent encounters between people of different cultural backgrounds will reduce their stereotypical views of each other, as well as leading, more or less

automatically, to an improved understanding of the other culture, is generally considered to be true. This is the case even though research in social psychology into the phenomena of prejudice and stereotypes raises considerable doubts about its validity. (Thomas, 1988: 79 (my translation); cf. Coleman, 1998: 59)

Intercultural continuities and discontinuities

The specific sampling strategy which was employed for this study (see Section II) allowed for a quasi-longitudinal analysis of the impact of the assistant experience on teachers' biographies (cf. Byram & Alred, 1996: 270ff.). Thus, the narratives of student teachers and qualified teachers shed light both on hopes and on realities with respect to the long-term intercultural benefits of the year abroad. All interviewees were convinced that their stay abroad has or will have a major impact on the way they present British, Irish or Australian culture to their German pupils. Yet, in the light of their narratives the quality and interculturality of this impact has to be questioned. For example, many of my informants did not seem to be fully aware of the potential danger inherent in the negative attitudes they developed towards the foreign school system. Ironically, they often mentioned 'school' as one of the topics of the cultural curriculum in order to illustrate how much more 'authentic' their teaching is or will be because, as they say, 'they know the system from inside'.

In general, my data suggest that the way many of them teach culture does not actually go beyond either a *Landeskunde* approach or a touristic approach. In order for them to be able to initiate genuine intercultural learning, teacher education has to provide them not only with conceptual frameworks for culture learning which support individual processes of cultural understanding before, during and after their year abroad, but also with adequate methodologies for intercultural learning and teaching as teachers in their classrooms (cf. Klippel, 1994).

Implications for Residence Abroad Within Teacher Education

The findings of this study show how both the experience of the assistant year itself and its evaluation are subject to a whole range of internal and external factors, making a clear-cut assessment of its educational and professional impact on teachers' lives impossible. For some informants, the assistantship proved to have a lasting effect on their professional as well as their personal biographies; for others it has faded into an episode of the past, leaving almost no traces in their present lives (cf. Byram & Alred, 2001: 8ff.). Within this diversity, some elements, however, have emerged which seem characteristic of many assistants' experiences.

Looking back on their year, for most of them, aspects of personal growth are of paramount importance, but this is often seen as only being relevant to their private lives, and no links seem to be established to the professional domain of teaching. The assistants' evaluations of the linguistic, cultural, and professional gains of their year reveal how little continuity there is between the potential benefits of residence abroad and the following stages of their education. Moreover, their accounts also show how aware they are of what is required of them academically and professionally in teacher education and how this, 'prospectively' as it were, influences the perceived benefit of their year.

The following implications for residence abroad within teacher education arise from this study. For foreign language teachers-in-training, residence abroad creates unique and potentially highly significant learning opportunities. More specifically, given a high degree of openness and initiative, teaching as an assistant really does seem to involve particularly relevant experiences for future language teachers. Therefore, the study confirms what teacher educators in Germany already suggested more than 100 years ago and what has long been a feature of modern foreign language courses in Britain and Ireland, namely the integration of residence abroad as a compulsory requirement. At the same time, the findings underline the need for careful curricular integration of such stays in terms of adequate preparation, monitoring and reflective evaluation (cf. Parker & Rouxeville, 1995; Roberts *et al.*, 2001). What is needed is a holistic as well as interculturally oriented teacher education, which not only helps students to maximise the potential benefits of residence abroad, but also seeks to systematically develop their professional skills with a view to their future tasks in the language classrooms, building on the individual linguistic, cultural (and teaching) skills acquired abroad.

II. RESEARCH METHODOLOGY – METHODS AND REFLECTIONS

In this Section I will discuss and reflect upon methodological issues and present facets of the 'natural history of my research' (Silverman, 2000: 236). The fact that this is done in consecutive steps may be slightly misleading to the reader. In practice, once the decision for a qualitative research design has been taken, changes, adjustments and re-conceptualisations may become necessary at virtually all stages of the research process, a fact which requires a general openness on the part of the researcher and which renders the course of action anything but linear (cf. Kvale, 1996: 83).

Why Qualitative Research?

I started out with the vague notion that not much is known either about the year abroad experiences of German assistants or about the way these experiences might influence their educational and professional biographies as foreign language teachers. At the same time I was quite certain that these issues deserved closer investigation. Reviewing the literature in the field confirmed both the gap and the need for more knowledge about the long-term processes at work in the year abroad experiences of prospective foreign language teachers (cf. Section I).

With my preliminary research idea in mind ('How/Does the assistantship influence teachers' biographies?'), I set out to explore what would be the best methodology for my study. As appropriateness of methodology is one of the key criteria for good research, thorough consideration of the choice of methods in the initial stages of research is imperative.

Quantitative and/or qualitative? This was one of the first questions which needed to be addressed. Quite clearly, a research project with a population of 500 to 600 students teaching as assistants in English-speaking countries each year seemed to lend itself to a quantitative research design, using standardised questionnaires which lead to 'objective' and 'representative' results in a strict quantitative sense. However, as '[s]tandardised methods need for the design of their data-collection instruments (for example, a questionnaire), some fixed idea about the subject of the investigation' (Flick *et al.*, 2004b: 5) such an approach seemed less than ideal. It has been shown in Section I that systematic academic research, especially in the areas of foreign language teacher education and the assistantship, is scarce and, instead, year abroad rhetoric and myths abound. Thus the prerequisites for a methodologically sound design of a quantitative investigation were not given.

If, on the other hand, 'qualitative research can be open to what is new in the material being studied, to the unknown in the apparently familiar' (Flick *et al.*, 2004b: 5) and also has the potential 'to describe life-worlds "from the inside out", from the point of view of the people who participate' (Flick *et al.*, 2004b: 3), adopting such an approach seemed more promising. The participants' perspectives on their everyday experiences both during their assistant year and in the following educational and professional contexts were central to the study. In the framework of a qualitative research design they would be seen as experts on the (research) subject and be invited to act as co-researchers, who help to co-construct the data-base for the phenomenon under investigation. In keeping with the epistemological principle of qualitative research, my task as a qualitative researcher was to arrive at a 'methodically controlled under-standing of otherness' (Flick *et al.*, 2004b: 8). In this process of understand-ing otherness my own personal background knowledge and experience would play an essential role at all stages of the research process, which is another characteristic of qualitative research.

In the course of thinking about my research design it became apparent that my initial idea, namely that of assessing the benefit of the assistant-ship with the help of normative standards such as those commonly found in teacher education curricula would be appropriate only after a thorough, empirically grounded (re)construction of the participants' sub-jective views of their assistantship and *their* conceptualisations of its long-term educational and professional impact.

The Research Questions

Bringing both my preliminary research idea and general principles of qualitative research practice together helped me to specify my research focus: Adopting a phenomenological approach, my primary purpose was to explore and describe the 'small social life-worlds' (Luckmann, 1970) of former foreign language assistants and their experiences. My aim of under-standing the subjectively intended meaning of those experiences and of reconstructing the inter-subjective meaning schemata of former assistants quite clearly suggested the need for an exploratory, qualitative research design which only later, in a second step, would be complemented by an evaluative perspective. Thus the research questions were as follows:

(1) How do former assistants describe their experience as an assistant? What are the internal and external factors shaping their stay abroad experiences?

(2a) How do former assistants describe the personal and educational impact of their assistant experience?

(2b) What (potential) value does the assistantship hold from the point of view of foreign language teacher education?

(3) What implications for foreign language teacher education in Germany emerge from a contrast of the two perspectives contained in 2a and 2b?

Quality Criteria

Last but not least, when doing qualitative research the question arises as to what quality criteria will be used to assess the quality of one's own study. Instead of re-interpreting traditional concepts such as 'validity' and 'reliability', I adopted as guidelines for my research the following two quality criteria: The first criterion concerns the 'indication of the research process' (*Indikation des Forschungsprozesses*; Steinke, 2004: 188ff.); all steps taken in the research process have to be justified in terms of their overall appropriateness, including the description of the qualitative procedure, the choice of method(s), of transcription rules, etc. The second criterion used as a guideline aims at 'inter-subject comprehensibility' (*Intersubjektive Nachvollziehbarkeit*), which involves detailed and transparent documentation of the research process and the use of (partly) codified procedures (Steinke, 2004: 186ff.).

Data Collection Procedures

Methodological options

No doubt, for the double purpose of my study, i.e. an investigation of the assistant experience *and* its long-term effects, a longitudinal study would have been ideal, following language teacher students from their assistantship through their final years at university and their teacher training to their first years on the job. However, for a single researcher doing her doctoral thesis, such a study is barely feasible as it requires several years of data collection. Other methodological ways of capturing the processes under investigation had to be found.

After having considered a whole range of methods for the collection of qualitative data (e.g. participant observation, analysis of diaries, reports or documents, questionnaires, interviews) and some potential combinations, I decided to carry out a cross-sectional study on the basis of retrospective data which would be gathered from a carefully structured sample of informants (see below 'Sampling and access to informants'). Of the two methodological options suitable for a cross-sectional retrospective study of this kind, questionnaires and interviews, I opted for the interview, since questionnaires containing open questions can be very time-consuming to fill in, and informants might feel less inclined to present complex ideas in detail in writing. Quite clearly, the quality of my study would thus depend both on the informants' capacity to remember, reflect on and talk about events and thoughts which possibly date back several years, and on the researcher's competence in conducting interviews and eliciting data, and in analysing these verbal data.

Interview design: Semi-structured interviews with 'narrative incentives'

The interview design had to fulfil the following set of requirements: it would have to generate retrospective and introspective data which are relevant to the research questions. While a certain degree of comparability was highly desirable, enough flexibility was needed for the informants to bring up unexpected aspects or formulate new insights gained in the course of the interview. Of course, the type of interview chosen would also have to be compatible with both the interviewee's and the interviewer's communicative skills. Finally, thinking about how to interview, i.e. collect data, always also involves thinking about how to analyse the data later. The challenge, therefore, was to strike the right balance between openness on the one hand, and thematic and communicative structuring on the other hand. Some form of semi-structured interview had to be developed, based on an interview guide, but at the same time allowing for narratives to shape the process of the interview.

Here, Flick's 'episodic interview' (2002: 104ff.) provided a useful starting point. In 'episodic interviews', the two forms of knowledge, narrative-episodic and semantic knowledge, are accessed via 'narrative incentives' (Flick, 2002: 106) and specific questions respectively. Thus, both narratives or descriptions of events and situations as well as argumentative and more abstract explications of developments and relationships are elicited in the course of an interview. Yet, it was also necessary to make 'implicit' knowledge accessible, i.e. aspects and links which participants had never considered or articulated before. Therefore, theory-driven questions – a type of question which is central in the *Forschungsprogramm Subjektive Theorien* (cf. Flick, 2002: 81) – were included in the interview guide as a methodological help for interviewees to generate and formulate ideas which they had hitherto hardly been aware of.

In general, the aim was to handle the interview conversation flexibly, leaving it to the interviewees whether to respond to certain questions and allowing them to take their time, to add something or revise earlier statements; strategies designed to generate fairly authentic impressions of how relevant certain topics actually are to individual interviewees.

Two elements of the 'problem-centred interview' developed by Witzel (cf. Flick, 2002: 85ff.) were included in order to contextualise and document the interview situation. The first was a short questionnaire collecting biographical and educational data, so called 'hard facts' or '"[o]bjective" life circumstances' (Flick *et al.*, 2004b: 7) which are indispensable for a solid analysis and interpretation of the material. In retrospect, the decision to complete this questionnaire together at the beginning of the interview conversation proved to be an excellent communicative warm-up phase for both interviewee and interviewer and it also provided me with useful references for the interview itself. The second element was a postscript, in which the interviewer writes down his or her overall impression of the interview situation and documents external influences, etc. for later reference.

The questions of the interview guide itself focused on five main topic areas: personal experiences, language, (inter)cultural learning, school and teaching, assistantship (i.e. pragmatic and administrative aspects of the exchange programme plus personal tips for future assistants). I started off all interviews with an *open introductory question* asking my informants about the most important experience in view of their assistant year. Questions following on from that would then be taken from the topic area which was addressed by the interviewee in response to that initial question, thus guaranteeing a subject-oriented procedure. The interview guide was piloted in four interviews with only minimal changes being necessary.

Following Silverman's (2000: 98ff.) critical remarks about the current multiple-method euphoria and the theoretical implications involved in any kind of methodological triangulation, I had made a deliberate choice to develop a theoretically consistent 'single-method' interview study, aiming at a well thought-out interview design and methodologically compatible methods of data analysis.

Sampling and access to informants

By giving careful consideration to the sampling procedure I sought to address two challenges inherent to this study. The first was the fact that, unlike in many other qualitative studies, there was no given group of potential informants (e.g. the students in a university seminar, etc.), which means that selection could not be constituted by 'accessibility' (cf. Merkens, 2004: 166). In fact, as one of the purposes of my study was to investigate specific features of the long-term impact of the assistantship in different stages of teachers' biographies, 'convenience sampling' (Flick, 2002: 68–69.) of any kind was not an option at all. The second challenge concerns the 'perennial worry' (Silverman, 2000: 103) of generalisability of qualitative research. For most qualitative studies obtaining generalisability via statistical sampling procedures is neither achievable nor desirable, and several suggestions as to how to deal with this challenge of scope in qualitative research are discussed in the literature (cf. Flick, 2002: 230; Silverman, 2000: 102ff.). Taking up some of Silverman's (2000: 103ff.) suggestions, the following three sampling strategies were combined for this study:

(1) 'combining qualitative research with quantitative measures of populations' (e.g. gender, host countries and regions),
(2) 'purposive sampling guided by time and resources' and
(3) 'theoretical sampling' (cf. Glaser & Strauss, 1967: 45), i.e. following up new aspects which appear in the course of data collection and preliminary data analysis (e.g. master students, negative memories of assistantship, early return).

22 participants	15 female participants			7 male participants	
Home federal state	Baden-Württemberg	Bavaria	Berlin	Brandenburg	North Rhine Westphalia
	7	12	1	1	1
Host country/ Host region	England	Wales	Scotland	N. Ireland	Ireland	Australia
	12	2	1	1	4	2
Residence in host country	city		town		boarding school campus	
	17		4		1	
Type of school/ university	secondary schools		adult education		higher education	
	21		2		1	
Year of assistantship	92/93	93/94	94/95	95/96	96/97	97/98	98/99	99/00	00/01
	1	1	3	2	4	5	2	2	2
Number of years btn assistantship and interview	8	7	6	5	4	3	2	1	–
Subjective evaluation of assistant year	positive or very positive		very critical about some areas of experience		negative	
	18		3		1	
Stage of teacher education or of teaching career at time of interview	teaching	non-teaching career	teacher training	university degree	final years at university/ degree exams	assistantship
	5	1	3	5	6	2

Figure 9.1 The group of participants in the study

Since it was not possible to carry out a 'fully-fledged' longitudinal study, I was hoping that with the help of a specific parameter, i.e. the different stages in study, training or teaching of the interviewees, it would be possible to reveal continuities and discontinuities in the spectrum of the different individual narratives and thus to gain a first set of generalisable insights into the long-term impact of the assistant experience in the course of language teachers' biographies. In the end, it was the following six parameters which guided the process of sampling:

(1) stage of teacher education or of teaching career at the time of the interview,
(2) gender,
(3) home federal state in Germany,

(4) host country or host region,
(5) personal evaluation of assistant experience and
(6) duration of their stay (full year or early return).

Access to informants was established through a multiple snowball method. The process of gradual selection of interview partners was finished after 22 interviews, when a high degree of 'theoretical saturation' (Glaser & Strauss, 1967: 61) was reached and the inclusion of new (sub)-groups of the population held little promise of new information (see Figure 9.1).

The Group of Participants in the Study

Interviews

Interviews were conducted between February 2001 and August 2001, in Germany and in Ireland, in my or the participants' homes or at university. The average length of the interviews was approximately 100 minutes. The interviewees provided me with open and detailed accounts of their experiences, not hesitating to express their ideas about existent or non-existent links between their assistantship and the following stages of their teacher education and career, data which proved to be highly relevant for the purpose of my study (cf. Section I). The use of different types of questions helped to gain access to different types of knowledge and perspectives. Strategies of communicative validation employed in the course of the interviews, (e.g. brief summaries, preliminary interpretation, clarifying requests) fulfilled the function of a 'within-method-triangulation' (Flick, 2004: 179–80), and thus the majority of interviews came close to Kvale's (1996: 145) ideal: 'The interview is "self-communicating" – it is a story contained in itself that hardly requires much extra descriptions and explanations.'

Data Analysis and Interpretation

Documentation of data

Interpretation starts (if not within the actual process of interviewing) with defining guidelines for transcription (Kvale, 1996: 160ff.). As the focus of my study was on the content of what was said, and to a lesser degree on details of discourse – though elements such as pauses, laughter, etc. were included in the transcription – the two main principles for transcribing were easy readability and, in keeping with standards of research ethics, loyalty towards my interviewees. Transcribing the interviews myself, though very time-consuming, provided me with a first close reading of, or rather, a 'multi-sensory' engagement (listening, writing, reading) with the texts, through which I gained a thorough knowledge of my data. Transcripts were then sent back to the interviewees for 'member check' in order to ensure their consent for the use and potential publication of quotes (cf. Kvale, 1996: 172ff.; Steinke, 2004: 185). The data gathered for this study thus consisted of interview transcripts (630 pages), short questionnaires containing socio-biographical data (33 pages), interview postscripts (37 pages) plus fieldnotes and my research diary.

As my personal 'PhD companion' this research diary served several purposes. An entry each day about my research activities helped me to keep track of my time management. At the same time, the diary also served as an 'information bank' in which I recorded details about all kinds of 'discoveries' concerning my topic (people, conferences, literature, websites, etc.). On a more reflexive level, most entries also contain extended notes about my reactions to central concepts and arguments in the literature as well as my reflections on the actual processes of interviewing, transcribing, analysing data, and writing. In addition to these notes, input and feedback by others was also documented and analysed. Pushing myself to spell out in writing the various reflective processes and the development of my own thinking certainly helped to maintain a critical stance throughout the project (Silverman, 2001: 193ff.).

Thinking about interview analysis

Developing their analytical tools, qualitative researchers have to make several fundamental choices. As I have pointed out, these should be considered at an early stage as the techniques used for data collection and the tools for data analysis have to be seen as closely linked elements of the research process (Kvale, 1996: 177) despite the fact that the two phases of gathering and analysing one's data may be months apart.

Qualitative data: Coding and/or sequential analysis?

Two general strategies for dealing with qualitative interview data can be adopted; researchers can either code their material according to theoretical or *a priori* categories, or use sequential analyses which take the temporal-logical sequence of the interview narrative as a starting point, aiming at reconstructing the individual case (Flick, 2002: 176). Methodological implications of my data collection procedure, i.e. semi-structured interviews with 'narrative incentives' (Flick, 2002: 106), but also pragmatic reasons meant that a combination of both approaches was necessary. Interview texts were coded, using both thematic and theoretical categories, while narrative episodes were analysed according to their internal structure.

In retrospect, having experienced how easily text passages, once isolated, 'gain a life of their own', I would claim that a high degree of context-sensitivity, though primarily a methodological feature of sequential approaches, must be paramount throughout the whole process of interview analysis. Fortunately, with the development of qualitative data analysis (QDA) software these issues are much easier to solve. (For this study, a software package called MAXQDA was used; cf. Kuckartz, 2001).

A modified version of Glaser and Strauss's (1967) grounded theory approach was adopted as the guiding principle for analysing my data, i.e. the analytical categories for coding and the evolving theory were developed on the basis of and grounded in my data. At the same time, however, keeping my research questions and the conceptual framework of the study in mind during the process of category formation, helped to reduce and thus limit the 'potential endlessness of options for coding and comparisons' (Flick, 2002: 185) implied in Glaser and Strauss's approach.

Representational or presentational view of language data?

With verbal data the question has to be considered as to how language data which have been co-constructed in the social event of an interview should be treated. Can we take interviewees 'at their word', as Freeman (1996) puts it? Discussing methodological implications of research based on qualitative interview data, Freeman (1996) and Block (2000) argue that an integrated approach is needed which takes into account both a representational and a presentational view of language data. A 'representational' view, on the one hand, looks at language data as a vehicle for thought and focuses on *what* is said in the interview. A 'presentational view', on the other hand, looks at the role(s) and voices a speaker adopts in the course of an interview and *how* something is said and of what this might be symptomatic. When both of these views are taken into account, inconsistencies in qualitative interview data are not a sign of a lack of validity but allow for an integrative analysis which actually provides a more comprehensive picture of the topic. Some of these ambivalences and the new insights gained from a close analysis utilising this methodological-conceptual approach have been illustrated in Section I.

Stages of Analysis and Interpretation

Data analysis consisted of five stages, of which the first three steps served to structure the material, facilitating the actual process of analysis and interpretation described in the last two steps.

Data-based formation of analytical categories and development of a summary format

Having acquired an intimate general knowledge of my material through transcribing, a second close reading and an interpretation of three interviews served as a starting point for determining analytical categories. Thematic units in the texts were identified and coded, using 'draft analytical categories'. These were mainly derived inductively, from aspects and concepts mentioned in the data; some drew on ideas included in my research and interview questions; some terminology was taken from the literature. A first network of categories was designed, trying to make relationships between categories and thematic clusters visible. Parallel to that, as a pragmatic supplement which facilitates quick orientation within each interview, a summary format was developed which comprised the following four elements: a table of contents, an overview of the sequence of topics covered, key words of answers plus references to potential quotations and, finally, a brief summary of the interview interpretation.

Constructing and testing of the code system

As a next step, the network of categories was transformed into an appropriate hierarchical system of codes and sub-codes, which was then imported into MAXQDA; so called 'code memos' containing definitions, and key examples were attached to some codes. By coding two more interviews, now electronically, the preliminary code system was tested for its scope and flexibility, necessary refinements were added and over-differentiations reduced.

Comparative analyses of single cases and coding of interviews

What followed was, for reasons of time economy, a highly multifunctional stage. All remaining interviews were analysed and coded and summaries for each interview were written. At the same time, first steps towards a comparative analysis of certain themes were taken; using Glaser and Strauss's motto 'stop and memo', preliminary results of cross-case comparisons, potentially relevant similarities and differences between text passages, ideas for interpretation, references to literature and open questions were stored in theoretical code memos.

Five thematic areas, taken from the interview guide as heuristic devices facilitating the first phase of the coding process, emerged gradually but clearly as core categories firmly grounded in the material. These were 'person', 'language', 'culture', 'school and teaching' and 'assistants', with the category 'assistants' (i.e. their socially shared knowledge and relevance system) proving to be a much more powerful and central category than had originally been envisaged. One formal category, 'methodology', containing references to the interview situation and the status of the 'ex post facto' data ('can't remember any more', 'now, it is all coming back again', pauses, etc.) had to be added to the core categories of the code system, which eventually consisted of a total of 350 codes and sub-codes. Kuckartz' (1997: 589–90) advice to invest sufficient time and effort into developing one's code system had proved salutary: after a good deal of reshuffling and revising in the initial phases of coding, the system proved to be a valid analytical tool for the rest of the interviews, and only minimal modifications to the system (and consequently to the previously coded interviews) had to be made.

Synoptic analysis of themes

With all interview texts coded, passages belonging to the same category (or categories) could easily be retrieved and compared. Thus, cross-case similarities and differences as well as distinct characteristics of certain phenomena as experienced by individuals became apparent and could then be analysed systematically and assessed in terms of their empirical relevance (cf. Kelle, 2004: 278ff.). Narrative passages were treated in their own right and complemented the code-based analysis.

It should be added that Oswald's (1997: 76–7) idea to actually use numbers, if possible and appropriate, when talking about the size of sub-groups in one's research report instead of 'hiding behind' quantifiers (e.g. much, few, a lot of), was more than helpful. No 'pseudo-quantification' of qualitative data was intended, but trying to follow this advice encouraged a more rigorous data-analysis, and in several instances, forcing myself to count cases helped to avoid rash conclusions.

Within-case and cross-case axial analysis of themes and theory building

In the above mentioned stages of analysis the following (sub-) categories had evolved as 'axial categories' (Strauss & Corbin, 1990: 114), being 'most relevant to the research question' (Flick, 2002: 182): 'mobility capital' and 'tertiary socialisation', 'own initiative', 'accommodation', 'contacts', 'key people', 'school arrangements', 'dis-continuities' (a sub-code of all four core categories 'person', 'language', 'culture' and 'school') and 'socially shared knowledge among assistants'. In a final analytical step, means-end and cause-and-effect or temporal relations between those phenomena and concepts as well as potentially relevant contextual factors were explored in detail through contrastive and complex retrievals of text segments assigned to the above mentioned 'axial categories'. Building on these interim results, central aspects and factors of a theory of the significance of the assistantship within teacher education and development gradually emerged (see discussion of findings in Section I).

Year Abroad Research: Looking Back and Looking Ahead

Looking back, I can say that once again, qualitative methodology has proven to be invaluable in terms of exploring the 'unknown in the apparently familiar' (Flick *et al.*, 2004b: 5), providing me with a wealth of surprises. Unexpected elements of the assistants' relevance system emerged and several of my preconceptions had to be discarded as 'wishful thinking'.

More specifically, the results of my study suggest that criteria-guided instead of convenience sampling (though not always possible) helps to further systematise one's research findings. All sampling parameters used turned out to be highly relevant variables influencing the specific quality of the individual assistant experience as well as the subjective evaluation of its educational significance, thus offering preliminary results and hypotheses for further investigation.

Conducting retrospective studies has its advantages and disadvantages. The phenomenology of the assistant year discussed in this study is, strictly speaking, a 'remembered phenomenology'. In methodological terms, however, the fact that the assistantship was presented by my informants as it was seen at the time of the interview was in fact highly compatible with the purpose of this study. It could be shown how former assistants never assess the educational and professional significance of their year independent of but always with reference to the specific requirements of the different stages of teacher education.

With respect to future year abroad research I would like to point out several implications arising from my study. First, further in-depth studies about the year abroad experiences of German students are needed, focusing on factors specific to German institutions and to the

German national-cultural context. Second, the research process and the findings of this study underline the fact that in the intercultural domain of year abroad research all types of *self*-assessment generate data of a highly ambivalent nature, which, if not analysed carefully, only serve to perpetuate the notion of apparently automatic benefits of residence abroad (cf. Laubscher, 1994: 8ff.). Third, the observation that students without previous experience of otherness (see the concepts of 'mobility capital', Murphy-Lejeune, 2002: 51ff.; and 'tertiary socialisation', Byram, 1997: 34; Doyé, 1992) seem to profit far less from going abroad than others, emphasises the powerful influence of this variable in shaping the individual quality of students' year abroad experiences, making detailed research of this aspect and its effects necessary. Helpful insights into the cause-and-effect relationships of successful intercultural learning in residence abroad contexts could also be gained if research reports included transparent documentation of this variable.

If our aim is to mobilise those students with little or no previous experience of otherness, we need to know more about those factors and what can be done within teacher education or higher education in general (cf. Isserstedt & Schnitzer, 2002: 58–9) to generate processes of 'tertiary socialisation' and thus help to maximise their learning experiences abroad.

Notes

1. I would like to thank Gill Woodman for her constructive comments and helpful suggestions on the manuscript.
2. All interviews were conducted in German; interview quotations used in this paper were translated by Susanne Ehrenreich.

Chapter 10
British Students in France: 10 Years On

GEOF ALRED and MIKE BYRAM

Introduction

The year abroad (YA) is a long standing example of the more recent trend for students of any subject in further and higher education to include residence abroad within their studies. For many years, students of languages in many western European countries have been encouraged or, in most British universities, obliged to spend a year immersed in a society whose language, society and literature they are studying. In Britain reciprocal arrangements have long existed with Austria, France, Germany and Spain, allowing students of these countries to work or study abroad. Generations of linguists have valued such experience as the one opportunity to spend a substantial period of time in a foreign country. In more recent decades, European Union ERASMUS and SOCRATES programmes have given students from other disciplines similar opportunities. All of these schemes represent a significant investment of time and money on the part of governments, institutions and individuals. The belief in their educational value is clearly evident in this commitment but evaluation of the policy has not been as rich as it might have been, either for students in general or languages students in particular. One purpose of our research was to contribute to evaluation of language students' experience and, by implication, of the wider issue of the value of study and work abroad as part of higher education.

Evaluation of learning during the YA has tended to focus on improved linguistic competence. The conclusions of systematic evaluations and research (Coleman, 1995) are not always sufficient on their own to justify the time, money and effort on the part of students and sending/ receiving institutions. However, the value placed on the experience by students themselves is an indication that dimensions other than the linguistic are involved.

The present study sought to examine these other dimensions to reveal a fuller picture of the personal meaning and educational significance of the YA undertaken by British modern languages students. It was a follow-up to a previous investigation of the nature of the YA experience and the learning that can result from this particular kind of sojourn abroad (Alred, 1998, 2000; Byram & Alred, 1992, 1995). Students interviewed 10 years previously, before and after their sojourn abroad as teaching assistants, were studied again.

The previous study provided an understanding of the experience of the YA from the students' perspective, British students in France and French students in England. They were beneficiaries of the tradition of reciprocal arrangements which gave them a post in a secondary school as 'language assistants' conducting conversation lessons in their mother tongue. One purpose of this study was to investigate the experience of being an assistant and a series of booklets was produced as aids to students and their advisers/mentors preparing for the assistantship (Byram, 1992; Byram & Alred, 1993a, b).

Another major focus was the development of knowledge of the culture of the host society and the relationship of that knowledge to the circumstances of residence. These two factors were linked by students' capacity to adjust to living abroad and the consequences for personal development.

The findings were positive. Students were challenged, generally enjoyed their sojourn and reported extensive cultural learning. By the end of the year, an initial emphasis on language *per se* had given way to attention to the use of language in social exchange and intercultural mediation. Experiences were varied, and several students described the YA as a major episode in their lives, affecting self-understanding and outlook on life. Many also reported marked changes in self-perception, personal development and maturity.

In the second study, which is the focus of this chapter, our theoretical position was articulated slightly differently and rather than focus on knowledge acquisition and the experience of being an assistant, we conceptualised the learning whilst living and working abroad – changes in self-concept, attitudes and behaviour – as the acquisition of 'intercultural competence' (Byram, 1995, 1997). Intercultural competence has been defined as 'the ability to behave appropriately in intercultural situations, the affective and cognitive capacity to establish and maintain intercultural relationships and the ability to stabilise one's self identity while mediating between cultures.' (Jensen *et al.*, 1995: 41). Although during their YA students had remained in some respects on the margins of the foreign society, nonetheless they conformed to certain institutional expectations, in the schools where they worked, which challenged their taken-for-granted understanding. The experience became a process of temporary re-socialisation into a foreign culture and its practices and beliefs.

This second study aimed to reveal the long-term significance of this process by re-interviewing as many of the British students as could be traced.

Ten Years On

We first decided to investigate the long term effects seven years after the first study and made our first attempt to trace the British group of whom there had originally been 30. At this point we managed to trace 16, and 15 of them said they would be willing to be re-interviewed. However the vagaries of research funding for what was described by one reviewer of our proposal as an 'arcane' project, meant that it was 10 years after the first project when we eventually managed to start and by this time we had lost contact with some of those who had volunteered. Others were known to us and willing to be involved but living in other countries and thus beyond the reach of our research funding. As a consequence, a total of 12 interviews were conducted, one by email. The latter is necessarily of a different quality and this was acknowledged in the data analysis. The group included just one male, whereas there had been three males in the original group of thirty.

Participants were interviewed at their home address, or a negotiated venue. One person normally resident abroad was interviewed during a visit to the UK. The interviews began in March 1999 and were completed in October, 2000. The interviews lasted approximately one and a half hours, and were audio recorded and transcribed.

In this second project, we had three main objectives:

(1) to compare former students' perceptions of residence abroad immediately after the sojourn and ten years later;
(2) to explore former students' perceptions of the sojourn as an educational experience occupying one quarter of the duration of their degree course, and what in practical terms influenced the lasting outcomes of the sojourn;
(3) to assess the long term significance and meaning of residence abroad, in terms of attitudes and personal qualities, career patterns and ways of life, with reference to the concept of intercultural competence.

This was to be, like the first study, a series of cases with no claim to generalisability, although we had carried out a survey of universities during the first project and were confident that the participants in our study had an experience similar to that of most students of French in British universities at the time.

As will be explained later, we used semi-structured interviews in both projects and our purpose was to understand the participants' experience, as individuals and as a group, to encourage them to articulate their own interpretation of the experience seen in retrospect, and to evaluate its significance for them. Thus our research questions were:

- In what terms do participants give meaning to the experience of living abroad in a European country 10 years earlier?
- Have they developed careers or ways of life that draw upon what they learned during the YA?
- How are the effects of the YA manifest in their lives in terms of the qualities inherent in intercultural competence?

The third question was motivated by the theory of intercultural competence mentioned earlier. We expected that the YA had allowed participants to gain intercultural competence and that this would be manifest in their lives in some way even 10 years later. We were looking for evidence of this in their accounts, their 'stories', which were the result of our research methods. Our findings can thus be presented as stories or narratives and in the next section we select two of these to illustrate the range of experience and interpretations participants put on their experience.

Narrative Analysis

Jane's Story

Ten years after her YA, Jane is a full time mother of three children. She will resume her career in a year or two's time (working for charities), and retains the desire to use her French in some way but is not sure how.

The YA was a useful experience in terms of clarifying Jane's ideas about teaching. Her parents were themselves teachers, and being a teaching assistant gave her a taste of this as a possible career. However, she concluded that she would not make a good teacher. Being in the classroom was often enjoyable but she realised she did not have the commitment required to make teaching a satisfying career: '(E)ven when sort of things were working better, I never really felt that it was something that I wanted to do particularly. I didn't dislike it but I wouldn't have said that I was particularly at home.'

Teaching aside, living in France was a very positive experience, and it got better and better, although it never felt like home. She enjoyed the richness of living in a large provincial French town. She led a full social life and was busy as a teaching assistant. At first, Jane was overwhelmed but gradually settled in and found support and comfort in a group of assistants, comprising other English students and two Spanish students. The YA contrasted with an earlier year as an au pair in a small French village, which was very good for learning French but was a lonely time.

The group of friends was very important. Her social life was carefree, especially in the later months. Being in the same situation as others and looking on the funny side of things were important factors. She remembers that the YA was a big thing to do in her early twenties. After initial excitement, the first term was hard, and the winter was a low point. She became dispirited but not homesick. It was miserable being apart from her boyfriend. She came home at Christmas and her boyfriend visited at Easter.

During the year as an au pair, she became fluent in French, and even dreamt in French, but the YA did not completely restore her fluency, although she still became a proficient French speaker once again. She acquired good friends, amongst the network of assistants, and some of the teachers, who would occasionally invite her into their homes. She can still remember the meals, and she came to appreciate the French attitude to food and hospitality. Overall, however, she didn't become a Francophile, and at the time, she recognised that the friendships were contextual, of that time and those circumstances.

She remembers feeling older on her return to studies in England. She felt out of kilter with other students, and was pleased to spend the year living with two friends who were then doing postgraduate courses.

Everybody's sort of young, undergraduates of 18 and there you are pushing 23, and you think really I feel a bit beyond this. And yet you still haven't graduated, you've still got this huge hurdle of finals to jump over. I still have nightmares that I haven't done my finals. . . . It's obviously something that's stuck with me that – I haven't read the books and it's a couple of months to finals and I haven't read the books. So you are in an odd situation when you come back.

In addition to learning that she does not have the commitment to teach, she also discovered she could survive in a situation not of her choosing:

> I definitely feel that it was a positive year and I did enjoy it generally but there were times when I thought this is not of my choosing. Like the place I was living, it was actually so grotty. I wasn't cut out to be a teacher of these particular kids. But it was fun overall. So that's quite a good thing to learn – that things can be not quite right or not as you would choose to have them, but you can still survive and you can still have fun. It doesn't all have to be perfect.

The YA helped her to become more confident and independent. Projecting a persona to fill a professional role was part of teaching and she has carried this forward in her working life as a fund raiser for charities. It also helped her be more confident in the final year of her undergraduate studies.

She does not think of living abroad again, although when asked, does not rule out the possibility. Her life since graduating has been focused on getting married, having a family, developing a career and supporting her husband's career. Now a major priority is her children's education and having stability for the family and the prospect of a reasonably certain future.

Looking back, the YA is located within an important period of her life. The YA was unique, challenging and enjoyable, but it does not stand out from other parts of the formative period during which she left home, gained her independence, went to university and whilst there met the person who later became her husband.

The only tangible link now with the YA is occasional correspondence and getting together with one of the Spanish teaching assistants. She has not been back to the place she lived, although she has made several visits to other parts of France.

The YA has been influential in the sense that she has lived abroad, has done that, and now wants to build a life in England, 'with all the commitments that that involves'. When asked if having lived aboard has influenced her way of life, she replies:

> I'm just thinking that the things I've said to you sound all terribly negative. Things like knowing I don't want to teach, and feeling that I'm quite content to be established in middle-class St. Albans with plans to educate my children here and all that sort of thing. I'm quite content to have that. It sounds a bit negative but I'm content to have

it because I feel I've done the living abroad experience and got that out of my system, really.

She concludes:

There are a lot of things about living in this country that are very important to me as well and I suppose you only find that out when you don't have them, when you miss them after sort of a few months living away from them.

Anne's Story

Ten years after her YA, Anne is teaching in a comprehensive school in central London. She has been there for eight years. After graduating, Anne worked in the retail sector for a year and found this deeply unsatisfying, and so decided to train as a teacher. She guards her free time and spends as much time as possible travelling, and recognises the importance of maintaining a good balance between work and her personal life.

She has been Head of Year and is now Head of Languages, an exciting and demanding position. Her school has a broad intake in terms of ability and background, including a strong ethnic mix, and promotes a positive ethos of hard work, high academic achievement and an emphasis on students' all round development.

Modern languages are popular in the school. Anne is proud of the students' and her department's achievements. The work is satisfying and Anne attributes student interest and motivation, in large part, to students living in an ethnically and linguistically diverse metropolitan city. The school has exchange arrangements with schools in Germany, dating since soon after the Second World War, and with schools in France. It is also developing links with Japanese schools. Japanese is beginning to be taught, and Anne herself has become a student with others in the school learning Japanese.

Anne is strongly committed to the students, referring to them as 'my children', but she is also beginning to think of moving on in her career. She gained promotion at a relatively young age and has been given opportunities to develop as a modern languages teacher. She has enjoyed being able to innovate and take managerial responsibility in a medium sized department. She is not quite sure what she is looking for next but it will be something which will challenge her to innovate again and is likely to have a strong community element and cultural diversity. Anne is a dedicated hard working teacher and an excellent role model:

I hope the children would tell you ... that I love them and I [try] to establish a happy environment ... I try to create an atmosphere of achievement that, you know, everybody can achieve something and feels positive about ... I think the children know that I love languages and that I love travelling ... [it's] infectious. ... I think the most important things are they know that I love them and ... that I want the best for them and that's the atmosphere that I think I create.

Anne recalls that when she was Head of Year, she was often affected emotionally by students' predicaments when these were difficult. She remembers needing to off-load with colleagues and also taking this emotional side of her work home. 'I think so long as you let them feel that you think they're wonderful even though they've done this that and the other ... it's important for them to feel accepted by you no matter what happens.'

Anne considers herself to be a good listener; she can be empathic and encouraging. These qualities were developed in the early years of teaching, through trial and error, hard work and sensitivity. She has had no formal management training, but is constantly learning and has been involved in setting up a mentor programme in the school. She remembers the support she received when first at the school – a space in which to cry, talk things through, and remind herself that she is a strong person.

She links many of the features of her present life and herself as a person to her YA. When she thinks back, she says 'I loved my year abroad'. And despite being disappointed initially with the location, she had a fantastic time. She made French friends who are still friends from 'a little slice of a different life'. It was a wonderful experience for a person in early adulthood, it taught her 'that things are possible, you know, ... it is possible to just get up and go and live in another country for a year'. During her YA, Anne travelled to many different places in Europe and travel became an important part of the experience, in the area where she lived and also further afield during vacations, rather than return to England.

Initial worries about accommodation and difficulties with bureaucracy were soon overcome. Getting to know another English student who shared an interest in the arts and who became a constant companion provided an early secure base for making the most of the year. With this friend, she entered into a full social life with local people of similar age and interests. This helped her to integrate into French life as a young teaching assistant, with ample free time, strong interests and a love of travel. The friend was the only English person she spent time with. She has since returned to the French town of her YA but not to her university town in the UK, and recalls: 'I really do have very happy memories. You've got time for doing things like sitting in cafés and, you know, watching the world go by and that was really lovely.' She took the teaching seriously and enjoyed it. It was a year like she had never had before. She had lived abroad as a child, in Belgium and America, but this was different, because she went on her own.

> (I)t really does help you, it makes you feel confident and it makes you feel things are possible and also the fact of just living in France and everything is very, very different there. You know, it's very close by but it's very, very different, you know, the way people think. ... (W)e'd have these huge philosophical discussions in cafés and you just think, gosh, this just doesn't happen in England. ... I did feel that it was, you know, really living in France and living as French people do.

Anne thrived on cultural difference, she went out and embraced it. She was glad to have a position as a teacher that required her to be an active, if temporary and peripheral, member of French society. She has ready for a 'proper job', and being a teaching assistant provided an exciting and challenging opportunity, after her earlier 'cosy' undergraduate years.

Anne remembers only a few difficult times. She remembers having to think carefully about a number of sensitive issues and take account of cultural and language differences, and her ability to be understood and understand in interpersonal matters. It was necessary to be focussed and, at times, to set her feelings to one side, as important issues were addressed. She doesn't remember being ever in low spirits or homesick. On the contrary, she felt at home abroad, and enjoyed family visits when she could introduce family members to her new life, situation and friends. Living abroad felt like something she had genuinely chosen, unlike other major decisions in her educational career. The YA felt like it was hers, she made it what it was, free of imposition or prescription. A difficult relationship with a teacher when Anne was in upper secondary school has left a lasting impression, and she felt this keenly when she was herself a teacher for the first time, in France. It increased her motivation to do the job to the best of her ability and to encourage and support students, the basis of what she tries to do now.

  Anne often thinks back to her YA, sometimes prompted by personal or school trips to France, and the experience of being a teaching assistant comes back to her. It was a very important year for her. Now she is in the position of being approached by former students who themselves are either anticipating or reflecting on their own YA. She is touched by this, and is often able to help.

When asked to sum up her YA, she says: '(I)t was kind of your own life, that was very nice and very important. It was really lovely to get to know French people and their culture. It was also really lovely to get to know France.' And it helped her realise how much she values travel:

> ... one of the most important things to me is travelling and getting to know different types of people ... the chance to go and discover places and that's very, very important to me ... what else? ... I mean it has led me to a job as well and to a job that I love. (I)t has shaped my career. So a very, very important time, also very happy, ... very free.

More generally, she recognises the YA reinforced her openness:

> I've always been quite open I think but it felt like the first time because you're old enough to do whatever you want to do, you don't have to get anybody's permission, it was the first time you really generally had the freedom to lead the kind the life you want to lead and it was just exciting to do that in another place. You know, you are learning lots of different things and meeting lots of new people, so I think it's a very important time.

She also remembers some unpleasant incidents when she was sexually harassed. The memory of these stays with her. At the time these incidents were disturbing but they did not stop her getting on with her life in France on her own terms. Her one friendship with an English person was a valued support at the time.

She remembers becoming more aware of herself as a person. Being on her own, she discovered things about herself. It was a process of redefining herself, of truly getting to know herself: 'I had a real test of who I really am.' She relates this to the impression her students have of her and believes that they, at their stage of life, do not truly understand what it means to know oneself. In contrast, the YA provided the conditions, of being alone and being in a foreign culture, of getting to know oneself and believing in oneself, away from the influence of family and the familiarity of one's own culture. And for Anne, this kind of honest self-understanding and knowledge is essential to being a good teacher.

She recalls how she had never thought of being a teacher, despite her mother thinking it would be a good career for her, and then suddenly making the decision to teach. The freedom to choose is very important to Anne – 'it is the most important thing actually I think'. The YA allowed her to experience freedom after years which, in retrospect, looked like following a conventional path that she had not truly chosen. In contrast, returning to regular undergraduate studies felt like having her freedom taken away. At the same time, the YA brought her final year of studies to life, and provided a context of memories and associations so that learning ceased to be narrowly theoretical and encouraged integration between different areas of her studies. When she left her French school, she was given a leather bound copy of works by Albert Camus and a watch that commemorated the bi-centenary of the French Revolution. These gifts represent her integration of the experience of living in another culture and the person she is. She stills agrees with a statement she made 10 years ago: 'I'm not going to wish this year away. I'm not going to wish my life away.'

Evaluating the Year Abroad

These two accounts could be complemented by others each with their own unique understanding of the experience, and each with a different degree and kind of relationship between present life and the YA. They demonstrate the long-term impact of the YA. In some cases, as with Jane, it seems to be in her words a 'negative' experience and one which she draws on only by contrast with her present life. In the case of Anne, there is an almost unbroken line between the YA and present life; only a brief diversion into the retail trade created a temporary break. Others talked of the intercultural competence they had acquired through the YA and which they call upon in their lives, as teachers, as personnel managers and in similar occupations.

The question of evaluation of the YA cannot be reported in quantitative terms and we cannot generalise from a sample which is not random, but the evidence can be accumulated through this kind of study. When the purpose of university education is under debate (Arthur & Bohlin, 2005) this kind of study shows how the YA is significant in personal development and also in professional competence. Whether as language teachers, which several students became, or as workers in a globalised economy co-operating with people from other countries, which was the choice of some others, there is evidence here that the YA provided an opportunity for acquiring learning experience not otherwise available in universities.

Research Design and Methods

The first study had arisen from previous research on the teaching of cultural knowledge and understanding in foreign language teaching in secondary schools (Byram *et al.*, 1991). It was argued that the main opportunity for language teachers in Britain to gain a knowledge and understanding of one of the countries where their language is spoken is through the YA. We were therefore interested in whether students' perceptions, understanding of and attitudes towards France and French people and culture changed during their period of residence.

Participants

Participants in the first study were found by inviting students in the French departments of two universities to volunteer for the project. The initial contacts were made through the university tutors responsible for the organisation of the YA in each department. In this way we found 30 volunteers. In the first study we also had a group of students from France who were spending their YA in the North East of England, the region where we work. In this case, we made contact through the inspectors/advisers responsible for language teaching in the local education authorities in the region. However, we did not try to contact this group again 10 years later both because it would have been very difficult and because our research funding would not have allowed travel to France to interview them. Contact with the English group was made seven and then 10 years later through the addresses we and their university French department still had. This meant in fact that letters were often forwarded to them through their parents, whose addresses they had given when they left university. As explained earlier, our second group consisted of 12 people from the original 30, an 'opportunity sample' for which we claim no generalisability.

Research instruments

In the first study, the main source of data was to be semi-structured interviews. However in order to ensure that that part of the interview which dealt with their perceptions or representations of France was derived from participants' perspectives rather than interviewers', a version of Kelly's (1955) Repertory Grid was developed. Prior to their period of residence, participants were asked to use the technique to develop an analysis of their perceptions of a number of nationalities, including the one they would experience. After the YA they completed the grid a second time to provide comparative data. Furthermore the technique was used to elicit participants' concepts representing their learning experiences during the year, and this formed the basis of a further interview to explore their types of experience and the nature of their learning.

The semi-structured interviews before and after the year had other purposes too. Participants were asked before the YA about their previous and current language learning experience, about their current perceptions of a range of issues concerning France and French people, and about their expectations of the YA. After the YA, they were asked about their work as assistants, about their perceptions of the same aspects of France and French people as before the YA, and about their experiences in addition to their work as assistants.

The second study had a different focus, as was explained earlier, and the approach taken to the interviews was also different. The use of semi-structured interviews in the previous study was extended by drawing on narrative theory (Polkinghorne, 1995; Thomas, 1995) and giving emphasis to the narrative character of interview data. In-depth interviews having two phases were carried out:

> Narrative generation. The interview began with an open 'generative narrative question' (Flick, 1998), inviting interviewees to tell the story of their lives around the focus of the YA, followed by more specific questions to further explore and clarify aspects of the narrative. This was followed by a 'balancing' phase of questioning to yield statements of the overall significance of the YA. A digest of the interviewee's interview from the previous research was used by the interviewer to prompt questions.

> Thematic phase. Interviewees were asked for their perceptions of the YA as an educational experience, and their learning from it, in terms of personal development, careers and ways of life. Following Chase (1995), the questions were adapted in the light of the narrative quality of the interview.

Steps were taken to ensure that consent to be interviewed was informed. A protocol stating the purpose and aims of the research was given to each interviewee, to sign to confirm consent. The protocol assured anonymity, contained the option to terminate the interview at any point, entitlement to exclude from the transcript anything the interviewee did not wish to be seen by others, and an undertaking to provide a copy of the final report if requested. Interviewees were sent a copy of the interview transcript for factual correction. This arrangement was consistent with our institutional guidelines. Three interviewees returned their transcript with corrections, and in one case, additional comment was given.

One of the issues which arose in this process was the use of interview transcripts from 10 years earlier. Some participants were surprised to know that we still had these and there was a risk of embarrassment if we gave the impression that we were 'challenging' them with their views from before, which they might no longer hold or have in any case forgotten. This technique had to be used sensitively. A second issue for some participants was that agreeing to be interviewed brought back memories which were not always pleasant, and in at least one case sent the participant to re-read her diary from 10 years previously. There is no doubt that being involved in research has consequences which are not often discussed in the literature on research methods (Byram, 1996).

Analysis

The analysis followed the two phases of the interview strategy, narrative and thematic:

Narrative analysis: following Polkinghorne (1995), data were analysed to provide descriptions of events, happenings and actions associated with the YA. This gave emphasis to an individual's social actions, and their meaning and significance.

Thematic analysis (Strauss, 1987) was combined with individual narratives to identify common themes and differences in the experiences and meanings associated with the YA. The set of research questions provided a framework for analysis.

The analysis was a collaborative undertaking by the two researchers. For each interview, data were coded using the research questions as codes. The questions overlap, and data segments were multiply coded where appropriate.

The results were initially organised in terms of the original objectives and research questions, the narrative and thematic phases of the interviews becoming parallel strands of analysed data. The stories presented in the first part of this article are a further and final stage of data presentation and interpretation.

The initial organisation according to the research objectives can be illustrated by extracts from our research report:

Objective 1: *to compare former students' perceptions of residence abroad immediately after the sojourn and ten years later.*

Narrative Accounts: two examples.

These accounts are written largely using the language and constructs employed by the interviewees, to reveal their 'narrative cognitions' and to capture the choices, actions, meanings and understandings that constitute narrative (Polkinghorne, 1995).

Lynn

Immediately after Lynn's YA, the picture that emerged is of an assistantship that went well, approximating an ideal (Alred, 1998, 2000). She returned a fluent, confident French speaker, and displayed renewed commitment and enthusiasm for her studies, and had acquired a clearer sense of herself. Three contributing factors were central:

- the favourable circumstances of her placement
- close relationships that developed amongst a group of mixed nationality assistants with whom she lived, a powerful base of support and sharing which helped her take full advantage of living and working abroad
- being an effective teacher

[...]

Lynn now lives in Brussels. She is married to a Belgian and has recently become a mother. She has worked for an American law firm for 10 years as office manager, dealing with human resource issues. The working language is English, but Lynn uses French daily. On graduating, she took a further course in economics, politics and law at the French speaking University in Brussels. She then began working in her present post and has made Brussels her home. She attributes her decision to live and work abroad to the YA.

Her contemporary life and its links with her YA can be summarised as follows:

- Her work involves mediating between people from several nationalities.
- She is intercultural in her rich working environment and living in a European city.
- At this stage she is settled in a career and marriage, and work has become less important. She describes a feature of an intercultural marriage as finding a middle ground of interests and activities.
- She has become interested in Belgian politics and history. She is putting down roots and looks forward to her daughter being bilingual and bicultural.

- Being a mother is adding a new dimension to being intercultural, that of maintaining her Britishness.
- Her cultural identity is more complex than ten years ago. A desire to live abroad has transformed into a comfortable way of being herself abroad that includes her Britishness.

[...] She concludes that the YA set in train changes that are now major themes of her life, and has led to her intercultural situation and outlook. She is conscious of still learning and becoming more bilingual and bicultural.

Sarah

In the interview after the YA, Sarah said she faced difficulties that were not easily overcome and her verdict on the year was not entirely positive (Alred, 1998, 2000). She felt she was an outsider, both as an assistant and as a member of French society, and discovered 'being foreign makes everything twice as hard'.

Sarah lived with other assistants, but did not find in communal living adequate support to fully overcome her difficulties. The group tended to converse in English which emphasised Sarah's separateness from the surrounding culture. She used this to explain her disappointment in her linguistic progress.Although difficult, the teaching was largely successful and satisfying. Sarah became more independent, patient and resourceful.

[...]

She didn't feel much different in herself after the YA, but did gain confidence. However, she discovered something about her identity – 'I feel a lot more patriotic' and the conviction that she belongs in Britain – 'I think definitely it's made me realise that I'd rather live in Britain than anywhere else'. The YA reinforced her initial ethnic identity. Immersion in French society did not bring Sarah closer to French culture, or to an intercultural outlook.

Nonetheless, she was glad to have completed a YA abroad, and described it as both an 'ordeal' and a 'great accomplishment'. Main effects were greater linguistic competence, greater self-sufficiency, and a reinforced cultural identity

Ten years later, Sarah is a manager in a building society, having started as a graduate trainee. The job requires initiative, tact and good communication. Sarah is organised and prepares well, and has an eye for detail. She enjoys good relationships with close colleagues.

Her memory of the YA has faded but she has returned to a diary kept at the time in order to prepare for the interview. She didn't enjoy teaching, felt isolated and wished she had had more support in the school. She remembers difficulties with accommodation, finance and French bureaucracy. The YA was spoilt by the lack of support. The diary reminded her of the frustrations of teaching, but also the many enjoyable things she did, especially travelling, and also that she spoke more French than she remembers.

Living with two other assistants is remembered as pleasurable and supportive, but she again referred to talking in English and the brake this placed on learning French.

The YA did not meet Sarah's expectations, but she now thinks these were high. She was disappointed with the area of her placement. She thinks now that she could have made more effort to socialise but she 'got into a routine of avoiding the staff room because I found it a bit embarrassing to go in'.

[...]

A theme of Sarah's YA is not feeling integrated. After ten years she is reassessing the reasons for this, and sees the trip to Scotland as a turning point, during which relationships with French teachers became more reciprocal and enjoyable. It was helpful to see her own country through French people's eyes, and to experience the relativity of cultural perception, something that was difficult in the circumstances of her YA.

She links being organised to how she coped with teaching, and thinks that the YA helped her with the transition to employment. It also has helped to take things in her stride, but does not figure prominently in her life now. – 'my developments all come from being at work rather than all those years ago'. She wonders if time has softened her memory.

[...]

Lynn's views of her YA have not changed substantially whereas those of Sarah have. The impact for Lynn was great. The YA has shaped her identity and way of life. There are continuities between then and now, visible threads in her career and sense of self. In contrast, the long-term effects for Sarah are a combination of positive and negative influences, a contribution to personal and professional development and a turning away from an overtly intercultural way of life. The YA is stored in a diary, rather than alive in her present life. An important factor is Sarah's felt lack of support, suggesting missed opportunities for learning and a consequent reduction in the educational impact of her YA. Both became proficient French speakers, but beyond that the differences in long-term significance are marked.

Objective 2: *to explore former students' perceptions of the sojourn as an educational experience occupying one quarter of the duration of their degree course, and what in practical terms influenced the lasting outcomes of the sojourn*

The first part of this objective – perceptions of the sojourn as an educational experience – is addressed throughout the narratives and the thematic analysis. In relation to helpful and unhelpful factors, we conclude that an important general feature influencing lasting outcomes is the combination of support and challenge that the YA presented. Successful sojourns, and continuing positive effects, are associated with circumstances in which meeting the challenge of living and working abroad was accompanied by some supportive part(s) within the whole experience. Most commonly mentioned are living with other assistants, the friendliness and hospitality of teachers, and visits to and from home. There was a degree of chance in the balance between support and challenge that evolved and it was not always optimal.

Hence, we argue that educational responses must be seen in this light and attend to both, providing learning opportunities and also facilitating students' reflection on intercultural experience and its effects. The potential for profound learning, and for developing intercultural competence, lies in a combination of support and challenge. New teachers in Britain benefit from mentoring when starting their teaching career, and this can be seen as a formal counterpart to what for many assistants abroad is left to chance.

This conclusion was already evident ten years ago, in relation to cultural learning and successful integration abroad. It is reinforced by examples of career trajectories and ways of life revealed in this study.

Objective 3: *to assess the long term significance and meaning of residence abroad, in terms of attitudes and personal qualities, career patterns and ways of life, with reference to the concept of intercultural competence*

The concept of the 'intercultural mediator' encompasses an individual's potential for social action in intercultural situations, drawing upon intercultural and linguistic competencies. The methods used allowed interviewees to describe what they do and did rather than make explicit underlying competencies (Polkinghorne, 1995). Awareness of the precise nature of their competencies is limited and it develops further as a consequence of being asked to reflect on their YA and the years since.

A central result of the thematic analysis is that the YA is an experience which confirms and strengthens a process of 'tertiary socialisation' (Doyé, 1992) which began as early as the start of secondary socialisation and in parallel with this.

A second result is that the YA is a major factor influencing interviewees to become *mediators* in their subsequent life, drawing on the intercultural competence they have acquired through tertiary socialisation.

A further result is that where tertiary socialisation has not already begun, the YA can have a counter-effect of reinforcing secondary socialisation and identification with the society/ies and culture(s) of origin.

[...]

The clearest indications of the effects of tertiary socialisation, i.e. the acceptance and juxtaposition of conflicting cultural concepts and values are to be found when someone learnt another language and lived in a bilingual/ bicultural environment from an early age (e.g. Lynn had lived in Wales since the age of four; Elizabeth described her parents' foreign friends and colleagues whom she met as a child). Our view is that these two factors are complementary and that 'time abroad' is an opportunity for developing not just attitudes, *savoir être*, but also the social action of the mediator, *savoir faire*.

An intercultural mediator is someone who, drawing upon their savoirs of intercultural competence, is able to perceive the origins of conflicting perspectives and to use that knowledge to explain one in terms of the other and, where possible, resolve the conflict. The role of mediator does not necessarily follow from tertiary socialisation and acquisition of intercultural competence, but the latter is a necessary condition to be able to take the role.

Although tertiary socialisation can begin early and is dependent on travelling to and living in another country with another language, the

YA may be the first opportunity to experience being a mediator. Some interviewees reported this after the YA and again ten years later.

[...]

One question which is raised by this mode of reporting the analysis as opposed to the narratives we have given in the first part of this chapter is whether one is more effective than the other. Unlike some other chapters in this book where the research was conducted for a doctoral degree, our project had public funding and there were certain requirements as a consequence. The process can be described briefly as follows:

- An application for funding is made to a national research council using their application forms which require detailed plans for the conduct of the research as well as the justification and methodology; these plans have then to be costed – number of journeys, cost of transcription, cost of hardware needed.
- The application is read and given a grading by anonymous referees; in our case there were three; the funding body makes a decision with the help of a committee of academic experts, who agreed to support us despite or because of one referee calling our research 'arcane' as mentioned above.
- The research is carried out and a report submitted also using the forms of the funding body; any changes from the original plan have to be explained and justified, and an account of expenditure given.
- This report is sent to anonymous referees who check whether the research has been carried out as planned, judge the results produced and give a grade to the report, a grade which will be taken into consideration in any future applications.
- The report is made available to the public but only if requested; there is no attempt to 'publish' the report.

This means that the research is reported in a way which is not in fact focused on the findings or methodology but rather on the degree to which the original plans have been carried out successfully, although as is evident from the extract above, there is a summary of findings. Researchers need to make their work known through academic journals, as we did (Byram & Alred, 2002), but the main readership of such journals is other researchers and not the participants in the research or people like them. To reach students about to go abroad who might find the long-term effects interesting, the internet and a website is probably the best solution. This requires however time and resources which were not included in our original application, and are not easy to find otherwise. This is a lesson to learn, namely that this kind of research should always include a plan for dissemination which is not only to other researchers through the routine of journal publication.

Drawing Conclusions

The narratives created in the interviews are indeed narratives, but at the same time they are accounts elicited by the interviewers with a certain number of research questions in mind. In particular we were asking interviewees to recount experiences and events which might provide direct or indirect evidence, either in the events themselves or how they were presented, for intercultural competence. Similarly we were framing questions to provide opportunity for interviewees to provide evidence that their intercultural competence was related to, or developed through, their YA. These questions were sometimes direct, asking interviewees if they attributed any present competencies or inter- ests to the YA. As we have seen, neither they nor we can be entirely sure, but there is often strong evidence of the significance of the YA in their lives. For example.

> I think, having, you know, sort of been able to say that you have actually lived in a different country – I always think it when people tell me that they've, you know – I've lived abroad – you think, oh well, you know that, and you respect them, sort of thing – so you know I'm pleased with myself really, you know, glad that I've had that opportunity and, you know – yes, it's this life experience, isn't it, that you draw on. (Alice)

Similarly, others felt strongly about their identity and how they relate to otherness and, as part of the same process, to their own self and environ- ment. Where the experience was a difficult one, especially being an assist- ant, this leads to conscious rejection of it.

Those who enjoyed the YA tend to follow careers which allow them to be intercultural mediators, but those who did not, find themselves in careers and circumstances where being interculturally competent is not a frequent demand. However, when circumstances demand it, the YA becomes a reference point, a 'strong experience' to which they turn.

The relationship between the YA, prior intercultural learning experi- ence and subsequent seeking for a career with intercultural potential is complex. This research demonstrates that the YA can become a lens through which to consider later experience, a force which leads someone in an unexpected direction, and the experience which created an awareness of otherness and how one relates to it. In marked contrast, it can also confirm a sense of belonging 'at home', rather than among others and 'otherness'. In both cases, and neither need be evaluated as better or worse than the other, it is the demanding and consuming nature of the YA which makes it such a powerful reference point.

However, although neither the effect of opening to otherness and becoming a mediator, nor the effect of closing back into oneself need be judged, it is probably the hope of those concerned with the YA, administratively and educationally, that the former outcome will dominate in the long term.

Chapter 11
Assessing Intercultural Competence in Study Abroad Students

DARLA K. DEARDORFF

One meaningful outcome of internationalization efforts at post-secondary institutions is the development of interculturally-competent students. Intercultural competence can be developed in numerous ways, including through the curriculum, through meaningful intercultural interactions on campus, and through other opportunities such as service learning. One of the primary ways, though, that post-secondary institutions seek to develop students' intercultural competence is by sending and receiving students who reside for study abroad. As such, post-secondary institutions in the United States are beginning to engage in research on outcomes of students' study abroad experiences. Yet, few universities address the development of interculturally-competent students as an anticipated outcome of internationalization in which the concept of 'intercultural competence' is specifically defined. This lack of specificity in defining intercultural competence is due presumably to the difficulty of identifying the specific components of this complex concept. Even fewer institutions have designated methods for specifically documenting and measuring intercultural competence. As Terenzini and Upcraft (1996: 217) observed, 'while assessing the purported outcomes of our efforts with students is probably the most important assessment we do, it is seldom done, rarely done well, and when it is done, the results are seldom used effectively'. Key questions arise: How do institutions of higher education measure the effectiveness of their internationalization efforts? And specifically, how can these institutions know if they are graduating interculturally competent students? Even more importantly, what does it mean to be interculturally competent? Furthermore, what works and what does not in the way of assessment, particularly in regard to assessing students' intercultural competence?

This chapter details a doctoral research study that was conducted to examine some of these questions through the collection and analysis of data on the identification and assessment of intercultural competence as a student outcome of internationalization in higher education. As one scholar wrote, 'Competence can be measured. But its measurement depends first on its definition' (Klemp 1979, p. 41). Scholars throughout the past 30 years have defined intercultural competence in its various iterations but there has not been agreement on how intercultural competence should be defined (Baxter Magolda, 2000; Beebe *et al.*, 1999; Bennett, 1993; Bradford *et al.*, 2000; Byram, 1997; Cavusgil, 1993; Chen, 1987; Chen & Starosta, 1996, 1999; Collier, 1989; Dinges, 1983; Dinniman & Holzner, 1988; English, 1998; Fantini, 2000; Fennes & Hapgood, 1997; Finkelstein *et al.*, 1998; Gudykunst, 1994; Gundling, 2003; Hammer *et al.*, 1978; Hampden-Turner & Trompenaars, 2000; Hanvey, 1976; Hess, 1994; Hett, 1992; Hoopes, 1979; Hunter, 2004; Kealey, 2003; Kim, 1992; Koester & Olebe, 1989; Kohls, 1996; Kuada, 2004; La Brack, 1993; Lambert, 1994; Lustig & Koester, 2003; Miyahara, 1992; Paige, 1993; Pedersen, 1994; Pusch, 1994; Rosen *et al.*, 2000; Ruben, 1976; Samovar & Porter, 2001; Satterlee, 1999; Spitzberg, 1989; Spitzberg & Cupach, 1984; Stewart & Bennett, 1991; Storti, 1997; Tucker, 2001; Wiseman, 2001; Yum, 1994, Zhong, 1998).

One study observed that there is 'a need for a clearer definition of the concept of intercultural competence' (Kuada, 2004: 10). The director of Educational Testing Service's Center for Assessment of Educational Progress concurred, noting that 'once a definition (of global competence) has been agreed upon, experts will have to decide what the components of the definition are' so that they can then be measured (Lapointe, 1994: 275). This study documents consensus among top intercultural experts and university administrators on what constitutes intercultural competence and the best ways to measure it, and thus represents the first crucial step towards measurement.

Theoretical Framework

Assessment of student outcomes of internationalization can be placed within the theoretical programme logic model (Rogers, 2000) in which outcomes become one step beyond outputs, which are defined as the citing of numbers as indicators of successful internationalization efforts. In addressing specific outcomes of internationalization efforts, long-term impact can be more fully determined. Figure 11.1 presents the model as it relates to this study, with the shaded area being the focus of this research.

INTERNATIONALIZATION
at institutions of higher education

Inputs/Resources
needed for implementation of components of internationalization
(i.e. interested students, funding, institutional leadership and support)

|

Activities/Components of Internationalization
(college leadership, faculty international involvement, curriculum, study abroad, international
students/scholars/faculty, international co-curricular units) (Ellingboe, 1998)

|

Outputs of Internationalization
(i.e. number of international students, number of study abroad programmes, number of students studying foreign
languages, etc.)

|

Outcomes of Internationalization
(i.e. interculturally competent graduates) (Knight, 1997)
Intercultural competence – what is it?
How do higher education administrators define it? intercultural experts?
How can it be assessed?

= Long-Term Impact of Internationalization

Figure 11.1 General program logic model applied to internationalization
(Deardorff, 2004)

Overview of Method

This study used a combination of two research methods: a questionnaire completed by US institutional administrators of internationalization
strategies and a Delphi technique used to develop consensus by a panel of
nationally and internationally-known intercultural experts on a definition
and components of intercultural competence, as well as recommended
ways for assessing intercultural competence. As Linstone and Turoff
(1975) describe it, the Delphi method is a process for structuring anonymous communication within a larger group of individuals in an effort
to achieve consensus among group members. As in the case of this
study, the Delphi technique can be used when there is a need for identified experts who are not geographically close to arrive at consensus on
a particular issue; the structured nature of the process allows all
members to contribute equally without dominance by a few.

A total of 73 US postsecondary institutions initially received invitations
through NAFSA: Association of International Educators and the American Council on Education (ACE) to participate in the first phase of this
study. These institutions were identified as those that were strongly committed to internationalization given either their participation in ACE's

Internationalization Collaborative or through their national recognition by NAFSA as being an internationalized institution. Twenty-four of the 73 institutions (33%) chose to participate representing a wide variety of institutions across the United States, from community colleges to large research universities. Table 11.1 shows a profile of the 24 institutions that participated, 54% of which were public and the other 46% private.

The 11-item questionnaire, completed by mid and senior level post-secondary administrators, included both closed and open-ended questions about how that institution addressed intercultural competence as a student outcome. Data from the informational questionnaires were analyzed using descriptive statistics for overall trends and patterns so as to give a 'snapshot' of what is currently being done in defining and assessing intercultural competence as an outcome of internationalization efforts at institutions of higher education in the United States.

The questionnaire also asked administrators to identify nationally/internationally known intercultural experts from the intercultural field for participation in the Delphi study. This was one method used to generate names of top intercultural experts who were later invited to participate in the second phase of the study. Names of top intercultural experts were also generated through recommendations of other experts, an extensive literature review, and from those scholars included in the International Academy of Intercultural Research. From the names generated through these lists, a total of 37 experts received multiple nominations and were invited to participate in the Delphi study. Selection of participants for a Delphi study is crucial to the overall validity of the study (Dalkey *et al.*, 1972), which is why a variety of means were used to generate the list of experts invited to participate as members of the

Table 11.1 Institutional size: Number of undergraduate students at institutions participating in study

Range of undergraduate students	Number of institutions	% of institutions in study
Under 1000	3	13%
1000–4999	8	33%
5000–9999	5	21%
10,000–14,999	2	8%
15,000–19,999	2	8%
20,000 +	4	17%

Delphi panel. Twenty-three intercultural experts (62%) accepted the invitation and participated in a three-round Delphi study.

Results and Discussion

Based on the data collected and analyzed in ways which will be described in the second part of this chapter, the following responses to research questions emerged:

Question 1

What is intercultural competence according to administrators at US institutions of higher education committed to internationalization?

There were a variety of opinions and definitions among administrators as to what constitutes intercultural competence. Most preferred a more general definition of the construct as opposed to specific, delineated components as to exactly what constitutes intercultural knowledge, for example. The reason most often cited for a more general definition of intercultural competence is that administrators need an institutional definition that works with all students in all situations, regardless of their majors.

Nine definitions of intercultural competence, culled from intercultural literature, were provided to administrators who participated in this study. The definition deemed most applicable to institutions' internationalization strategies was one derived from Byram's (1997) work on intercultural competence. It received an average rating of 3.5 out of 4.0 and was summarized as follows: 'Knowledge of others; knowledge of self; skills to interpret and relate; skills to discover and/or to interact; valuing others' values, beliefs, and behaviors; and relativizing one's self. Linguistic competence plays a key role' (Byram, 1997). The second highest-rated definition received an average rating of 3.3 and can be summarized as follows: 'Five components: World knowledge, foreign language proficiency, cultural empathy, approval of foreign people and cultures, ability to practice one's profession in an international setting' (Lambert, 1994). Table 11.2 provides a summary of administrators' ratings of the nine definitions of intercultural competence presented to them in the survey.

In addition, one of the survey questions provided the opportunity for administrators to write other definitions of intercultural competence currently being used at their institutions. Several schools had developed institutional definitions of intercultural competence that were general in

Table 11.2 Administrators' ratings of existing definitions of intercultural competence

Mean	SD	ICC definition
3.5	(0.7)	Knowledge of others; knowledge of self; skills to interpret and relate; skills to discover and/or to interact; valuing others' values, beliefs, and behaviors; and relativizing one's self. Linguistic competence plays a key role (Byram, 1997)
3.3	(0.8)	Five components: World knowledge, foreign language proficiency, cultural empathy, approval of foreign people and cultures, ability to practice one's profession in an international setting (Lambert, 1994)
3.0	(0.7)	One's adaptive capacity to suspend/modify old cultural ways, learn/accommodate to new cultural ways, and creatively manage dynamics of cultural difference/ unfamiliarity and accompanying stress (Kim, 1992)
3.0	(0.9)	Five key competencies: Mindfulness, cognitive flexibility, tolerance for ambiguity, behavioral flexibility, cross-cultural empathy (Gudykunst, 1994; Pusch, 1994)
2.9	(0.9)	Eight components: Display of respect, orientation to knowledge, empathy, interaction management, task role behavior, relational role behavior, tolerance for ambiguity, and interaction posture (Koester & Olebe, 2003)
2.9	(0.6)	Ability to effectively and appropriately execute communication behaviors in a culturally diverse environment (Chen & Starosta, 1996). Includes intercultural sensitivity (affective process), intercultural awareness (cognitive process), and verbal/nonverbal skills (Fantini, 2000). May include motivation dimension (Wiseman, 2001)
2.8	(0.7)	Comprised of six factors: Knowledge of target culture, one's personal qualities, behavioral skills, self-awareness, technical skills, and situational factors (Paige, 1993)
2.7	(0.8)	The expandability, flexibility, and adaptability of one's frame of reference/filter (Fennes & Hapgood, 1997)
2.2	(0.9)	Not comprised of individual traits or characteristics but rather the characteristic of the association between individuals. Dependent on the relationships and situations within which the interaction occurs. No prescriptive set of characteristics guarantees competence in all intercultural situations (Lustig & Koester, 2003)

Note: Ratings were based on a 4-point Likert-type scale with 4.0 being most applicable to the institution's internationalization strategies.

nature and contained several common elements. The top three common elements were the awareness, valuing and understanding of cultural differences, experiencing other cultures, and self-awareness of one's own culture.

Question 2

What is intercultural competence according to intercultural experts?

There was an even greater breadth of definitions among intercultural experts than among the administrators, with a wide variety of definitions put forward. Based on the data generated from intercultural experts through the Delphi study, the top-rated definition was one in which intercultural competence was defined as 'the ability to communicate effectively and appropriately in intercultural situations based on one's intercultural knowledge, skills, and attitudes'. There were numerous other statements developed by the experts regarding intercultural competence which received 80% or higher agreement including the ability to shift one's frame of reference appropriately, the ability to achieve one's goals to some degree and behaving appropriately and effectively in intercultural situations. These are summarized in Table 11.3. The definitions seemed to focus primarily on individuals' communication and behavior in intercultural situations.

Of the specific components of intercultural competence noted, many of them addressed an individual's personal attributes such as curiosity, general openness, and respect for other cultures. Other delineated components involved cultural awareness, various adaptive traits, and cultural knowledge – both culture-specific knowledge as well as deep cultural knowledge, often defined as the underlying, out-of-awareness elements of culture, such as attitudes, values, and beliefs, and the system of decision-making which manifests through individuals' behaviors (Paige *et al.*, 2002).

One surprising result of this study was the specific skills that emerged through consensus which included skills to analyze, interpret, and relate as well as skills to listen and observe. Cognitive skills emerged including comparative thinking skills and cognitive flexibility. These skills point to the importance of *process* in acquiring intercultural competence and the attention that needs to be paid to developing these critical skills. This finding confirms the writing of Yershova *et al.* (2000) in which they argue that the intercultural perspective along with intellectual competencies is integral to developing intercultural competence.

Table 11.3 Intercultural competence definitions with 80%–100% agreement among top intercultural experts

				Intercultural competence (ICC) is:
ACC.	*REJ.*	*Mean*	*SD*	*Item*
19	1	3.8	(0.5)	Ability to communicate effectively and appropriately in intercultural situations based on one's intercultural knowledge, skills, and attitudes.
19	1	3.6	(0.8)	Ability to shift frame of reference appropriately and adapt behavior to cultural context; adaptability, expandability, and flexibility of one's frame of reference/filter.
19	1	3.4	(0.7)	Ability to identify behaviors guided by culture and engage in new behaviors in other cultures even when behaviors are unfamiliar given a person's own socialization.
18	2	3.4	(1.0)	Behaving appropriately and effectively in intercultural situations based on one's knowledge, skills, and motivation.
17	3	3.4	(0.8)	Ability to achieve one's goals to some degree through constructive interaction in an intercultural context.
16	4	3.6	(0.6)	Good interpersonal skills exercised interculturally; the sending and receiving of messages that are accurate and appropriate.
16	4	3.1	(1.0)	Transformational process toward enlightened global citizenship that involves intercultural adroitness (behavioral aspect focusing on communication skills), intercultural awareness (cognitive aspect of understanding cultural differences), and intercultural sensitivity (focus on positive emotion towards cultural difference).

Question 3

What are the best ways to assess students' intercultural competence according to administrators at institutions of higher education committed to internationalization?

All institutions in this study agreed that it is important to assess students' intercultural competence. Thirty-eight percent already assess students' intercultural competence, and there was surprising consistency among methods used. Top assessment methods currently being used include student interviews (used by eight out of nine institutions), followed by student papers/presentations, student portfolios, observation of students by others/host culture, professor evaluations (in courses), and pre/post tests (see Figure 11.2). It is important to note that these institutions used a variety of methods to assess students' intercultural competence, with an average of five different assessment methods used per institution.

The results of the administrators' participation in the last round of the Delphi study indicated that administrators achieved 100% agreement on four specific assessment methods: Observation by others/host culture, case studies, judgment by self and others, and student interviews. Administrators were nearly unanimous (95%) in using a mix of qualitative and quantitative measures to assess students' intercultural competence. The following assessment methods also received 95% acceptance

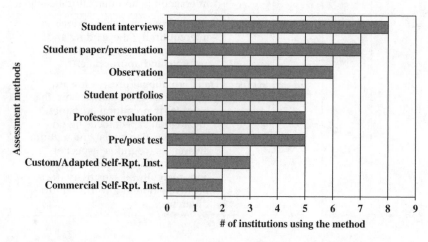

Figure 11.2 Intercultural competence assessment methods used by institutions

among administrators: analysis of narrative diaries, self-report instruments, other-report instruments, triangulation (multiple methods), and a bottom-up approach involving such techniques as focus groups, dialogues, and workshops.

Question 4

What are the best ways to assess intercultural competence according to intercultural experts?

According to the intercultural experts, the best way to assess intercultural competence is through a mix of qualitative and quantitative measures (rated 3.7 out of 4.0). Specifically, case studies and interviews received the strongest agreement (90%) followed by analysis of narrative diaries, self-report instruments, observation by others/host culture, and judgment by self and others (all at 85% agreement). Table 11.4 contains further details.

Question 5

Do higher education administrators agree with intercultural experts in regard to the identification and assessment of intercultural competence?

Generally, intercultural experts and higher education administrators agreed on the definitions, components and assessment methods for intercultural competence that emerged through this study. However, administrators accepted a larger percentage of the items pertaining to the definition and assessment of intercultural competence areas, with the experts rejecting 19 items that were accepted by the administrators, based on a 70% acceptance rate by both groups. Those items upon which there was disagreement between administrators and experts included the following components of intercultural competence: accomplished language and cultural learner, gaining trust and confidence of others, comparative thinking skills, operating within the rules of the host culture, and cross-cultural scholarship.

Assessment methods rejected by experts but accepted by administrators included quantitative measurements, pre-post tests, other-report measures, and critical incidents and essays. In fact, it is important to note that only 65% of the experts felt that pre/post testing should be used as a way to assess intercultural competence, while administrators (90%) overwhelmingly agreed on the use of pre/post tests.

Both administrators and experts rejected seven items including statements about placing the concept within a theoretical frame, measuring intercultural competence holistically as well as within a specific situation

Table 11.4 Assessment items with 80%–100% agreement among top intercultural experts

				Ways to assess intercultural competence include:
ACC.	*REJ.*	*Mean*	*SD*	*Item*
18	2	3.2	(0.9)	Case studies
18	2	2.9	(1.0)	Interviews
17	3	3.7	(0.8)	Mix of quantitative and qualitative measures
17	3	3.4	(0.7)	Qualitative measures
17	3	3.2	(0.9)	Analysis of narrative diaries
17	3	3.2	(0.9)	Self-report instruments
17	3	3.2	(0.9)	Observation by others/host culture
17	3	3.1	(1.0)	Judgment by self and others
16	4	3.1	(1.1)	Developing specific indicators for each component/dimension of ICC and evidence of each indicator
16	4	3.0	(1.2)	Triangulation (use of multiple data-collection efforts as corroborative evidence for validity of qualitative research findings)
				Issues raised by experts in assessing intercultural competence include:
ACC.	REJ.	Mean	SD	Item
19	1	3.6	(0.5)	ICC assessment involves more than just observable performance.
19	1	3.4	(0.6)	It is important to consider the cultural and social implications of assessing ICC.
17	3	3.6	(0.6)	It is important to determine who measures ICC, who is the locus of evaluation, in what context, for what purpose, to what benefit, the time frame involved, the level of cooperation, and the level of abstraction.
16	4	3.2	(0.9)	It is important to measure the degrees of ICC.
16	4	3.1	(0.7)	When assessing ICC, it is important to analyze the impact of situational, social, and historical contexts involved.

or context, and avoiding the use of standardized competency instruments. Both groups agreed that assessment of intercultural competence involves more than observable performance, that it is important to measure the degrees of competence, and that it is important to consider the cultural and social implications when assessing intercultural competence.

While 65% of both the administrators and intercultural experts accepted the statement 'Measuring intercultural competence is specific to context, situation, and relation' (65% was defined as not constituting consensus), there was general agreement on the importance of analyzing the situational, social, and historical contexts when assessing intercultural competence.

Conclusions

Defining and modeling intercultural competence

Intercultural experts and higher education administrators did not define intercultural competence in relation to specific components (i.e. what specifically constitutes intercultural knowledge, skills, and attitudes). Instead, both groups preferred definitions that were broader in nature. While this may be a surprising conclusion, this is actually in keeping with the literature in that most definitions are more general. However, it is important to note that a key criticism of existing definitions is that they are either too general or provide a disjointed list of attributes. This criticism may be responsible, in part, for the lack of specificity on the part of the intercultural experts.

One of the key motivations for initiating this research was the assumption that specific components of intercultural competence needed to be delineated for institutions to assess students' intercultural competence. The findings actually run contrary to this initial assumption. Since both administrators and intercultural experts preferred more general conceptions of intercultural competence, it appears that further research is needed on the development of this definition. In reviewing the specific components developed by the experts in this study, it can be concluded that even these components are more general in nature (e.g. culture-specific knowledge, flexibility).

Based on the literature review and the findings, what can be concluded about intercultural competence? It is important to note that 80% or more of the intercultural experts and administrators were able to reach consensus on essential elements of intercultural competence. Those key elements primarily involved communication and behavior in intercultural contexts.

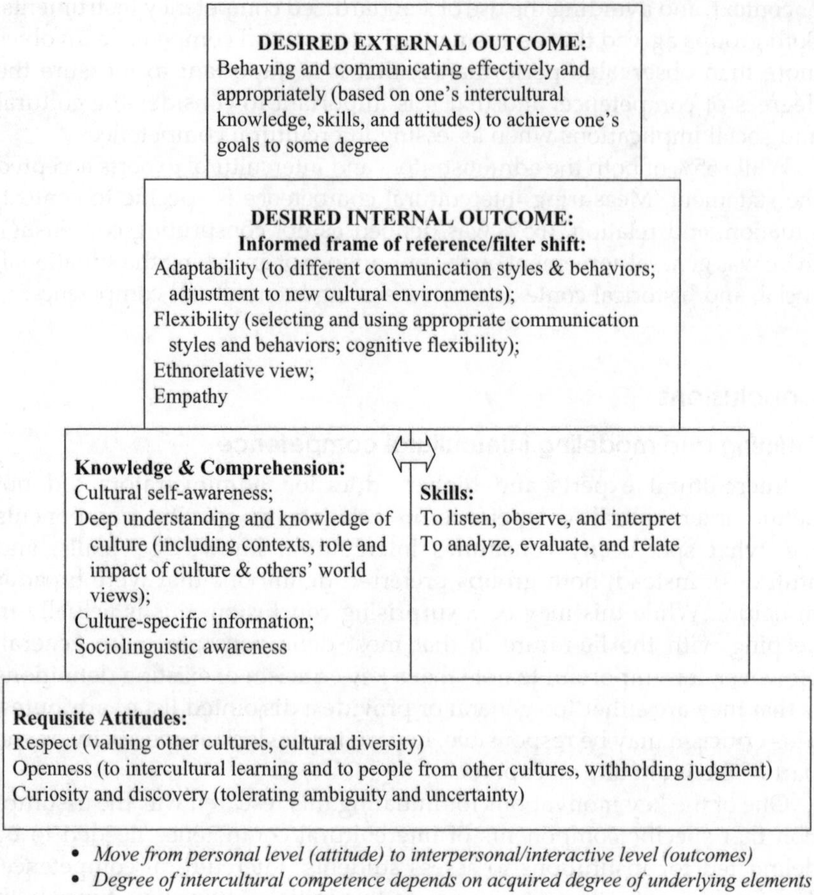

DESIRED EXTERNAL OUTCOME:
Behaving and communicating effectively and
appropriately (based on one's intercultural
knowledge, skills, and attitudes) to achieve one's
goals to some degree

DESIRED INTERNAL OUTCOME:
Informed frame of reference/filter shift:
Adaptability (to different communication styles & behaviors;
    adjustment to new cultural environments);
Flexibility (selecting and using appropriate communication
    styles and behaviors; cognitive flexibility);
Ethnorelative view;
Empathy

Knowledge & Comprehension:
Cultural self-awareness;
Deep understanding and knowledge of
    culture (including contexts, role and
    impact of culture & others' world
    views);
Culture-specific information;
Sociolinguistic awareness

Skills:
To listen, observe, and interpret
To analyze, evaluate, and relate

Requisite Attitudes:
Respect (valuing other cultures, cultural diversity)
Openness (to intercultural learning and to people from other cultures, withholding judgment)
Curiosity and discovery (tolerating ambiguity and uncertainty)

- *Move from personal level (attitude) to interpersonal/interactive level (outcomes)*
- *Degree of intercultural competence depends on acquired degree of underlying elements*

Figure 11.3 Pyramid model of intercultural competence (Deardorff, 2004)

The representation (Figure 11.3) of intercultural competence places
components of intercultural competence within a visual framework that
can be entered from various levels. However, having components of the
lower levels enhances upper levels. Process orientation throughout is
key – this means being aware of the learning that takes place at each
level and the necessary process skills that are needed for acquisition of
intercultural competence.

Though individuals can enter these frameworks at any particular
point, attitude is a fundamental starting point (Byram, 1997) as

illustrated in this visual representation. It has been referred to as the affective filter in other models (Krashen, 1982, as cited in Hadley, 2001). The model in Figure 11.3 concurs with these scholars in emphasizing the importance of attitude to the learning that follows. Specifically, the attitudes of openness, respect (valuing all cultures), and curiosity and discovery (tolerating ambiguity) are viewed as fundamental to intercultural competence.

This pyramid model of intercultural competence (Figure 11.3) allows for degrees of competence (the more components acquired/developed increases probability of greater degree of intercultural competence as an external outcome), and while it provides some delineation of the definition, it is not limited to those components included in the model. This model enables the development of specific assessment indicators within a context/situation while also providing a basis for general assessment of intercultural competence, thus embracing both general and specific definitions of intercultural competence. This model of intercultural competence moves from the individual level of attitudes/personal attributes to the interactive cultural level in regard to the outcomes. The specific skills delineated in this model are skills for acquiring and processing knowledge about other cultures as well as one's own culture. The model also emphasizes the importance of attitude and the comprehension of knowledge (Bloom, 1965).

A unique element of this pyramid model of intercultural competence is its emphasis on the internal as well as external outcomes of intercultural competence. The internal outcome which involves an internal shift in frame of reference, while not requisite, enhances the external (observable) outcome of intercultural competence. The external outcome can be described as essentially 'Behaving and communicating appropriately and effectively in intercultural situations.' Definitions of *effective* and *appropriate* are taken from Spitzberg's work (1989) where appropriateness is the avoidance of violating valued rules and effectiveness is the achievement of valued objectives.

It is interesting to compare this pyramid model of intercultural competence to the four developmental stages developed by the American Council on International Intercultural Education (1996). The four developmental stages of the global competence development process were listed as follows: (1) Recognition of global systems and their interconnectedness (including openness to other cultures, values, attitudes), (2) intercultural skills and experiences, (3) general knowledge of history and world events, and (4) detailed areas studies specialization (i.e. language). The administrators who developed these stages recognized that the first stage was most important to all global learners. The first stage stressed the importance of openness which is the same starting point as the visual model presented in this chapter. Intercultural skills and general knowledge are also noted in the developmental stages which are accounted for in this model.

The definition of intercultural competence continues to evolve, which is perhaps one reason why this construct has been so difficult to define. The panel experts' opinions and definitions have changed over the years so what was written 10–15 years ago may not be considered valid anymore by the author and in fact, several panelists expressed this explicitly to the researcher. Definitions and assessment methods need to be re-assessed on an on-going basis. Just as culture is ever-changing, scholars' opinions on intercultural competence change over time. It is important for research and practice to stay current with scholars' research and thought processes on this construct.

Measuring intercultural competence

Based on the overall consensus of both the experts and administrators, it can be concluded that intercultural competence can indeed be measured. Furthermore, it is important to measure degrees (levels) of intercultural competence (as discussed in Pottinger, 1979). Given the findings of this study, it is best to use multiple assessment methods and not just one method such as an inventory. In fact, it is important to note that an inventory alone is not a sufficient measurement of intercultural competence according to our results. Recommended assessment methods are primarily qualitative in nature including the use of interviews, observation, and case studies as well as the possible use of standardized competency instruments. Quantitative methods of measurement are somewhat controversial with administrators and intercultural experts, despite administrators' overwhelming preference for pre/post testing, and there is much stronger agreement between both groups on the use of qualitative measures. Both groups agree that intercultural competence can be measured in its separate components and not holistically, as some of the literature had indicated.

In measuring intercultural competence, it is important first to determine who is engaged in the actual measurement (including identifying their cultural biases), who is the locus of evaluation, in what context, for what purpose, to what benefit, the time frame involved (e.g. ongoing assessment), the level of cooperation, and the level of abstraction. Furthermore, it is important to determine how the assessment will be used and how measurement methods will account for multiple competencies and multiple cultural identities within individuals. It is vital for the assessment method to match the definition devised for intercultural competence (i.e. more specific methods for more specific definitions and more general methods for more general definitions). This leads to the importance of developing indicators (perhaps in specific contexts) and delineated objectives and criteria for measurement if definitions and assessment methods are more specific. An assessment guide for intercultural competence has been developed based on the results of this study and can be obtained from the researcher.

Research Methodology

This study involved a multiple method, descriptive research approach that was primarily exploratory in nature. The research methods used were a questionnaire and a Delphi study and these were selected based on the focus of this study. The 11-item questionnaire, completed by university administrators, was designed to find out what is currently known and done in assessing intercultural competence as a student outcome of internationalization. The second method involved the use of experts in a Delphi study in which nationally-known experts in the intercultural field served as consultants to determine the specific nature of intercultural competence through consensus. Respondents from both methods participated in the final round of questions in which they were asked to accept or reject the data that emerged through the earlier rounds of questions in the Delphi study. In this section we will report on the use of the Delphi study in particular.

Delphi study

The Delphi method was selected for this study since a geographically-diverse group of experts in the intercultural field was to reach consensus on what specifically constitutes intercultural competence. The Delphi method was developed in 1953 by Dalkey and Helmer for use by the military in forecasting bombing targets. The method was later used by government, industry, and eventually by academia in a variety of other ways including forecasting trends, decision-making, and consensus-building (Linstone & Turoff, 1975). The method slowly gained popularity so that by the 1990s, the method had grown immensely in use, with the corporate world seeing its value in predicting trends. Educational uses of the Delphi method include curriculum design, campus planning, and policy development. As Linstone and Turoff (1975) describe it, the Delphi method is a process for structuring anonymous communication within a larger group of individuals in an effort to achieve consensus among group members. It can be used when there is a need for identified experts who are not geographically close to arrive at consensus on a particular issue and the structured nature of the process allows all members to contribute equally without dominance by a few. Other advantages of using a Delphi process include the logical process in which participants reflect on a selected topic, the written format of responses, and the use of descriptive statistics to analyze group responses (Oakley, 2001).

The structured interactive process between researcher and respondents begins with the careful identification of the respondents, known as experts. The multi-stage interactive process consists of questions submitted to the panel of experts by the researcher (Linstone & Turoff, 1972). It usually takes at least three rounds of questioning for the experts to arrive at consensus, with the first round consisting of exploration of the subject under discussion, usually through a few open-ended questions which generate data. The data are then coded, categorized and utilized in the second round of closed-ended questions. The purpose of the second phase involves reaching an understanding of how the group views the issues, usually through the use of closed-ended questions to begin to generate feedback and consensus from the panel, with the respondents using a Likert-type-scale to respond to each question. This process is repeated for the third round at which time respondents may be asked to provide further feedback in any number of ways including specific feedback on their individual answers to the questions and in ranking the findings of Round 2. A fourth round of questions may be included in which participants provide final feedback on collected data, usually by being asked to accept or reject each of the items found as a result of the previous rounds of the study. These phases of the study are all designed to achieve consensus among the panelists with interest in the 'opinion of the group rather than in that of individuals' (Scheibe *et al.*, 1975: 277). Delphi scholars write that 'in most Delphis, consensus is assumed to have been achieved when a certain percentage of the votes fall within a prescribed range' (Scheibe *et al.*, 1975: 277). Similarly, the Merriam-Webster Collegiate Dictionary indicates consensus as 'the judgment arrived at by most of those concerned' (p. 279).

In regard to this Delphi study, the initial proposal called for four rounds with Round 1 consisting of two open-ended questions, Round 2 consisting of items from Round 1 that would be rated by the experts, Round 3 being the ranking of the items from Round 3 and Round 4 consisting of the accept/reject phase of the study. Based on experts' responses and feedback following Round 2 of this study, it was determined by the researcher that Round 3 involving the ranking of data would not yield any further consensus on the data and may, in fact, prove detrimental to the study if experts refused to engage in ranking the items. The literature supported using only three rounds of the Delphi process as noted by Linstone and Turoff (1975: 229): 'Most commonly, three rounds proved sufficient to attain stability in the responses; further rounds tended to show very little change and excessive repetition was unacceptable to participants.' In this case, four rounds would have been excessive and unacceptable to participants. Following completion of the second round of the Delphi, the researcher then moved directly to implementing the final round in which the Delphi panelists, as well as higher education administrators, simply rejected or accepted the items from Round 2 of the Delphi study.

Sample size

Delphi studies have been conducted with groups ranging from 10 to 30 experts or more. In an early study on the Delphi method, it was shown that reliability of group responses increases with group size (Dalkey *et al.*, 1972). However, reliability increases only slightly with groups of over 30 experts (Dalkey, 1969). Thus, it was proposed to use 20–30 experts in this study, depending on the results of the expert identification process. In the end, 37 experts were identified as potential participants in this Delphi study and invitations were issued to the 37 individuals via e-mail. Twenty-three (62%) accepted the initial invitation and submitted responses to Round 1 of the study. Five (14%) declined to participate and nine (24%) never responded to the invitation to participate, despite repeated follow-up via phone and e-mail.

Selection of participants of the Delphi study/expert qualifications

Selection of participants for a Delphi study is crucial to the overall validity of the study (Dalkey *et al.*, 1972). Intercultural experts for the Delphi study were identified through a variety of means. Qualitative means of expert identification consisted of a 'leadership identification approach' which was manifested in several ways:

(1) Practitioner Recommendation: The final item on the questionnaire distributed to higher education administrators asked administrators to list up to five nationally or internationally known experts in the intercultural field. This method generated 31 names that were compiled and ranked based on frequency count. Recommendations from those in the pilot study were also included. These recommendations from

administrators thus ensured that the experts included in the study were those considered to be experts by the practitioners in the field.

(2) Expert Recommendation: In addition to administrators' recommendations, nine experts, including four higher education administrators, were specifically contacted and asked for their recommendations as to possible participants in this Delphi study.

(3) The membership list for the International Academy of Intercultural Research (available through the Internet) was also consulted for names of intercultural experts.

Individuals whose names occurred multiple times from these lists were invited to participate in this Delphi study. Those whose names had the highest number of recommendations (11) were invited first and then progressed downward to those whose names were mentioned twice. This resulted in the issuance of 37 invitations via e-mail. The e-mail invitation included the following attachments: A one-page overview of the doctoral study and two letters of support, one from the Associate Executive Director of NAFSA: Association of International Educators and one letter of support from the Past-President of the Society for Intercultural, Training, and Research in the United States (SIETAR-USA). There was no compensation offered as an incentive to participate in this study.

There were phone and email follow-up to non-respondents to the initial invitation. It was hoped that 20–30 experts would emerge through this identification process. As noted previously, this number was to improve reliability of the study. Of the 37 invitations issued, 23 intercultural experts accepted the invitation to participate in the Delphi study. Since 23 fell within the ideal range of 20–30 experts, the process of identifying and selecting the panelists was complete. Two of the experts declined to participate beyond the first round, resulting in 21 experts (91%) who actually completed the Delphi study.

Biographies of these initial 23 individuals were acquired through the Internet or through publications in order to obtain more detailed information on the experts' backgrounds. The 23 experts included those with doctorates in a variety of disciplines including communication (9), political science, education (3), international relations, anthropology, political science, psychology, and business. All have written books and/or articles on intercultural topics. Several are active cross-cultural trainers and two have been involved directly in international education administration. One is currently a university president, as well as an expert on intercultural competence. Twenty-one were from the United States, one was in Canada, and one was in the United Kingdom. All are known nationally or internationally in the intercultural field. The participants remained anonymous to each other throughout the process so as to reduce respondent bias. Permission was sought from each participant to reveal his/her identity at the end of the study.

After this identification process was complete, further research uncovered an article written by William Hart (1999) that identified the most influential scholars and books in the interdisciplinary field of intercultural relations. With influence defined as the number of citations received in the International Journal of Intercultural Relations from 1983 to 1996, a list of 20 most cited authors was generated. Of the 20 names on the list, 12 (60%) names were ones that also appeared on the list of 37 experts who were invited to participate in this study. Seven of those 12 accepted the invitation to participate in the Delphi study, which constituted one-third of the Delphi participants. Two of the top three most influential authors in the intercultural field participated in this study. Among those on the top 20 list who gave permission to acknowledge their participation in this study are Triandis, Hammer, Spitzberg, Collier, and Kealey.

Instrumentation

All 23 participants had access to e-mail, allowing the study instruments to be administered via e-mail. In order to maintain the anonymity of respondents, e-mail communication was sent out individually each time to each expert. Participants were advised that all individual answers would remain confidential and would not be linked to individuals. Round 1 simply involved presenting two open-ended questions within the text of the e-mail. Round 2 and Round 3 instruments were sent as attachments to the e-mail. Panelists could reply by e-mail or could send their response via facsimile. Before panelists began their actual participation in the Delphi study, they were given instructions about the Delphi process including a statement that their participation in the study constituted their consent to participate fully in the Delphi study.

Monitoring team

When implementing the Delphi technique, it is recommended to use a monitoring team to help ensure the reliability of the data and to guard against researcher bias in the Delphi process. In this study, three higher education administrators with doctoral degrees agreed to be members of the monitoring team. The monitoring team agreed to review the data and instruments for each round of the Delphi process.

Procedure, data collection and analysis

The goal of the Delphi study was to gain consensus among the experts as to what it means to be interculturally competent as well as to gain consensus on some key ways to measure this competence. To that end, the second and third rounds in the Delphi study were in the form of closed-ended surveys derived from the data collected and analyzed from the previous rounds of the study. The questions in Rounds 2 and 3 were reviewed and tested with the monitoring team before distributing them to the experts electronically. The actual items in the second round consisted of statements and lists derived from the initial data collected, coded, and categorized. The monitoring team reviewed the raw data to make sure the items on the instrument were an accurate reflection of the data. Round 3 was a reiteration of the same data from Round 2. The data analysis used in the three rounds of this Delphi study were chosen based on analysis procedures used in previous Delphi studies and based on literature on Delphi methodology (Clark, 1997; Dalkey, 1969; Leibowitz, 2002; Linstone & Turoff, 1975). The study was conducted over a three-month period from December 2003 through February 2004. The first round, which required the most time and thought from panelists, took a little over one month to complete. Subsequent rounds took approximately two to three weeks to complete for each round, including response time, follow up, and data recording, monitoring, and analysis.

Round 1

Once the experts were secured for the Delphi study, the first round of open-ended questions was e-mailed to participants and consisted of the two key research questions in this study:

(1)   What constitutes intercultural competence?
(2)   What are the best ways to measure intercultural competence?

These two questions elicited a wide range of responses and generated a large quantity of qualitative data. The data from the first round of questions were coded and categorized based on emerging patterns; the coding process was similar to that previously described for coding data in the questionnaire. Given the large amount of data generated, the emerging patterns were placed in a matrix to aid in the analysis of the data. The monitoring team reviewed the raw data, codes, and subsequent categorization to ensure that the process had been done correctly by the researcher as well as to help reduce any researcher bias that may have contaminated the data analysis from Round 1.

Round 2

The data from Round 1 were coded and categorized into 98 items in four different sections on the Round 2 instrument. Sections 1 and 2 were responses to the first question of what constitutes intercultural competence. Section 3 was a list of specific ways to assess intercultural competence and Section 4 was comprised of issues raised by experts in the assessment of intercultural competence. Expert panelists were asked to rate each of the 98 items on a four-point Likert-type scale.

Experts were allowed to add items under each of the four sections. Experts were asked to submit their completed Round 2 instrument within one week. Follow-up was made by the researcher via e-mail and telephone. Of the 23 participants in Round 1, 18 participated in Round 2 (78%). Two of the remaining five did not submit completed responses and the other three expressed frustration with the Delphi process itself, with two of three stating their wish to no longer participate in the study.

Data from Round 2 were entered into an Excel spreadsheet. Descriptive statistics were used to analyze the data with means and standard deviations calculated for each item. Additional items were added by experts under section 1 only and those were coded for possible inclusion on the Round 3 instrument. However, since there was no overlap on the tems added, these additional items were not included in Round 3. Those items from the Round 2 instrument with a mean value of 2.5 or higher were retained for Round 3 (Clark & Wenig, 1999), resulting in the retention of 76 items for the Round 3 instrument. The mean value of 2.5 was established as the cut-off since it represented the neutral response on the four-point scale.

Round 3

Based on the statistical analysis of Round 2 responses, the questions for Round 3 were compiled, tested, and distributed in a similar manner as Round 2. In Round 3, respondents had the opportunity to accept or reject each of the items retained from Round 2 with the intended goal of gaining final approval from the panel to determine areas of consensus. The Round 3 instrument contained the mean and standard deviation for each of the 76 item so that the experts could see how consensus was evolving within the group and to allow each expert to see if their opinion agreed or disagreed with the majority of the group (Clark, 1997; Oakley, 2001). However, experts were encouraged not to let these statistics influence their final response. In addition, the final list of items was distributed to the administrators who completed the initial institutional questionnaire to determine whether they accepted or rejected the expert panel's collective opinions. This instrument was distributed to administrators without the means or standard deviations for each item so as not to influence their response. Again, all participants were asked to respond within one week. Follow up was made by phone and e-mail.

Twenty-one experts participated in the final round, with 20 usable responses. Similarly, all 24 of the institutional participants responded with 21 usable responses, resulting in 21 tallied responses from institutions on the last round.

Data from Round 3 were entered into an Excel spreadsheet and analyzed using two different methods, frequency distribution and Pearson's chi-squared test, in an effort to determine the prescribed range for group consensus. To determine the frequency distribution, frequencies were first tabulated for each item from each group. A summary of the frequencies per item per group was tabulated in respective bar charts. Through analysis of the bar charts, it was observed that the 80% agreement mark was the appropriate prescribed range for reaching consensus for both groups.

Pearson's chi-squared test was used to analyze the results of this final round as yet another way to determine the items on which consensus was obtained through a prescribed range established by the probability value calculated through Pearson's chi-squared test. One purpose of Pearson's chi-squared test is to compare expected frequencies to actual, obtained frequencies (Fraenkel & Wallen, 1993: 201). Pearson's chi-squared test was performed for each item to which panelists responded and again for each item to which the practitioners responded. Responses were placed in a contingency table for each item and a probability value was calculated for each against the null hypotheses of equal probability of response. Those items with a probability value of 0.05 or less were retained from Round 3. Those with a probability value of higher than 0.05 were discarded as items that did not have consensus.

The results of both the frequency distribution and Pearson's chi-squared test were used to compare responses of expert participants and practitioner participants, as well as to assess overall areas of consensus by both. A final listing of accepted items was established based on the results of this last round.

Given the purpose of this study, the Delphi method was an ideal method to achieve consensus among top intercultural experts and university administrators in diverse geographic locations. Technology, through the use of electronic mail, greatly aided in the timely completion of the data collection. On the other hand it is important to be aware of the limitations and criticisms of the Delphi technique, including the fact that it relies solely on the opinions of experts, albeit the results of the Delphi are a collective opinion that gives strength to the findings. Another limitation is in the very nature of the initial questions posed to the experts. The first question (What constitutes intercultural competence?) assumes that intercultural competence can be defined and delineated. The second question (What are the best ways to measure intercultural competence?) assumes that intercultural competence can be measured. These questions also contain cultural bias.

Furthermore, the Delphi study is subject to respondents' biases, including cultural bias from expert panelists. In this case, panelists in the group were primarily from Western cultures, which could lead to a distinctive Western bias in responses. There could have also been respondent biases regarding specific wording of statements or terminology used which led to responses that may have been different had specific words/terms not been used or had they been further defined. For example, Spitzberg noted in an article in 1989 that each expert has different concepts in mind for components such as empathy or flexibility and thus may 'imply consensus that does not exist' (Spitzberg, 1989: 245). Conversely, due to some of these study limitations, there should also be limited emphasis placed on items that were ultimately rejected.

Another limitation is the pressure to gain consensus in the Delphi study. This forced consensus is one of the main criticisms of the Delphi technique. Given the nature of the technique, it would be challenging for experts to arrive at consensus on more specific items, so the Delphi lends itself to more general results. Due to the nature of the data received, some terms were not defined so respondents may have had different conceptualizations of the terms used in the Delphi instruments or may have felt that the terminology was unclear. More specifically, the participation of well-known, published experts with well-formed opinions and experts' careful discernment in responses led to greater diversity in responses that inhibited the achievement of consensus on certain items.

The instruments used in the Delphi relied solely on the data collected from the participants. In addition, the quality of the Delphi data resides heavily with the experts and the time and thought they gave in responding. Since superficial response and analysis can be one weakness of a Delphi study, this could be one of the key limitations, depending on the time and thought given by the experts (Linstone & Turoff, 1975). There also exists the possible skewing of answers in the Delphi study given the particular wording of questions by the researcher or responses from experts that were not clear to other expert panelists. Several experts also noted that there were some items that contained more than one thought which made it difficult to rate those items and may have led to cognitive dissonance for some respondents.

Summary

This chapter summarizes the first research study to document consensus among top intercultural experts, as well as university administrators, on the definition and assessment methods of intercultural competence. It is hoped that this study's findings, along with the pyramid model of intercultural competence developed from the results of the study, will benefit university administrators in assessing student outcomes of internationalization, and specifically of study abroad experiences. All too often, programs cite outputs of study abroad programs (i.e. numbers of students residing abroad) as measures of success. While these numbers are important, it is equally important to assess the meaningful outcomes of sending students abroad. How do students benefit from study abroad? What are the measurable outcomes of their experiences? Through the assessment of students' intercultural competence, post-secondary institutions will be able to evaluate the effectiveness of programs which send and receive students who reside for study abroad.

References

Adelman, M.B. (1988) Cross-cultural adjustment: A theoretical perspective on social support. *International Journal of Intercultural Relations* 12, 183–205.

Adler, P. (1975) The transitional experience: An alternative view of culture shock. *Journal of Humanistic Psychology* 15 (4), 13–23.

Adler, P. (1977) Beyond cultural identity: Reflections upon culture and multicultural man. In R. Brislin (ed.) *Cultural Learning: Concepts, Applications, and Research* (pp. 24–41). Hawaii: East-West Center.

Adler, P.A. and Adler, P. (1987) *Membership Roles in Field Research*. Newbury Park, CA: Sage.

Adler, P.S. (1987) Culture shock and the cross-cultural learning experience. In L.F. Luce and E.C. Smith (eds) *Toward Internationalism*. Cambridge, MA: Newbury House.

Agar, M. (1980) *The Professional Stranger: An Informal Introduction to Ethnography*. New York: Academic Press.

Agar, M. (1994) *Language Shock. Understanding the Culture of Conversation*. New York: William Marrow and Co.

Agar, M. (1996) *The Professional Stranger*. San Diego, CA: Academic Press.

Allport, G.W. (1954) *The Nature of Prejudice*. Reading: Addison-Wesley.

Alptekin, C. (1983) Target language acquisition through acculturation: EFL learners in English-speaking environments. *Modern Language Review* 39 (4), 818–26.

Alred, G. (1998) Being abroad – Becoming a linguist: A discussion of the psychosocial effects of living abroad. *CRILE Working Papers: Research Issues in the Year Abroad*. Centre for Research in Language Education, Lancaster University.

Alred, G. (2000) L'année à l'étranger: une mise en question de l'identité. *Recherche et Formation Pour les Professions de l'Education: Mobilité Internationale et Formation – Dimensions Culturelles et Enjeux Professionnels* 33, 27–44.

Alred, G. and Byram, M. (1992) *Residence Abroad and the Cultural Perceptions of Foreign Language Students in Higher Education*. Report to the Economic and Social Research Council (mimeo).

Alred, G. and Byram, M. (2002) Becoming an intercultural mediator: A longitudinal study of residence abroad. *Journal of Multilingual and Multicultural Development* 23 (5), 339–52.

American Council on International Intercultural Education (ACIIE). (1996, November). *Educating for the Global Community: A Framework for Community Colleges*. Proceedings from conference convened at Airlie Center, Warrenton, VA. Retrieved August 21, 2003 from http://www.theglobalcommunitycollege.org/reports.html.

Amir, Y. (1969) Contact hypothesis in ethnic relations. *Psychological Bulletin* 71, 319–42.

Anderson, L.E. (1994) A new look at an old construct: Cross-cultural adaptation. *International Journal of Intercultural Relations* 18 (3), 293–328.

Appel, J. (2000) *Erfahrungswissen und Fremdsprachendidaktik*. München: Langenscheidt-Longman.

Arthur, J. and Bohlin, K.E. (eds) (2005) *Citizenship and Higher Education. The Role of Universities in Communities and Society*. London: RoutledgeFalmer.

Arthur, N. (2001) Using critical incidents to investigate cross-cultural transitions. *International Journal of Intercultural Relations* 25 (1), 41–53.

Atkinson, P. (1994) *The Ethnographic Imagination: Textual Constructions of Reality*. London: Routledge.

Babiker, I.E., Cox, J.L. and Miller, P.M.C. (1980) The measurement of culture distance and its relationship to medical consultation, symptomatology and examination performance of overseas students at Edinburgh University. *Social Psychiatry* 15, 109–16.

Bailey, K.M. and Ochsner, R. (1983) A methodological review of the diary studies: Windmill tilting or social science? In K.M. Bailey, M. Long and S. Peck (eds) *Second Language Acquisition Studies* (pp. 188–98). Rowley, MA: Newbury House.

Bailey, K.M. (1981) *Some Illustrations on Murphy's Law from Classroom Centred Research on Language Use*. Detroit: TESOL.

Barker, M., Child, C., Gallois, C., Jones, E. and Callen, V. (1991) Difficulties in overseas students in social and academic situations. *Australian Journal of Psychology* 43, 79–84.

Barnes, J.A. (1979) *Who Should Know What?* Harmondsworth: Penguin.

Barro, A., Jordan, S. and Roberts, C. (1998) Cultural practice in everyday life: The language learner as ethnographer. In M. Byram and M. Fleming (eds) *Language Learning in Intercultural Perspective: Approaches Through Drama and Ethnography* (pp. 76–97). Cambridge: Cambridge University Press.

Barth, F. (1994/1969) Introduction. In F. Barth (ed.) *Ethnic Groups and Boundaries*. Oslo: Pensumtjeneste/Universitetsforlaget.

Baxter Magolda, M.B. (ed.) (2000) *Teaching to Promote Intellectual and Personal Maturity: Incorporating Students' Worldviews and Identities into the Learning Process*. San Francisco: Jossey-Bass.

Beebe, S.A., Beebe, S.J. and Redmond, M.V. (1999) *Interpersonal Communication*. Boston: Allyn and Bacon.

Bennett, M. (1993) Towards ethnorelativism: a developmental model of intercultural sensitivity. In R.M. Paige (ed.) *Education for the Intercultural Experience* (pp. 21–71). Maine: Intercultural Press.

Bennett, M.J. (1986) A developmental approach to training for intercultural sensitivity. *International Journal of Intercultural Relations* 10, 179–96.

Bennett, J.M. (1993) Cultural marginality: Identity issues in intercultural training. In R.M. Paige (ed.) *Education for the Intercultural Experience*. Yarmouth, ME: Intercultural Press.

Benveniste, E. (1966) *Problèmes de Linguistique Générale*, 1. Paris: Gallimard.

Benzécri, J.-P. (ed.) (1981) *Pratique de l'Analyse des Données: Linguistique and Lexicologie*. Paris: Dunod.

Berger, P.L. and Luckmann, T. (1966) *The Social Construction of Reality*. Garden City, New York: Anchor Books.

Bernard, H.R. (1995) *Research Methods in Anthropology: Qualitative and Quantitative Approaches to Ethnographic Research* (2nd edn). Walnut Creek, CA: AltaMira.

Berry, J. (1980) Acculturation as varieties of adaptation. In A. Padilla (ed.) *Acculturation: Theory, Models and Some New Findings* (pp. 9–25). Washington, DC: AAAS.

Berry, J. (1990) Psychology of acculturation. In R. Brislin (ed.) *Applied Cross-cultural Psychology* (pp. 232–53). California: Sage Publications.

Berry, J.W., Kim, U., Minde, T. and Mok, D. (1987) Comparative studies of acculturative stress. *International Migration Review* 21, 491–511.

Berwick, R.F. and Whalley, T.R. (2000) The experiential bases of culture learning: A case study of Canadian high schoolers in Japan. *International Journal of Intercultural Relations* 24 (3), 325–40.

Block, D. (2000) Problematizing interview data: Voices in the mind's machine? *TESOL Quarterly* 34, 757–63.

Block, D. (2001) Foreign nationals on a PGCE modern languages course: Questions of national identity. *European Journal of Teacher Education* 24, 291–311.

Bloom, B.S. (1965) *Taxonomy of Education Objectives: The Classification of Educational Goals.* New York: David McKay.

Blumer, H. (1998) *Symbolic Interactionism.* Berkeley, CA: University of California Press.

Bochner, S. (1982) The social psychology of cross-cultural relations. In S. Bochner (ed.) *Cultures in Contact: Studies in Cross-cultural Interaction.* Oxford: Pergamon.

Bochner, S., Hutnic, N. and Furnham, A. (1986) The friendship patterns of overseas and host students in an Oxford Student Residence. *Journal of Social Psychology* 125 (6), 689–94.

Bochner, S., McLeod, B.M. and Lin, A. (1977) Friendship patterns of overseas students: A functional model. *International Journal of Psychology* 12 (4), 277–94.

Bolden, R. and Moscarola, J. (2000) Bridging the quantitative-qualitative divide: The lexical approach to textual data analysis. *Social Science Computer Review* 19 (4), 450–60.

Bond, M. (1996) Preface. In M. Bond (ed.) *The Handbook of Chinese Psychology* (pp. viii–ix). Hong Kong: Oxford University Press.

Bourdieu, P. (1986) *Distinction: A Social Critique of the Judgement of Taste.* London: Routledge and Kegan Paul.

Bourdieu, P. (1991) *Language and Symbolic Power.* (J.B. Thompson, ed.) (G. Raymond and M. Adamson, trans.). Cambridge: Polity Press.

Boyatzis, R.E. (1998) *Transforming Qualitative Information: Thematic Analysis and Code Development.* Thousand Oaks, CA: Sage Publications.

Bradford, L., Allen, M. and Beisser, K.R. (2000) Meta-analysis of intercultural communication competence research. *World Communication* 29 (1), 28–51.

Brecht, R. and Robinson, J. (1995) On the value of formal instruction in study abroad: Student reactions in context. In B. Freed (ed.) *Second Language Acquisition in a Study Abroad Context* (pp. 317–34). Amsterdam: John Benjamins Publishing Co.

Brewer, J.D. (2000) *Ethnography.* Buckingham: Open University Press.

Brewer, M.B. (1996) When contact is not enough: Social identity and intergroup cooperation, *International Journal of Intercultural Relations.* 20, 291–303.

Brislin, R. (1986) Wording and translation of research instruments. In W. Lonner and J. Berry (eds) *Field Methods in Cross-cultural Research* (pp. 137–64). California: Sage Publications.

Brislin, R. (2000) *Understanding Culture's Influence on Behavior* (2nd edn). Florida: Harcourt College.

Broadbent, D.E., Cooper, P.F., FitzGerald, P. and Parkes, K.R. (1982) The Cognitive Failures Questionnaire (CFQ) and its correlates. *British Journal of Clinical Psychology* 21, 1–16.

Brown, J.D. (1995) *The Elements of Language Curriculum: A Systematic Approach to Program Development*. Boston: Heinle and Heinle Publishers.

Burgoon, J.K. (1995) Cross-cultural and intercultural applications of expectancy violations theory. In R. Wiseman (ed.) *Intercultural Communication Theory*. Thousand Oaks, CA: Sage.

Byram, M. (1992) *The 'Assistant(e) d'Anglais': Preparing for the Year Abroad*. Durham: University, School of Education.

Byram, M. (1995) Acquiring intercultural competence. A review of learning theories. In Sercu, L. (ed.) *Intercultural Competence: A New Challenge for Language Teachers and Trainers in Europe* (Vol. 1). The Secondary School. Aalborg: Aalborg University Press.

Byram, M. (1996) Framing the experience of residence abroad: the pedagogical function of the informal interview. *Language, Culture and Curriculum* 9 (1), 84–98.

Byram, M. (1997) *Teaching and Assessing Intercultural Communicative Competence*. Clevedon: Multilingual Matters.

Byram, M. and Alred, G. (1992) *Residence Abroad and the Cultural Perceptions of Foreign Language Students in Higher Education*. Report to the Economic and Social Research Council.

Byram, M. and Alred, G. (1993) *'Paid to be English'. A Book for English Assistants and their Advisers in France*. Durham: University, School of Education.

Byram, M. and Alred, G. (1996) Language assistants' experience of a 'familiar' culture. *Actes du colloque 'Réciprocités'* (pp. 269–80). GREAM. Le Mans: Université du Maine.

Byram, M. and Alred, G. (2001) *A Narrative Study of the Long-term Educational Significance of the 'Year Abroad'*. Report to the Economic and Social Research Council (mimeo).

Byram, M. and Alred, G. (2002) Becoming an intercultural mediator: A longitudinal study of residence abroad. *Journal of Multilingual and Multicultural Development* 23 (5), 339–52.

Byram, M. and Zarate, G. (1997) Defining and assessing intercultural competence: Some principles and proposals for the European context. *Language Teaching* 29, 14–18.

Byram, M., Nichols, A. and Stevens, D. (eds) (2001) *Developing Intercultural Competence in Practice*. Clevedon: Multilingual Matters.

Byram, M., Esarte-Sarries, V. and Taylor, S. (1991) *Cultural Studies and Language Learning: A Research Report*. Clevedon: Multilingual Matters.

Campbell, J.K. (1988) Inside lives: The quality of biography. In R.S. Sherman and R.D. Webb (eds) *Qualitative Research in Education: Focus and Methods*. Lewes, East Sussex: The Falmer Press.

Carlson, J.S. and Widaman, K.F. (1988) The effects if study abroad during college on attitudes toward other cultures. *International Journal of Intercultural Relations* 12, 1–18.

Caspari, D. (2003) *Fremdsprachenlehrerinnen und Fremdsprachenlehrer. Studien zu ihrem beruflichen Selbstverständnis*. Tübingen: Narr.

Cavusgil, S.T. (ed.) (1993) *Internationalizing Business Education: Meeting the Challenge*. East Lansing: Michigan State University.

Chase, S. (1995) Taking narrative seriously: Consequences for method and theory in interview studies. In R. Josselson and A. Leiblich (eds) *Interpreting Experience: The Narrative Study of Lives*. Thousand Oaks, CA: Sage.

Chen, G.M. (1987) Dimensions of intercultural communication competence. Unpublished doctoral dissertation, Kent State University, OH.

Chen, G.-M. and Chung, J. (1993) *The Impact of Confucianism on Organisational Communication*. ERIC Document Reproduction Service No. 366023.

Chen, G.M. and Starosta, W.J. (1996) Intercultural communication competence: A synthesis. *Communication Yearbook* 19, 353–83.

Chen, G.-M. and Starosta, W. (1998) *Foundations of Intercultural Communication*. Massachusetts: Allyn and Bacon.

Chen, G.M. and Starosta, W.J. (1999) A review of the concept of intercultural awareness. *Human Communication* 2, 27–54.

Church, A.T. (1982) Sojourner adjustment. *Psychological Bulletin* 91 (3), 540–72.

Christ, H. (1993) Schüleraustausch zwischen Verstehen und Mißverstehen. In L. Bredella and H. Christ (eds) *Zugänge zum Fremden* (pp. 181–202). Giessen: Verlag der Ferberschen Buchhandlung.

Cirius (2004) *Internationalisering og Uddannelse*. At http://www.ciriusonline.dk.

Clark, A.C. (1997) Identification of quality characteristics for technology education programs in North Carolina. Unpublished doctoral dissertation, North Carolina State University, Raleigh.

Clark, A.C. and Wenig, R.E. (1999) Identification of quality characteristics for technology education programs: A North Carolina case study. *Journal of Technology Education* 11 (1), 18–26.

Clarke, M. (1976) Second language acquisition as a clash of consciousness. *Language Learning* 26 (2), 377–89.

Clifford, J. (1988) *The Predicament of Culture: Twentieth-Century Ethnography, Literature, and Arts*. Cambridge, MA: Harvard University Press.

Coleman, J.A. (1995) The current state of knowledge concerning student residence abroad. In G. Parker and A. Rouxeville (eds) *The Year Abroad: Preparation, Monitoring, Evaluation, Current Research and Development* (pp. 17–42). London: AFLS/CILT.

Coleman, J.A. (1996) *Studying Languages. A Survey of British and European Students*. London: CILT.

Coleman, J.A. (1997) Residence abroad within language study. *Language Teaching* 30 (1), 1–20.

Coleman, J.A. (1998) Evolving intercultural perceptions among university language learners in Europe. In M. Byram and M. Fleming (eds) *Language Learning in Intercultural Perspective* (pp. 45–75). Cambridge: Cambridge University Press.

Coleman, J.A. (2002) Translating research into disseminated good practice: The case of student residence abroad. In R. MacDonald and J. Wisdom (eds) *Academic and Educational Development: Research, Evaluation, and Changing Practice in Higher Education* (pp. 87–98). London: Kogan Page Ltd.

Collier, M.J. (1989) Cultural and intercultural communication competence: Current approaches and directions for future research. *International Journal of Intercultural Relations* 13, 287–302.

Condon, J. (1974) Introduction: A perspective for the conference. In J.C. Condon and M. Saito (eds) *Intercultural Encounters with Japan: Communication – Contact and Conflict.* Tokyo: Simul Press.

Cook, I. and Crang, M. (1995) Concepts and techniques in modern geography 58: Doing ethnographies.

Cook, S.W. (1984) Cooperative interaction in multiethnic contexts. In N. Miller and M.B. Brewer (eds) *Groups in contact* (pp. 155–85). New York: Academic Press.

Coolican, H. (1990) *Research Methods and Statistics in Psychology.* London: Hodder and Stoughton.

Corbett, J. (2003) *An Intercultural Approach to English Language Teaching.* Clevedon: Multilingual Matters.

Corbin, J. and Strauss, A. (1990) Grounded theory research: Procedures, canons, and evaluative criteria. *Qualitative Sociology* 13 (1), 3–21.

Cortazzi, M. (2001) Narrative analysis in ethnography. In P. Atkinson, A. Coffey, S. Delamont, J. Lofland and L. Lofland (eds) *Handbook of Ethnography* (pp. 384–94). Thousand Oaks, CA: SAGE Publications.

Crew, V. and Bodycott, P. (eds) (2001) *Language and Cultural Immersion: Perspectives on Short-term Study and Residence Abroad.* Hong Kong: Hong Kong Institute of Education.

Culioli, A., Fuchs, C. and Pécheux, M. (1970) *Considérations Théoriques à Propos du Traitement formel du Langage. Tentatives d'Application au Problème des Déterminants.* Paris: Dunod.

Dalkey, N.C., Rourke, D.L., Lewis, R. and Snyder, D. (1972) *Studies in the Quality of Life: Delphi and Decision-Making.* Lexington, MA: Lexington Books.

Dalkey, N.C. (1969) *The Delphi Method: An Experimental Study of Group Opinion* (RM-5888-PR). Santa Monica, CA: Rand Corporation.

Dalley, T. (1984) *Art as Therapy.* New York, Routledge.

Deardorff, D.K. (2004) *The Identification and Assessment of Intercultural Competence as a Student Outcome of Internationalization at Institutions of Higher Education in the United States.* Unpublished dissertation, North Carolina State University, Raleigh, NC.

Denscombe, M. (2003) *The Good Research Guide for Small-Scale Social Research Projects.* Philadelphia: Open University Press.

Diesing, P. (1971) *Patterns of Discovery in the Social Sciences.* Chicago: Aldine.

Dinges, N. (1983). Intercultural competence. In D. Landis and R.W. Brislin (eds) *Handbook of Intercultural Training Volume 1: Issues in Theory and Design* (pp. 176–202). New York: Pergamon Press.

Dinniman, A. and Holzner, B. (eds) (1988) *Education for International Competence in Pennsylvania.* Pittsburgh: University Center for International Studies, University of Pittsburgh.

Dion, K.L. and Dion, K.K. (1996) Chinese adaptation to foreign cultures. In M. Bond (ed.) *A Handbook of Chinese Psychology* (pp. 457–78). Hong Kong: Oxford University Press.

Douglas, M. (1966) *Purity and Danger.* London: Routledge and Kegan Paul.

Doyé, P. (1992) Fremdsprachenunterricht als Beitrag zu tertiärer Sozialisation. In D. Buttjes, W. Butzkamm and F. Klippel (eds) *Neue Brennpunkte des Englischunterrichts* (pp. 280–95). Frankfurt a.M.: Peter Lang.

Ehrenreich, S. (2004) *Auslandsaufenthalt und Fremdsprachenlehrerbildung: Das assistant-Jahr als ausbildungsbiographische Phase.* München: Langenscheidt.

Ellingboe, B.J. (1998) Divisional strategies to internationalize a campus portrait: Results, resistance, and recommendations from a case study at a US university. In J.A. Mestenhauser and B.J. Ellingboe (eds) *Reforming the Higher Education Curriculum: Internationalizing the Campus* (pp. 198–228). Phoenix, AZ: Oryx Press.

English, S.L. (1998) Internationalization through the lens of evaluation. In J.A. Mestenhauser and B.J. Ellingboe (eds) *Reforming the Higher Education Curriculum* (pp. 179–97). Phoenix, AZ: Oryx Press.

European Commission (1996) *Socrates, Guidelines for Applicants 1997*. Luxembourg: Office for Official Publications of the European Communities.

'Excellent students: experience is more important than a degree from a prestigious university' (2000, December 20) *Ming Pao*, p. E8.

Fantini, A.E. (2000). *A Central Concern: Developing Intercultural Competence*. Retrieved March 2003 from http://www.sit.edu/publications/docs/compe tence.pdf.

Farag, V. (1997) Erfahrungen mit Sprachen und interkulturelles Lernen im Auslands-studium. *Französisch heute* 28, 158–65.

Fazio, A.F. (1977) A concurrent validational study of the NCHS General Well-Being Schedule. (Dept. of H. E. W. Publ. HRA-78-1347). Hyattsville, MD: National Center for Health Statistics.

Fennes, H. and Hapgood, K. (1997). *Intercultural Learning in the Classroom: Crossing Borders*. London: Cassell.

Ferraro, G. (2001) *Methods in Cultural Anthropology*. Belmont, CA: Wadsworth Thomson Learning.

Fetterman, D. (2001) Ethnographic educational evaluation. In A. Bryman (ed.) *Ethnography. Vol. III* (pp. 304–27). Thousand Oaks, CA: SAGE Publications.

Finkelstein, B., Pickert, S., Mahoney, T. and Douglas, B. (1998). *Discovering Culture in Education: An Approach to Cultural Education Program Evaluation*. Washington DC: ERIC Clearinghouse on Assessment and Evaluation.

Fischler, C. (1988) Food, self and identity. *Social Science Information* 27 (2), 275–92.

Fisher, S. (1989) *Homesickness, Cognition, and Health*. Hove: Lawrence Erlbaum Associates.

Fisher, S. and Hood, B. (1987) The stress of the transition to university: A longitudinal study of psychological disturbance, absent-mindedness and vulnerability to homesickness. *British Journal of Psychology* 78, 425–41.

Flick, U. (1998) *An Introduction to Qualitative Research*. London: Sage.

Flick, U. (2002) *An Introduction to Qualitative Research* (2nd edn). London: Sage.

Flick, U. (2004) Triangulation in qualitative research. In U. Flick, E. von Kardorff and I. Steinke (eds) (pp. 179–83). London: Sage.

Flick, U., von Kardorff, E. and Steinke, I. (eds) (2004a) *A Companion to Qualitative Research*. London: Sage.

Flick, U., von Kardorff, E. and Steinke, I. (2004b) What is qualitative research? An introduction to the field. In U. Flick, E. von Kardorff and I. Steinke (eds) (pp. 3–11). London: Sage.

Forbes, D. (2004) Ethnic conflict and the contact hypothesis. In Y.-T. Lee, C. McCauley, F. Moghaddam and S. Worchel (eds) *Psychology of Ethnic and Intercultural Conflict*. Westport, CN: Praeger.

Fraenkel, J.R. and Wallen, N.E. (1993) *How to Design and Evaluate Research in Education*. New York: McGraw-Hill.

Freed, B. (1995) *Second Language Acquisition in a Study Abroad Context*. Amsterdam: John Benjamins Publishing Co.

Freed, B. (1998) An overview of issues and research in language learning in a study abroad setting. *Frontiers: The International Journal of Study Abroad* 1V, 1–18.

Freeman, D. (1996) 'To take them at their word': Language data in the study of teachers' knowledge. *Harvard Educational Review* 66, 732–61.

Freeman, D. and Johnson, K.E. (1998) Reconceptualizing the knowledge-base of language teacher education. *TESOL Quarterly* 32, 397–417.

Furnham, A. and Bochner, S. (1982) Social difficulty in a foreign culture: An empirical analysis of culture shock. In S. Bochner (ed.) *Cultures in Contact: Studies in Cross-cultural Interaction* (pp. 161–98). Oxford: Pergamon.

Furnham, A. and Bochner, S. (1986) *Culture Shock: Psychological Reactions to Unfamiliar Environments*. London: Metheun.

Furham, A. and Bochner, S. (1994) *Culture Shock: Psychological Reactions to Unfamiliar Environments*. London: Routledge.

Furnham, A. and Erdmann, S. (1995) Psychological and socio-cultural variables as predictors of adjustment in cross-cultural transitions. *Psychologia* 38, 238–51.

Furnham, A. (1988) The adjustment of sojourners. In Y. Kim and W. Gudykunst (eds) *Cross-cultural Adaptation: Current Approaches* (pp. 42–61). California: Sage Publications.

Furth, G. (1988) *The Secret World of Drawings: Healing Through Art*. Boston, Sigo.

Gall, M.D., Borg, W.R. and Gall, J.P. (1996) *Educational Research: An Introduction*. White Plains, NY: Longman.

Gareis, E. (2000) Intercultural friendship: Five case studies of German students in the USA. *Journal of Intercultural Studies* 4, 67–91.

Geertz, C. (1973, 2000) *The Interpretation of Cultures*. New York: Basic Books.

Gibbs, G. (2002) *Qualitative Data Analysis Explorations with NVivo*. Buckingham, UK: Open University Press.

Giddens, A. and Pierson, C. (1998) *Samtaler med Anthony Giddens*. København, Denmark: Reitzels Forlag.

Giddens, A. (1979) *Central Problems in Social Theory*. London: The Macmillan Press.

Giddens, A. (1997) *The Constitution of Society*. Cambridge: Polity Press.

Giles, H.W. and Smith, P. (1979) Accommodation theory: Optimum levels of convergence. In H. Giles and R.N. St.Clair (eds) *Language and Social Psychology*. Baltimore, MD: University Park Press.

Ginsberg, R. and Miller, L. (2000) What do they do? Activities of students during study abroad. In R. Lambert and E. Shohamy (eds) *Language Policy and Pedagogy: Essays in Honor of A. Ronald Walton* (pp. 237–60). Philadelphia: John Benjamins Publishing Co.

Glaser, B. and Strauss, A. (1967, 1999) *The Discovery of Grounded Theory: Strategies for Qualitative Research*. Chicago: Adeline.

Glaser, B.G. (1978) *Theoretical Sensitivity*. Mill Valley, CA: The Sociology Press.

Glaser, B.G. (1992) *Basics of Grounded Theory Analysis*. Mill Valley, CA: Sociology Press.

Glaser, B.G. (2002) Conceptualisation. In A. Bron and M. Schemmann (eds) *Social Science Theories in Adult Education Research* (pp. 313–35). Münster: LIT Verlag.

Goffman, I. (1967) *Interaction Ritual. Essays in Face-to-face Behaviour*. New York: Pantheon.

Greene, J. (2003) Understanding social programs through evaluation. In N. Denzin and Y. Lincoln (eds) *Collecting and Interpreting Qualitative Materials* (pp. 590–618). Thousand Oaks, CA: Sage Publications.

Grossman, L. (1996) *The World on a Plate*. London: BBC.

Guba, E.G. (1978) *Towards a Methodology of Naturalistic Inquiry in Educational Evaluation*. Los Angeles: UCLA, Centre for the Study of Evaluation, CSE Monograph Series in Evaluation, 8.

Gudykunst, W.B. (1994) *Bridging Differences: Effective Intergroup Communication* (2nd ed). London: Sage.

Gudykunst, W.B. (1979) The effects of an intercultural communication workshop on cross-cultural attitudes and interaction. *Communication Education*, 28, 179–87.

Gudykunst, W.B. (1983) Toward a typology of stranger host relationships. *International Journal of Intercultural Relations* 7, 401–13.

Gudykunst, W.B. (1998) *Bridging Differences: Effective Intergroup Communication*. London: Sage Publications.

Gudykunst, W.B. and Hammer, M.R. (1987) Strangers and hosts: An uncertainty reduction based theory of intercultural adaptation. In Y.Y. Kim and W.B. Gudykunst (eds) *Cross-Cultural Adaptation: Current Approaches* (Vol. 11). Newbury Park, CA: Sage.

Gudykunst, W. and Kim, Y.Y. (1997) *Communicating with Strangers. An Approach to Intercultural Communication*. New York: McGraw-Hill.

Gundling, E. (2003) *Working GlobeSmart: 12 People Skills for Doing Business Across Borders*. Palo Alto: Davies-Black.

Hadley, A.O. (2001) *Teaching Language in Context* (3rd edn). Boston, MA: Heinle and Heinle.

Hall, E.T. (1982/1966) *The Hidden Dimension*. New York: Anchor/Doubleday.

Hammer, M.R., Gudykunst, W.B. and Wiseman, R.L. (1978) Dimensions of intercultural effectiveness: An exploratory study. *International Journal of Intercultural Relations* 2, 382–93.

Hammersley, M. and Atkinson, P. (1983) *Ethnography: Principles in Practice*. London: Tavistock Publications.

Hammersley, M. (ed.) (1994) *Controversies in Classroom Research: A Reader*. Buckingham: Open University Press.

Hammersley, M. and Atkinson, P. (1995) *Ethnography: Principles in Practice*. London: Routledge.

Hampden-Turner, C.M. and Trompenaars, F. (2000) *Building Cross-Cultural Competence: How to Create Wealth from Conflicting Values*. New Haven: Yale University Press.

Hanvey, R.G. (1976) *An Attainable Global Perspective*. New York: Global Perspectives in Education.

Hargreaves, D. (1994) Whatever happened to symbolic interactionism? In M. Hammersley (ed.) *Controversies in Classroom Research: A Reader* (pp. 135–152). Buckingham: Open University Press.

Hart, W.B. (1999) Interdisciplinary influences in the study of intercultural relations: A citation analysis of the International Journal of Intercultural Relations. *International Journal of Intercultural Relations* 23 (4), 575–89.

Hayashi, S. (2000). Study abroad and change of self: An interview study of vocational school students. *Jinbun Ronso: Bulletin of the Faculty of Humanities and Social Sciences, Mie University of Japan* 17, 59–83.

Heath, S. (1982) Ethnography in education: Defining the essentials. In P. Gillmore and A. Glatthorn (eds) *Children In and Out of School* (pp. 33–58). Washington, DC: Center for Applied Linguistics.

Hess, J.D. (1994) *Whole World Guide To Culture Learning*. Yarmouth, ME: Intercultural Press.

Hett, E.J. (1992). Development of an instrument to measure global-mindedness. Unpublished doctoral dissertation, University of San Diego.

Higher Education Statistics Agency (HESA) (2004) *Students in Higher Education Institutions*. Cheltenham: Higher Education Statistics Agency Ltd.

Hitzler, R. and Eberle, T.S. (2004) Phenomenological life-world analysis. In U. Flick, E. von Kardorff and I. Steinke (eds) *A Companion to Qualitative Research* (pp. 67–71). London: Sage.

Hofstede, G. (1994) *Cultures and Organisations. Intercultural Co-operation and Its Importance to Survival. Software of the Mind*. London: Harper Collins.

Hoopes, D.S. (1979) Intercultural communication concepts and the psychology of intercultural experience. In M. Pusch (ed.) *Multicultural Education: A Cross-Cultural Training Approach* (pp. 9–38). Yarmouth, ME: Intercultural Press.

Hunter, W. (2004) Knowledge, skills, attitudes, and experiences necessary to become globally competent. Unpublished dissertation, Lehigh University, Bethlehem, PA.

Hutchinson, S. (1988) Education and grounded theory. In R.S. Sherman and R.D Webb (eds) *Qualitative Research in Education: Focus and Methods*. Lewes, East Sussex: The Falmer Press.

Hymes, D. (1974) *Foundations in Sociolinguistics: An Ethnographic Approach*. London: Tavistock Publications Ltd.

ICS Kokusai Bunka Kyoiku Senta. (n.d.) Saikin no ryugaku jijo. (Recent report of study abroad) *Ryugaku Janal (Journal of Study Abroad)*. Retrieved 3 April 2002, from http://www.ryugaku.co.jp/report/recently.html.

Interculture Project (1997–2000). Lancaster University, Dept of European Languages and Cultures, Lonsdale College, Lancaster University, Lancaster LA1 4YN. On www at http://www.lancs.ac.uk/users/interculture/about.htm.

Ishiyama, F.I. (1988) A model of visual case processing using metaphors and drawings. *Counsellor Education and Supervision* 28, 153–61.

Isserstedt, W. and Schnitzer, K. (2002) *Internationalisierung des Studiums: Ausländische Studierende in Deutschland. Deutsche Studierende im Ausland*. Bonn: BMBF.

Jackson, J. (2004a, December) Ethnographic groundwork for language and cultural immersion. Paper presented at the International Language in Education (ILEC) Conference, Hong Kong Institute of Education, Hong Kong.

Jackson, J. (2004b, November) English only: Sojourner reflections, reactions, and resistances to a language policy. Paper presented at the International Association for Languages and Intercultural Communication (IALIC) 5th Annual Conference: Politics, Plurilingualism and Linguistic Identity. Dublin City University, Dublin, Ireland.

Jackson, J. (2004c, May) Barriers to intercultural harmony: A case study of Hong Kongers in England. Paper presented at the Third Biennial International Conference on Intercultural Research (IAIR); Theme: Harmonizations between within-cultural diversities and cross-cultural commonalities, National Taiwan Normal University, Taipei, Taiwan.

Jackson, J. (2004d, April) Ethnographic preparation for study and residence abroad. Paper presented at the Teachers of English to Speakers of Other Languages Convention, Long Beach, CA, USA.

Jeffrey, B. and Craft, A. (2003) *An Intercultural Approach to English Language Teaching*. Clevedon: Multilingual Matters.

Jeffrey, B. and Craft, A. (2004) Teaching creatively and teaching for creativity: distinctions and relationships. *Educational Studies* 301, 77–87.

Jensen, A. A., Jaeger, K. and Lorentsen, A. (eds) (1995) *Intercultural Competence: A New Challenge for Language Teachers and Trainers in Europe. Vol II: The Adult Learner*. Aalborg: Aalborg University Press.

Jordan, S. and Barro, A. (1995) The effect of ethnographic training on the year abroad. In G. Parker and A. Rouxeville (eds) *'The Year Abroad': Preparation, Monitoring, Evaluation: Current Research and Development* (pp. 76–90). London: CILT.

Jordan, S. and Roberts, C. (2000) *Introduction to Ethnography* (Language and Residence Abroad (LARA) Project). Oxford: Oxford Brookes University.

Jurasek, R. (1995) Using ethnography to bridge the gap between study abroad and the on-campus language and culture curriculum. In C. Kramsch (ed.) *Issues in Language Program Direction* (pp. 85-101). Boston: Heinle and Heinle.

Jurasek, R., Lamson, H. and O'Maley, P. (1996). Ethnographic learning while studying abroad. *Frontiers: The Interdisciplinary Journal of Study Abroad* II, 1–25.

Kaës, R.R., Correa, O.R., Douville, O., Eiguer, A., Moro, M.-R., Revah-Lévy, A., Sinatra, F., Dahoun, Z. and Lecourt, E. (1998) *Différence Culturelle et Souffrances de l'Identité*. Paris: Dunod.

Kauffmann, N., Martin, J., Weaver, H. and Weaver, J. (1992) *Students Abroad: Strangers at Home: Education for a Global Society*. Yarmouth, ME: Intercultural Press.

Kealey, D.J. (2003) *The Intercultural Living and Working Inventory: History and Research*. Retrieved 12 December 2003 from http://www.dfait-maeci.gc.ca/cfsa-icse/cil-cai/ilwi-ici-background-en.asp.

Kelle, U. (2004) Computer-assisted analysis of qualitative data. In U. Flick, E. von Kardorff and I. Steinke (eds) (2004a) *A Companion to Qualitative Research* (pp. 276–83). London: Sage.

Kelleher, A. (1996) Earlham College. In *Learning from Success: Campus Case Studies in International Program Development* (pp. 75–95). New York: Peter Lang.

Kellogg, R. (1970) *Analysing Children's Art*, California; National Press Books.

Kelly, G. (1955) *The Psychology of Personal Constructs*. New York: Norton.

Kelman, H.C. (1975) International interchanges: Some contributions from theories of attitude change. In W. Coplin and J.M. Rochester (eds) *A Multi-Method Introduction to International Politics*. Chicago: Markham.

Kerbrat-Orecchioni, C. (1999) *L'Énonciation*. (4th ed). Paris: Armand Colin.

Kim, Y.Y. (1988) *Communication and Cross-Cultural Adaptation*. Clevedon: Multilingual Matters.

Kim, Y.Y. (1992). Intercultural communication competence: A systems-thinking view. In W.B. Gudykunst and Y.Y. Kim (eds) *Readings on Communicating with Strangers: An Approach to Intercultural Communication* (pp. 371–81). New York: McGraw-Hill.

Kim, Y. (1997) Adapting to a new culture. In L. Samovar and R. Porter (eds) *Intercultural Communication: A Reader* (8th edn.) (pp. 404–16). California: Wadsworth Publishing Company.

Klemp, G.O. Jr. (1979). Identifying, measuring and integrating competence. In P.S. Pottinger and J. Goldsmith (eds) *Defining and Measuring Competence* (pp. 41–52). San Francisco: Jossey-Bass.

Klineberg, O. (1981) The role or international university exchanges. In S. Bochner (ed.) *The Mediating Person*. Cambridge, MA: Schenkman.

Klineberg, O. (1982) Contact between ethnic groups: A historical perspective of some aspects of theory and research. In S. Bochner (ed.) *Cultures in Contact: Studies in Cross-Cultural Interaction*. Oxford: Pergamon.

Klineberg, O. and Hull, F. (1979) *At a Foreign University: An International Study of Adaptation and Coping*. New York, Praegar.

Klippel, F. (1994) Cultural aspects of foreign language teaching. *Journal for the Study of British Cultures* 1, 49–61.

KMK-PAD/Kultusministerkonferenz – Pädagogischer Austauschdienst (ed.) (2002) *Jahresbericht 2001/2002*. Bonn: KMK-PAD.

Knapp, M. (1999) Ethnographic contributions to evaluation research: The experimental schools program evaluation and some alternatives. In A. Bryman and R. Burgess (eds) *Qualitative Research. Vol. IV* (pp. 160–79). Thousand Oaks, CA: SAGE Publications.

Knight, J. (1997). A shared vision? Stakeholders' perspectives on the internationalization of higher education in Canada. *Journal of Studies in International Education* 1 (1), 27–44.

Koester, J. and Olebe, M. (1989) The behavioral assessment scale for intercultural communication effectives. *International Journal of Intercultural Relations*, 12, 233–46.

Kohls, L.R. (1996) *Survival Kit for Overseas Living* (3rd edn). Yarmouth, ME: Intercultural Press.

Kohonen, V., Jaatinen, R., Kaikkonen, P. and Lehtovaara, J. (2001) *Experiential Learning in Foreign Language Education*. London: Longman.

Kottak, C.P. (2002) *Anthropology: The Exploration of Human Diversity*. Boston: McGraw Hill.

Kuada, J. (2004) *Intercultural Competence Development of Danish Managers*. Retrieved 12 April 2004 from www.business.aau.dk/ivo/publications/working/wp33.pdf

Kübler-Ross (1988) Foreword. In G. Furth, (ed.) *The Secret World of Drawings: Healing through Art* (pp. ix–x). Boston: Sigo.

Kuckartz, U. (1997) Qualitative Daten computergestützt auswerten: Methoden, Techniken, Software. In B. Friebertshäuser and A. Prengel (eds) *Handbuch Qualitative Forschungsmethoden in der Erziehungswissenschaft* (pp. 584–95). Weinheim: Juventa.

Kuckartz, U. (2001) *MAXQDA Introduction* (trans. John Poppe). Berlin. On www at http://www.maxqda.com/maxqda-eng/download/mxintro.pdf. Accessed 28 1.05.

Kudo, K. and Simkin, K. (2003) Intercultural friendship formation: the case of Japanese students at an Australian university. *Journal of Intercultural Studies* 24 (2), 91–114.

Kvale, S. (1996) *InterViews: An Introduction to Qualitative Research Interviewing*. London: Sage.

L'Ecuyer, R. (1987) L'analyse de contenu: notion et étapes. In J.-P. Deslauriers (dir.) *Les méthodes de la Recherche Qualitative* (pp. 49–65). Québec: Presses universitaires du Québec.

La Brack, B. (1993) The missing linkage: The process of integrating orientation and reentry. In R.M. Paige (ed.) *Education for the Intercultural Experience* (pp. 241–80). Yarmouth, ME: Intercultural Press.

Lambert, R.D. (ed.) (1994) *Educational Exchange and Global Competence*. New York: Council on International Educational Exchange.

Lapointe, A.E. (1994) Measuring global competence. In R.D. Lambert (ed.) *Educational Exchange and Global Competence* (pp. 275–76). New York: Council on International Educational Exchange.

Laubscher, M. (1994) *Encounters with Difference: Student Perceptions of the Role of Out-of-Class Experiences in Education Abroad*. Westport, CT: Greenwood Press.

Lawes, S. and Barbot, M.-J. (2001) The intercultural problems involved in setting up a joint teacher training programme. In M. Kelly, L. Fant and I. Elliott (eds) *Third Level, Third Space: Intercultural Communication and Language in Higher Education* (pp. 105–17). Frankfurt a.M.: Lang.

Layder, D. (1998) *Sociological Practice, Linking Theory and Social Research*. London: Sage.

Layton, R. (1998) *An Introduction to Theory in Anthropology*. Cambridge: Cambridge University Press.

Le Page, R.B. and Tabouret-Keller, A. (1985) *Acts of Identity: Creole Based Approaches to Language and Ethnicity*. Cambridge/New York: Cambridge University Press.

Lecompte, M. and Schensul, J. (1999) *Designing and Conducting Ethnographic Research*. Walnut Creek, CA: AltaMira Press.

Lee, W. (1996) The cultural context for Chinese learners. In D. Watkins and J. Biggs (eds) *The Chinese Learner* (pp. 25–42). Hong Kong: CERC.

Leibowitz, S.L. (2002) Determining curricular components of living-learning programs: A Delphi study. Unpublished doctoral dissertation, North Carolina State University, Raleigh.

Leonard, M. and Davey, C. (2001) *Thoughts on the Eleven Plus: A Research Report Examining Children's Experiences of the Transfer Test*. Belfast: Save the Children.

Leung, K. (1996) The role of beliefs in Chinese culture. In M. Bond (ed.) *A Handbook of Chinese Psychology* (pp. 247–63). Hong Kong: Oxford Univeristy Press.

Levi-Strauss, C. (1968) *L'Origine des Matieres de Table. Mythologiques* 1V. Paris: Seuil.

Lillie, E. (1994) *Abroad Alone? Student Experience on Study Placements in Continental Europe*. Paper presented to Society for Research in Higher Education Conference, University of York.

Lincoln, Y.S. and Guba, E.G. (1985) *Naturalistic Inquiry*. Beverly Hills, CA: Sage

Linstone, H.A. and Turoff, M. (1975) *The Delphi Method: Techniques and Applications*. London: Addison-Wesley.

Long, M.H. (1980) Inside the black box: Methodological issues in classroom research on language Learning. *Language Learning* 30 (1), 1–42.

Luckmann, B. (1970) The small life-worlds of modern man. *Social Research* 4, 580–96.

Lustig, M.W. and Koester, J. (2003). *Intercultural Competence: Interpersonal Communication Across Cultures* (4th edn). Boston: Allyn and Bacon.

Lynch, B. (1996) *Language Program Evaluation: Theory and Practice*. Cambridge: Cambridge University Press.

Lysgaard, S. (1955) Adjustment in a foreign society: Norwegian Fullbright grantees visiting the United States. *International Social Science Bulletin* 7, 45–51.

Magri, V. (1995) *Le Discours sur l'Autre à Travers Quatre Récits de Voyage en Orient*. Paris: Honoré Champion éditeur.

Markus, H. and Kitayama, S. (1991) Culture and the self: Implications for cognition, emotion and motivation. *Psychological Review* 98, 224–53.

McKinlay, N.J., Pattinson, H.M. and Gross, H. (1996) An exploratory investigation of the effects of a cultural orientation on the psychological well-being of international university students. *Higher Education* 31, 379–95.

Merkens, H. (2004) Selection procedures, sampling, case construction. In U. Flick, E. von Kardorff and I. Steinke (eds) *A Companion to Qualitative Research* (pp. 165–71). London: Sage.

Miyahara, A. (1992) Cross-cultural views on interpersonal communication competence: A preliminary study proposal. *Human Communication Studies (Journal of the Communication Association of Japan)* 20, 129–143.

Morgan, C. (1993) Attitude change and foreign language culture learning. In *Language Teaching* Vol. 26 (pp. 63–75). Cambridge: Cambridge University Press.

Morgan, G. (1996) *Images of Organization*. Thousand Oaks: Sage.

Morse, M. (1994) What do cyborgs eat? Oral logic in an information society. In G. Bender and T. Druckrey (eds) *Culture on the Brink: Ideologies of Technology*. Boston: Bay Press.

Murphy-Lejeune, E. (2002) *Student Mobility and Narrative in Europe – The New Strangers*. London: Routledge.

Murphy-Lejeune, E. (2003) *L'Étudiant Européen Voyageur: Un Nouvel Étranger*. Paris: Didier.

Nesdale, D. and Todd, P. (1993) Internationalizing Australian universities: The intercultural contact issue. *Journal of Tertiary Education Administration*, 15; 189–202.

Oakley, B.L. (2001) *A Delphi Study of Accounting Major Attrition and Retention in the North Carolina Community College System: Identification of the Problems and Possible Remediation*. Unpublished dissertation, North Carolina State University, Raleigh, NC.

Oberg, K. (1960) Culture shock: adjustment to new culture environments. *Practical Anthropology* 7, 177–182.

Ochs, E. and Capps, L. (1996) Narrating the self. *Annual Review of Anthropology* 25, 19–43.

Oswald, H. (1997) Was heißt qualitativ forschen? Eine Einführung in Zugänge und Verfahren. In B. Friebertshäuser and A. Prengel (eds) *A Companion to Qualitative Research* (pp. 71–87). Weinheim: Juventa.

Paige, R.M. (ed.) (1993) *Education for the Intercultural Experience*. Yarmouth, ME: Intercultural Press.

Paige, R.M., Cohen, A.D., Kappler, B., Chi, J.C. and Lassegard, J.P. (2002) *Maximizing Study Abroad: A Students' Guide to Strategies for Language and Culture Learning and Use*. Minneapolis, MN: University of Minnesota.

Papatsiba, V. (2003) *Des Étudiants Européens. Erasmus et l'Aventure de l'Altérité*. Bern: Peter Lang.

Papatsiba, V. (2005) Political and individual rationales of student mobility. A case-study of ERASMUS programme and a French regional scheme. *European Journal of Education* 40 (2), 173–88.

Parker, G. and Rouxeville, A. (eds) (1995) *'The Year Abroad': Preparation, Monitoring, Evaluation*. London: CILT.

Parkinson, B. and Howell-Richardson, C. (1990) Learner diaries. In C. Brumfit and R. Mitchell (eds) *Research in the Language Classroom, ELT Documents 133*. Oxford: Modern English Publications.

Pearson-Evans, A. (1998) 'With a little help from your friends': Relationship networks during the Year Abroad. In D. Killick and M. Parry (eds) *Languages for Cross-Cultural Capability*. Conference Proceedings, Leeds. Metropolitan University, 12–14 December 1998. Leeds: Centre for Language Study, Metropolitan University.

Pearson-Evans, A. (1999) Sushi for breakfast? The role of food in cross-cultural adjustment. In A. Cuk and F. Del Campo (eds) *One Community and Many Identities. On the Crossroads of a New Europe*. SIETAR Europa Congress Proceedings, 1999. Trieste: Battello Stampatore.

Pearson-Evans, A. (2000) A grounded theory approach to the analysis of cross-cultural adjustment: Case studies based on the diaries of six Irish university students in Japan. Unpublished doctoral dissertation. University of Dublin, Trinity College, Ireland.

Pearson-Evans, A. (2001) Beyond *kotoba* to *kokoro*: Exploring the dimensions of intercultural learning during study abroad. In D. Killick, M. Parry and A. Phipps (eds) *Poetics and Praxis of Languages and Intercultural Communication*. Glasgow: University of Glasgow French and German Publications.

Pedersen, P. (1994) *A Handbook for Developing Multicultural Awareness* (2nd edn). Alexandria, VA: American Counseling Association.

Pedersen, P. (1995) *The Five Stages of Culture Shock: Critical Incidents Around the World*. Westport, CT: Greenwood Press.

Pellegrino, V. (1998) Student perspectives on language learning in a study abroad context. *Frontiers: The International Journal of Study Abroad* IV, 1–17.

Pelto, P.J. and Pelto, G.H. (1978) *Anthropological Research: The Structure of Inquiry* (2nd edn). Cambridge, UK: Cambridge University Press.

Perelman, C. and Olbrechts-Tyteca, L. (1970) *Traité de l'Argumentation, La Nouvelle Rhétorique*. Bruxelles: Editions de l'Université de Bruxelles.

Pettigrew, T.F. (1971) *Racially Separate or Together?* New York: McGraw-Hill.

Piaget, J. (1971) *Science of Education and the Psychology of the Child*. New York: Grossman Publishers, A Division of the Viking Press.

Polkinghorne, D.E. (1995) Narrative configuration in qualitative analysis. In J.A. Hatch and R. Wisniewski (eds) *Life History and Narrative*. London: Falmer.

Posavac, E. and Carey, R. (2003) *Program Evaluation: Methods and Case Studies*. Upper Saddle River, NJ: Prentice Hall.

Pottinger, P.S. (1979) Competence assessment: Comments on current practices. In P.S. Pottinger and J. Goldsmith (eds) *Defining and Measuring Competence* (pp. 25–40). San Francisco: Jossey-Bass.

Pusch, M. (1994) The chameleon capacity. In R.D. Lambert (ed.) *Educational Exchange and Global Competence* (pp. 205–10). New York: Council on International Educational Exchange.

Rampton, M.B.H. (1991) Second language learners in a stratified multilingual setting. *Applied Linguistics* 12 (3), 229–48.

Reissman, C.K. (2002a) Analysis of personal narratives. In J. Gubrium and J. Holstein (eds) *Handbook of Interview Research: Context and Method* (pp. 695–710). Thousand Oaks, CA: SAGE Publications.

Reissman, C.K. (2002b) Narrative analysis. In M. Huberman and M. Miles (eds) *The Qualitative Researcher's Companion* (pp. 217–70). Thousand Oaks, CA: Sage Publications.

Richards, L. (2002) *NVivo: Using NVivo in Qualitative Research*. Melbourne: QSR International.

Ritzer, G. (1996) *Modern Sociological Theory*. Singapore: McGraw-Hill Companies.

Roberts, C. (1995) Language and cultural learning: An ethnographic approach. In A. Jensen *et al.* (eds) *Intercultural Competence. Vol. 2. The Adult Learner* (pp. 53–69). Aalborg: Aalborg University Press.

Roberts, C. (1997) The year abroad as an ethnographic experience. In M. Byram (ed.) *Face to Face: Learning Language-and-Culture Through Visits and Exchanges* (pp. 62–76). London: CILT.

Roberts, C., Byram, M., Barro, A., Jordan, S. and Street, B. (2001) *Language Learners as Ethnographers*. Clevedon: Multilingual Matters.

Robinson, J.P., Shaver, P.R. and Wrightsman, L.S. (eds) (1991). *Measures of Personaligy and Social Psychological Attitudes*. San Diego: Academic Press.

Robson, C. (2002) *Real World Research: A Resource for Social Scientists and Practitioners – Researchers*. Oxford: Blackwell Publishers.

Rogers, P.J. (2000) Program theory: Not whether programs work but how they work. In D.L. Stufflebeam, G.F. Madaus, and T. Kellaghan (eds) *Evaluation Models: Viewpoints on Educational and Human Services Evaluation* (2nd edn), (pp. 209–32). Boston: Kluwer Academic.

Rosen, R., Digh, P., Singer, M. and Phillips, C. (2000) *Global Literacies: Lessons on Business Leadership and National Cultures*. New York: Simon and Schuster.

Rossman, G. and Rallis, S. (1998) *Learning in the Field: An Introduction to Qualitative Research*. Thousand Oaks, CA: Sage Publications.

Rossman, G. and Rallis, S. (2003) *Learning in the Field: An Introduction to Qualitative Research* (2nd edn). Thousand Oaks, CA: Sage Publications.

Rossmann, P. (1896) Ein Studienaufenthalt in Paris. *Die Neueren Sprachen* 4, 257–95.

Rothbart, M. and John, O.P. (1985) Social categorization and behavioral episodes: A cognitive analysis of the effects of intergroup contact. *Journal of Social Issues*, 41, 81–104

Rowles, D., Carty, M. and McLachlan, A. (1998) *Foreign Language Assistants: A Guide to Good Practice*. London: CILT.

Royse, D., Thyer, B., Padgett, D. and Logan, T. (2001) *Program Evaluation: An Introduction*. Belmont, CA: Wadsworth/Thomson Learning.

Ruben, B.D. (1976) Assessing communication competence for intercultural communication adaptation. *Group and Organization Studies* 1 (3), 334–54.

Rudenberg, S., Jansen, P. and Fridjhon, P. (2001) Living and coping with ongoing violence. A cross-national analysis of children's drawings using structured rating indices, *Childhood* 8 (1), 31–55.

Saddlemire, J.R. (1996) Qualitative study of white second-semester undergraduates' attitudes toward African American undergraduates at a predominantly white university. *Journal of College Student Development* 37 (6), 684–91.

Saldana, J. (2003) *Longitudinal Qualitative Research: Analyzing Change through Time*. Walnut Creek, CA: AltaMira Press.

Samovar, L.A. and Porter, R.E. (eds) (2001) *Communication Between Cultures* (4th edn). Belmont, CA: Wadsworth.

Satterlee, B. (1999). The acquisition of key executive skills and attitudes required for international business in the third millennium. (ERIC Document Reproduction Service No. ED432175).

Scheibe, M., Skutsch, M. and Schofer, J. (1975) Experiments in Delphi methodology. In H.A. Linstone and M. Turoff (eds) *The Delphi Methods: Techniques and Applications* (pp. 262–87). Reading, MA: Addison-Wesley.

Schensul, J., LeCompte, M., Hess, A., Nastasi, B., Berg, M., Williamson, L., Brecher, J. and Glasser, R. (1999a) *Using Ethnographic Data: Interventions, Public Programming, and Public Policy*. Walnut Creek, CA: AltaMira Press.

Schensul, S.L., Schensul, J.J. and LeCompte, M.D. (1999b) *Essential Ethnographic Methods*. Walnut Creek, CA: AltaMira Press.

Schocker-von Ditfurth, M. (2001) *Forschendes Lernen in der fremdsprachlichen Lehrerbildung: Grundlagen, Erfahrungen, Perspektiven*. Tübingen: Narr.

Schumann, F. and Schumann, J. (1977) Diary of a language learner: An introspective study of second language learning. In H. Brown, C. Yorio and R. Crymes (eds) *On TESOL '77: Teaching and learning English as a Second Language: Trends in Research and Practice*. Washington: TESOL.

Schutz, A. (1987) L'étranger. Essai de psychologie sociale, In A. Schutz (ed.) *Le Chercheur et le Quotidien. Phénoménologie des Sciences Sociales*. Paris: Méridiens Klincksieck.

Schwandt, T.A. (1994) Constructivist, interpretivist approaches to human inquiry. In N.K. Denzin and Y.S. Lincoln (eds) *Handbook of Qualitative Research* (pp. 118–137). Thousand Oaks, CA: SAGE Publications.

Searle, W. and Ward, C. (1990) The prediction of psychological and sociocultural adjustment during cross-cultural transitions. *International Journal of Intercultural Relations* 14, 449–64.

Sherman, R.S. and Webb, R.D. (1988) Qualitative research in education: A focus. In R.S. Sherman and R.D. Webb (eds) *Qualitative Research in Education: Focus and Methods*. Lewes, East Sussex: The Falmer Press.

Shimahara, N. (1988) Anthroethnography: A methodological consideration. In R.S. Sherman and R.D. Webb (eds) *Qualitative Research in Education: Focus and Methods*. Lewes, East Sussex: The Falmer Press.

Siegal, M. (1996) The role of learner subjectivity in second language sociolinguistic competency: Western women learning Japanese. *Applied Linguistics* 17 (3), 356–82.

Siegelman, E.Y. (1990) *Metaphor and Meaning in Psychotherapy*. New York: Guilford Press.

Silverman, D. (2000) *Doing Qualitative Research: A Practical Handbook*. London: Sage.

Simmel, G. (1950/1908) The stranger. In K. Wolff (ed.) *The Sociology of George Simmel*. New York: Free Press of Glencoe.

Simmel, G. (1979) Digressions sur l'étranger. In Y. Grafmeyer and I. Joseph (eds) *L'École de Chicago: Naissance d'une Écologie Urbaine*. Paris: Champ Urbain.

Spitzberg, B.H. (1989) Issues in the development of a theory of interpersonal competence in the intercultural context. *International Journal of Intercultural Relations* 13 (3), 241–68.

Spitzberg, B.H. and Cupach, W.R. (1984) *Interpersonal Communication Competence*. London: Sage.

Spradley, J.P. (1979) *The Ethnographic Interview*. New York: Holt, Rinehart and Winston.

Spradley, J.P. (1980) *Participant Observation*. New York: Holt, Rinehart and Winston.

Spradley, J. and McCurdy, D. (1988) *The Cultural Experience: Ethnography in Complex Societies*. Chicago: Waveland Press.

Stangor, C., Klaus, J., Stroebe, W. and Hewstone, M. (1996) Influence of student exchange on national stereotypes, attitudes and perceived group variability. *European Journal of Social Psychology* 26, 663–75.

Steinke, I. (2004) Quality criteria in qualitative research. In U. Flick, E. von Kardorff and I. Steinke (eds) *A Companion to Qualitative Research* (pp. 184–90). London: Sage.

Stephan, W.G. (1985) Intergoup relations. In G. Lindzey and E. Aronson (eds) *Handbook of Social Psychology* (pp. 599–658) New York: Random House.

Stewart, A. (1998) *The Ethnographer's Method*. Thousand Oaks, CA: Sage Publications.

Stewart, E.C. and Bennett, M.J. (1991) *American Cultural Patterns*. Yarmouth, ME: Intercultural Press.

Stier, J. (2003) Internationalisation, ethnic diversity and the acquisition of intercultural competencies, *Intercultural Education* 14 (1), 77–91.

Storti, C. (1997) *Culture Matters: The Peace Corps Cross-Cultural Workbook*. Washington, DC: Peace Corps Information Collection and Exchange.

Strauss, A. and Corbin, J. (1990) *Basics of Qualitative Research: Grounded Theory Procedures and Techniques*. London: Sage.

Strauss, A. and Corbin, J. (1994) Grounded theory methodology: An overview. In N.K. Denzin and Y.S. Lincoln (eds) *Handbook of Qualitative Research* (pp. 273–85). Thousand Oaks, CA: Sage.

Strauss, A.L. (1987) *Qualitative Analysis for Social Scientists*. Cambridge: Cambridge University Press.

Strauss, A.L. (1996) *Qualitative Analysis for Social Scientists*. Cambridge: Cambridge University Press.

Stroebe, W., Lenkert, A. and Jonas, K. (1988) Familiarity may breed contempt: The impact of student exchange on national stereotypes and attitudes. In W. Stroebe, A.W. Kruglanski, D. Bar-Tal and M. Hewstone (eds) *The Social Psychology of Intergroup Conflict. Theory, Research and Applications* (pp. 167–87). Berlin: Springer.

Tanaka, T., Takai, J., Kohyama, T., Fujihara, T. and Minami, H. (1997) Effects of social networks on cross-cultural adjustment. *Japanese Psychological Research* 39 (1), 12–14.

Tarp, G. (2004) Listening to agent agendas in student exchanges – A grounded theory study, PhD thesis, Aalborg University, Denmark. On www at http://www.learning.aau.dk/dk/forskning/publikationer/phd-afhandlinger.htm.

Terenzini, P.T. and Upcraft, M.L. (1996) Assessing programs and service outcomes. In M.L. Upcraft and J.H. Schuh (eds) *Assessment in Student Affairs: A Guide for Practitioners* (pp. 217–39). San Francisco: Jossey-Bass.

Terhart, E. (2001) *Lehrerberuf und Lehrerbildung: Forschungsbefunde, Problemanalysen, Reformkonzepte*. Weinheim: Beltz.

The Ministry of Education (2001) *Heisei 12 nendo waga kuni no bunkyo shisaku: 2- 9(4) Sogo rikai o susumeru kokusai koryu.*(International interactions which facilitate mutual understanding, *Educational policy of Japan for 2000, 2-9(4)*) Retrieved 4 April 2002, from Japan, Ministry of Education Website: http://www.npb.go.jp/ja/books/whitepaper/aracontents/bunkyo/010124/siry0124.htm.

The Ministry of Justice, Immigration Control Office (2001). *Heisei 12 nen ni okeru gaikokujin oyobi nihonjin no shutsu nyukokusha tokei ni tuite. (Statistics of immigration of foreigners and the Japanese in 2000)* Retrieved 2 April 2002, from Japan, Ministry of Justice Website: http://www.moj.go.jp/PRESS/010330-2/010330-2.html.

Thomas, A. (1988) Psychologisch-pädagogische Aspekte interkulturellen Lernens im Schüleraustausch. In A. Thomas (ed.) *Interkulturelles Lernen im Schüleraustausch* (pp. 77–99). Saarbrücken: Breitenbach.

Thomas, D. (1995) *Teachers' Stories*. Buckingham: Open University Press.

Ting-Toomey, S. (1999) *Communicating Across Cultures*. New York: The Guilford Press.

Todorov, T. (1986) Le croisement des cultures. *Communications* 43; 5–24.

Torbiorn, I. (1982) *Living Abroad – Personal Adjustment and Personnel Policy in the Overseas Setting*. New York: Wiley and Sons.

Tucker, M. (2001) Selecting an international workforce: Elusive best practices. *Intercultural Management Quarterly* 2 (1), 1–3.

Tung, C.W. (1997) *Chief Executive's Policy Address 1997* (Paragraph 95). Hong Kong: Printing Department.

Tung, C.W. (1998) *Chief Executive's Policy Address 1998* (Paragraph 103). Hong Kong: Printing Department.

Turner, J.C. (1987) *Rediscovering the Social Group: A Self-Categorising Theory*. London: Basil Blackwell.

Van Maanen, J. (1988) *Tales of the Field*. Chicago: The University of Chicago Press.

Vasil, R. and Yoon, H.K. (1996) *New Zealanders of Asian Origin*. Wellington, New Zealand: Institute of Policy Studies.

Volet, S. and Ang, G. (1998) Culturally mixed groups on international campuses: An opportunity for inter-cultural learning. *Higher Education Research and Development*, 17 (1), 5–23.

Wagner, K. and Magistrale, T. (1997) *Writing Across Culture, an Introduction to Study Abroad and the Writing Process*. New York: Peter Lang.

Ward, C., Bochner, S. and Furnham, A. (2001) *The Psychology of Culture Shock*. Hove, UK: Routledge.

Ward, C., Okura, Y., Kennedy, A. and Kojima, T. (1998) The U-Curve on trial: A longitudinal study of psychological and sociocultural adjustment during cross-cultural transition. *International Journal of Intercultural Relations* 22 (3), 277–291.

Watson-Gegeo, K. (1988) Ethnography in ESL: Defining the essentials. *TESOL Quarterly* 22 (4), 575–92.

Whalley, T. (1997) Culture learning as transformative learning. In M. Byram (ed.) *Face to Face: Learning 'Language and Culture' Through Visits and Exchanges*. London: CILT.

Whorf, B.L. (1998) Science and linguistics. In M.J. Bennett (ed.) *Basic Concepts of Intercultural Communication*. Yarmouth, ME: Intercultural Press.

Wierzbicka, A. (1997) The double life of a bilingual. In M. Bond (ed.) *Working at the Interface of Cultures* (pp. 110–125), London: Routledge.

Wilkinson, S. (1998) Study abroad from the participants' perspective: A challenge to common beliefs. *Foreign Language Annals* 31, 23–39.

Wiseman, R.L. (2001) *Intercultural communication competence*. Retrieved 11, December 2001 from http://commfaculty.cullerton.edu/rwiseman/ICCCpaper.htm.

Wolf, R.L. and Tymitz, B. (1977) Towards more natural inquiry in education. *CEDR Quarterly*, 10 (3), 7–9.

Woodman, G. (2003) The Intercultural Project: An innovation at Ludwig-Maximilians-Universitaet (LMU), Munich. *Englisch* 38, 111–17.

Yershova, Y., DeJeagbere, J. and Mestenhauser, J. (2000). Thinking not as usual: Adding the intercultural perspective. *Journal of Studies in International Education* 4 (1), 59–78.

Yokota, M. (1991) Jiko kaiji kara mita ryugakusei to nihonjin-gakusei no yujin-kankei. (Research on friendship between foreign and Japanese students from the perspective of self-disclosure). *Hitotsubashi Ronso (Hitotsubashi Review)* 105 (5), 57–75.

Yoshikawa, M. (1987) The double-swing model of intercultural communication between the East and the West. In L. Kincaid (ed.) *Communication Theory*, (pp. 319–30). San Diego: Academic Press.

Yoshikawa, M. (1988) Cross-cultural adaptation and perceptual development. In Y. Kim and W. Gudykunst (eds) *Cross-Cultural Adaptation: Current Approaches*, (pp. 140–48). California: Sage Publications.

Yum, J.O. (1994) The impact of Confucianism on interpersonal relationships and communication patterns in East Asia. In L.A. Samovar and R.E. Porter (eds) *Intercultural Communication: A Reader* (pp. 75–86). Belmont, CA: Wadsworth.

Yum, J.O. (1988) Multidimensional analysis of international images among college students in Japan, Hong Kong, and the United States. *Journal of Social Psychology* 128, 765–77.

Zheng, X. and Berry, J. (1991) Psychological adaptation of Chinese sojourners in Canada. *International Journal of Psychology* 26 (4), 451–70.

Zhong, M. (1998) Perceived intercultural communication competence in cross-cultural interactions between Chinese and Americans. *Critical Studies* 12, 161–79.

Zydatiss, W. (ed.) (1998) *Fremdsprachenlehrerausbildung – Reform oder Konkurs*. München: Langenscheidt.